THE STATE AND
EDUCATION POLICY

MODERN EDUCATIONAL THOUGHT
Series Editor: Professor Andy Hargreaves,
           Ontario Institute for Studies in Education

This important new series contains some of the very best of modern educational thought that will stimulate interest and controversy among teachers and educationalists alike.

It brings together writers of distinction and originality within educational studies who have made significant contributions to policy and practice. The writers are all scholars of international standing who are recognized authorities in their own particular field and who are still actively researching and advancing knowledge in that field.

The series represents some of their best and most distinctive writing as a set of provocative, interrelated essays addressing a specific theme of contemporary importance. A unique feature of the series is that each collection includes a critical introduction to the author's work written by another influential figure in the field.

Current titles:

Roger Dale: *The State and Education Policy*
Andy Hargreaves: *Curriculum and Assessment Reform*

Forthcoming titles include:

Michael Fullan: *Implementation and Change in Education*
Ivor Goodson: *Pupils, Pedagogy and Power*
David Hargreaves: *Teaching*
Jean Rudduck: *Innovation, Independence and Involvement*

The State and Education Policy

ROGER DALE

OPEN UNIVERSITY PRESS
Milton Keynes · Philadelphia

Open University Press
12 Cofferidge Close
Stony Stratford
Milton Keynes MK11 1BY

and
1900 Frost Road, Suite 101
Bristol, PA 19007, USA

First Published 1989

British Library Cataloguing in Publication Data

Dale, Roger
   The State and education policy. — (Modern
   education thought)
   1. Educational. Policies
   I. Title   II. Series
   379.1'54

   ISBN 0–335–09553–4
   ISBN 0–335–09552–6 (pbk)

Library of Congress Cataloging-in-Publication Data

Dale, Roger
   The state and education policy / by Roger Dale.
       p.   cm. — (Modern educational thought)
   Bibliography: p.
   Includes index.
   ISBN 0–335–09553–4   ISBN 0–335–09552–6 (pbk)
   1. Education and state — Great Britain.   2. Politics and education —
Great Britain.   I. Title.   II. Series
LC135.G7D35   1989
379.41—dc20   89-32657   CIP

Typeset by Inforum Typesetting, Portsmouth
Printed in Great Britain by St Edmundsbury Press,
Bury St Edmunds, Suffolk

Contents

Acknowledgements   vii
Preface   ix
Critical Introduction: Ideology and the State in Education Policy   1
Michael W. Apple

Part 1   The State and Education
1 Education and the Capitalist State: Contributions and
   Contradictions   23
2 Implications for Education   45

Part 2   Education as a State Apparatus
3 What is the State?   53
4 From Expectations to Outcomes in Education Systems   58
5 The Scope of Education: Mandate and Capacity in TVEI   65

Part 3   Politics and Education
6 Thatcherism and Education   77
7 Political Change, Educational Change and the State in England,
   1944–88   94

Part 4   Two Cases
8 The Case of William Tyndale   125
9 The Technical and Vocational Education Initiative   147

References   165
Author index   171
Subject index   173

Acknowledgements

The author and publishers thank the following publishers for permission to reprint material in which they hold copyright:

Routledge for permission to reproduce extracts from 'Education and the State: Contributions and contradictions', first published in Michael Apple (ed.), *Economic and Cultural Reproduction in Education* (1981).

The Open University for permission to reproduce extracts from 'Education and the State: Some theoretical approaches' (E353 Unit 3) (1981).

Ontario Institute for Studies in Education for permission to reproduce extracts from 'From expectations to outcomes in education systems', published in *Interchange*, 12, 2/3 (1981).

A. Hargreaves and D. Reynolds for permission to reproduce extracts from 'TVEI: A policy hybrid', first published in A. Hargreaves and D. Reynolds (eds), *Controversies and Critiques in Education* (1989).

Croom Helm for permission to reproduce 'Thatcherism and Education', first published in J. Ahier and M. Flude (eds), *Contemporary Education Policy* (1983).

Falmer Press for extracts from 'Control, accountability and William Tyndale', first published in Roger Dale *et al.* (eds), *Education and the State: Vol. 2, Politics, Patriarchy and Practice* (1981).

Studies in Education Ltd, for permission to reproduce extracts from 'The politicization of school deviance: The case of William Tyndale', first published in L. Barton and R. Meighan (eds), *Schools, Pupils and Deviance* (1979).

Pergamon Press for permission to reproduce extracts from 'The background and inception of TVEI', first published in R. Dale (ed.), *Education, Training and Employment* (1986).

Preface

The chapters making up this book were written over the course of the last 10 years. Their unity and coherence are based in a continuing project attempting to trace the contexts, nature and consequences of state involvement in education.

This project was originally stimulated by a desire to retain and build on the insights of the neo-Marxist theories of education that were prominent at that time. The most important of these was Bowles and Gintis's *Schooling in Capitalist America* (1976), which had been instrumental in my contribution to the Open University course *Schooling and Society* for which it was a set book. Bowles and Gintis's central proposition that the functions and processes of education correspond to the needs and processes of industry was clearly very important, and a major contribution to our understanding of education policies and practices (though its original impact is often overlooked now). However, what crucially seemed to be missing was any account of the link between industry's needs and schools' daily practices, and it was the search for this link that led eventually to my focusing on the State.

My first response to the correspondence principle was developed through two working papers written in 1976. One, 'Education in the crisis and the crisis in education', was very long, discursive and rather indecisive, but it did serve to sharpen my focus on the nature of education in capitalism; one thought first expressed in that paper has remained influential (though often rather remotely) on my subsequent work – that schooling in capitalist societies is fundamentally about the reproduction of class structure without the reproduction of class consciousness.

The other working paper led more directly to the interest in the State. It was written with John Trevitt-Smith, then a graduate student, and was entitled 'From mystique to technique: Completing the bourgeois revolution in education'. That title is unusually revealing, for what we were arguing in the paper was that education was and always had been class based, legitimating class rule by the mystique (which is hard to fathom and hence to replicate) of a classical liberal education, and the technique (which is patent and easily reproduced) of elementary and vocational education. (It may be interesting to note that John – who is now working with me once again on the evaluation of TVEI – and I presented 'From mystique to technique' to the TVEI Study Group at the Open University recently where it could still shed useful light on the continuing tension between liberal and vocational education.) We were still at this stage (and influenced especially by Poutantzas) essentially seeking, as it were, to derive education from capitalism. The advance came with the introduction in this paper of the idea of the conditions of existence of capitalism. This set me wondering how these conditions of existence were met and about the State's and education's role in this – and thence eventually to the first chapter in this book.

One other experience was critical in shaping my approach. This was visiting Portugal in 1976, 2 years after the revolution. My first brief visit (to make an Open University television programme) quickly showed that none of my social science knowledge could give me any effective purchase on understanding what was happening there. It was clear that in order to understand Portugal in 1976 I needed to know more about Portugal's place in the world economy and about Portuguese history. I returned for a longer stay as soon as I was able, and in the meantime began reading all I could on theories of the world economy. I have continued to pursue my interests in the world economy and Portugal separately, but the comparative context, the recognition of the role of the world economy in all national economies and the national/historical nature of the resources that nation-states draw on to tackle their problems have remained absolutely crucial in my subsequent work on the State and education. They show a State doubly constrained, in that control of fundamental economic problems is not in its hands alone, and that its ability to respond to those problems is determined by the strengths and limitations of its existing apparatuses.

All these influences lay behind the development of the first chapter, which was written in 1979. The central ideas outlined there, that there are three key items on the agenda of education systems in the capitalist states – directly supporting capital accumulation, contributing to a context not inimical to its continuing development, and providing legitimation for its activities, and that the solutions to them are as likely to be mutually contradictory as mutually complementary – remain a key theoretical resource on which all the chapters in the book draw. Its basic premises are further developed in Chapters 2 and 3. The chapters in Part 2 explore the nature of the educational state apparatus and how it operates. Chapter 4 is a somewhat speculative attempt at devising a means of examining the process of education policy making. Chapter 5 is a much more recent piece on the nature of the educational state apparatus. It uses the opportunity provided by the joint sponsorship of the Technical and Vocational Education Initiative by the different departments of state, the Department of Education and Science, and the Department of Employment (through the Manpower Services Commission*) to compare their different views of the scope of education, and what it could and should be doing. It develops the concepts of mandate and capacity (which can be seen in more rudimentary and implicit forms in chapters written earlier) and focuses on how they frame the expectations of, and set limits to, what can be achieved by state apparatuses and the organizations within them.

Part 3 makes the idea of politics more central. Chapters 6 and 7 are both concerned with the politics of education, rather than education politics, i.e. broadly with how education's share of the national cake is determined and directed rather than with how it is divided among competing interests within the education system. They also place considerable emphasis on the role of political ideology. It is a commonplace that education is necessarily political, but that 'political' has typically a resolutely small 'p'. The last 10 years in the politics of English education have made that increasingly difficult to sustain and Chapters 6 and 7 both reflect this. Chapter 6 was written after Mrs Thatcher's first term in office and was an attempt to understand the sources and likely future of Thatcherite education policy. Chapter 7 was specially written for this volume. It attempts to chart the changing place of the politics of education since the 1944 Act, and points to the creation of a new education settlement replacing the remaining vestiges of that created by the 1944 Act. This chapter also seeks to show the limitations of pluralist analyses of education policy making. It may, indeed, be regarded as a summary of many of the themes that have characterized my work on the State and education policy.

The final part of the book looks at two 'critical' cases: William Tyndale and TVEI. These are not case studies in the sense that they have an empirical focus and nothing else. They were, in fact, deliberately chosen immediately they came to public notice, as key turning points in the politics of education. Tyndale represented the final defeat of the post-war progressive consensus, TVEI the first sign of the settlement that would eventually replace it. The choice of these two cases for detailed empirical study was very much 'theory led'. Both cases represented opportunities to ground theory in areas which would provide both the greatest test and the most substantial pay off from, and development of, that theory.

The chapters appear almost exactly as they were first published. The only changes I have made have been to eliminate repetition and to tidy up editing. I resisted the temptation to make more substantial changes because that would have set in motion a process that would potentially never end. I am also quite happy, on the whole, for the chapters to appear in their original form. They contain a few passages that make me blush, and a few that make me cringe, but some that make me think and will I hope stimulate others to do so.

Inevitably, in the course of writing the chapters I have been influenced by a

---

* The Manpower Services Commission changed its name in 1988 to the Training Commission, which very soon afterwards became the Training Agency. It is referred to throughout this book as the MSC, the name by which it was known while the chapters mentioning it were being written.

large number of people, though often neither they nor I realized it at the time. In particular, I have benefited from the Open University system of course production which encourages both giving and accepting constructive criticism of colleagues' drafts. Geoff Esland was particularly helpful at the time I was writing the earlier chapters. Madeleine Arnot, Rosemary Deem, Ross Fergusson and Ann Wickham contributed much to those in the middle phase, while Jenny Ozga has helped me a great deal since I started thinking about education policy as such. Friends abroad have given me a great deal of encouragement, support and advice. Michael Apple has demonstrated all these qualities in abundance, though by no means uncritically as his introduction demonstrates. Paul Olson and Gordon West made my times at OISE in Toronto intellectually stimulating and profitable. Gordon West deserves especial thanks for comments and encouragement that contributed so much to the first chapter, and for the warmth of his sustaining friendship. More recently, Liz Gordon's epistolary urgings and suggestions from New Zealand have forced me to clarify some of my more entrenched views about the State and education policy. Two other groups of colleagues should be mentioned. The students whose Ph.D. theses I have supervised have never, I am glad to say, regarded the supervisor–student relationship as one-way traffic. Richard Bowe, Kevin Brehony, Tricia Broadfoot, John Fitz, Chris Shilling, Steve Stoer and John Trevitt all gave as good as they got and I was as much a beneficiary as they were. Finally, the loose-knit group known as the Open University TVEI Study Group, made up in addition to some already mentioned in other categories, of Mark Loveys, David Harris, Robert Moore (with whom I have had especially useful conversations), Simon Sandberg, Pat Sikes and Vicki Valsecchi, have worked with me on TVEI for 4 years, and made major contributions to Chapter 5 in particular.

My gratitude to all these people does not stop with what I have received from them intellectually. They have all shown that constructive criticism and comment cannot only survive but enrich friendship, even when they disagree with the outcomes.

I must admit that in my more cynical moments when I have tended to regard the traditional final acknowledgement to family as a bit of a ritual incantation. Now that I have come to do it, I know better – at least if my case is at all typical. Jo, Nicholas, Charlotte and Patrick have had to put up with me being 'away' even when I was not absent, and I can only thank them for being so tolerant of missing too much of what they might have expected of me. Jo Dale's contributions to this book have been greater than even she knows. They are by no means confined to taking on burdens that would have interfered with me writing the pieces that make up this book, or even to producing insights from her practical experience to temper and modify my wilder theoretical excesses. She, more than anyone, has challenged me to clarify and justify what I was saying throughout, and I have regretted ignoring her comments more than those of any other individual, as their truth and value became apparent. I cannot express the extent of my gratitude for this continuing intellectual challenge.

Critical Introduction: Ideology and the State in Educational Policy

MICHAEL W. APPLE

Introduction

For two decades now, the realization that education is not a neutral set of institutions but is inextricably connected to the forms of domination and subordination in a society – and to the conflicts over altering these forms – has come centre stage in educational scholarship. While relationship between formal schooling and social inequality has generated considerable debate at the level of history, policy and practice for decades, the search for the specific connections between schooling and capitalism has dominated critically oriented work in the sociology of education more in the recent past than ever before. In Britain, the United States and elsewhere, the control of the curriculum and teaching, the goals and policies that guide education, and the cultural policy and economic outcomes of the school have been placed under a microscope labelled 'Who benefits?'

Marx and Engels wrote of capitalism that it constantly revolutionized production. It led to 'everlasting uncertainty'. As they put it in some of their most famous lines: 'All fixed, fast-frozen relations . . . all swept away, all new-formed ones become antiquated before they can ossify. All that is solid melts into air, all that is holy is profaned.'[1]* What is true for capitalism is just as true for scholarship about it. Our understandings of the intricate and immensely contradictory relationships between education and the larger society have themselves been dramatically altered. From theories of correspondence – where schooling is seen to reproduce the division of labour through the teaching of a hidden curriculum,[2] and where the overt curriculum is seen as only reproducing the cultural capital of dominant classes[3] – we have moved to more subtle approaches that are less determined and less

---

* Superscript numerals refer to numbered notes at the end of each chapter.

reductive. Not only is our understanding of class relations and the role of the school in responding to them and forming them more subtle,[4] but we have moved toward a greater understanding of the utter importance and irreducibility of gender and race relations as well.[5] Further, from an earlier position in which everything of importance in schooling was seen to stem from the workings of the capitalist economy, the joint construction and mutual interdependence of (and contradictory relations among) the economic, political and cultural/ideological 'spheres' of society have now increasingly been recognized as well.[6]

Thus, what started out as a simple question – 'Who benefits?' – has become decidedly less simple. For in order to think about that question in relevant and non-reductive ways and in ways that make a difference in policy and practice *in education*, we have had to focus on what actually happens in schools, on the agency of teachers and students, on how policies are actually made in the political area, and on what the contradicting tensions are in the reality of schools. And even though some of the work has once again taken a somewhat economistic and class-reductionist turn,[7] there can be no doubt that – like the social relations of capitalism – theories and research on these relations are not 'fast-frozen'. 'They melt away' to be built upon or replaced by increasingly sophisticated understandings.

One of the most thoughtful writers about these issues has been – and of course continues to be – Roger Dale. There are few individuals who have so consistently advanced our understanding of the political nature of education. I, personally, happily acknowledge the influence his work on the State has had on my own efforts over the years. Others in Britain, the United States, Spain, Portugal, Australia, Canada and elsewhere would willingly do the same I am certain. His work takes on increasing importance during what has been called the 'conservative restoration',[8] with its ideological attacks on all things public so that what is private is now good and what is public is now the root of all evil.[9] What also adds to the current significance of Roger Dale's writings is the reconstruction of what education is *for* that is proceeding rapidly in the United States and Britain and the concomitant acceptance of portions of this reconstruction by large segments of 'the public'. We are in the midst of widespread, rightist-inspired, economic, political and ideological changes in which forms of domination and subordination are being built and rebuilt. Education has become one of the arenas in which this is occurring.

I want to first describe this situation in general, paying particular attention to the ideological reconstruction in which the right is engaged. I will then return to the selection of Roger Dale's corpus of work that is presented here and will situate it within both this situation and our altered understanding of it that I noted earlier.

Reconstructing education

The conventional approach to understanding how ideology operates assumes by and large that ideology is 'inscribed in' people simply because they are in a particular class position. The power of dominant ideas is either a given in which dominance is guaranteed or the differences in 'inscribed' class cultures and ideologies will generate significant class conflict. In either case, ideology is seen as something that somehow makes its effects felt on people in the economy, in politics, in culture and education, and in the home, without too much effort. It is simply *there*. The common sense of people becomes common sense 'naturally' as they go about their daily lives, lives that are prestructured by their class position. If you know someone's location in the class structure, you know their sets of political, economic and cultural beliefs, and you do not really have to inquire into *how* dominant beliefs actually do become dominant. It is usually not assumed that these ideas 'should positively have to *win* ascendency (rather than being ascribed it) through a specific and contingent (in the sense of open-ended, not totally determined) process of ideological struggle'.[10]

Yet the current political situation in many Western capitalist nations presents us with evidence that such a conventional story is more than a little inadequate in understanding the shifts that are occurring in people's common sense. We are seeing a pattern of conflicts within dominant groups that has led to significant changes in their own positions and, even more importantly, we are witnessing how elements of ideologies of groups in dominance become truly *popular*. There is a rupture in the accepted beliefs of many segments of the public who have historically been less powerful,[11] a rupture that has been worked upon and expanded by economically and politically strong forces in the society. And these ideological shifts in common sense are having a profound impact on how a large portion of the public thinks about the role of education in that society.

As I have argued at considerably greater length elsewhere, what we are witnessing today is nothing less than the recurrent conflict between *property rights* and *person rights* that has been a central tension in our economy.[12] Gintis defines the differences between property rights and person rights in the following way.

A *property right* vests in individuals the power to enter into social relationships on the basis and extent of their property. This may include economic rights of unrestricted use, free contract, and voluntary exchange; political rights of participation and influence; and cultural rights of access to the social means for the transmission of knowledge and the reproduction and transformation of consciousness. A *person right* vests in individuals the power to enter into these social relationships on the basis of simple membership in the social collectivity. Thus, person rights involve equal treatment of citizens, freedom of expression and movement, equal access to participation in decision-making in social institutions, and reciprocity in relations of power and authority.[13]

It is not surprising that in our society dominant groups 'have fairly consistently defended the prerogatives of property', while subordinate groups on the whole have sought to advance 'the prerogatives of persons'.[14] In times of severe upheaval, these conflicts become even more intense and, given the current balance of power in society, advocates of property rights have once again been able to advance their claims for the restoration and expansion of their prerogatives not only in education but in all of our social institutions.

The United States and British economies are in the midst of one of the most powerful structural crises they have experienced since the depression. In order to solve it on terms acceptable to dominant interests, as many aspects of the society as possible need to be pressured into conforming with the requirements of international competition, reindustrialization, and (in the words of the National Commission on Excellence in Education in the United States) 'rearmament'. The gains made by women and men in employment, health and safety, welfare programmes, affirmative action, legal rights, and education must be rescinded since 'they are too expensive', both economically and ideologically.

Both of these latter words are important. Not only are fiscal resources scarce (in part because current policies transfer them in many countries to the military), but people must be convinced that their belief that person rights come first is simply wrong or outmoded given current 'realities'. Thus, intense pressure must be brought to bear through legislation, persuasion, administrative rules, and ideological manoeuvring to create the conditions right-wing groups believe are necessary to meet these requirements.[15]

In the process, in the United States, Britain and Australia, the emphasis of public policy has materially changed from issues of employing the State to overcome disadvantage. Equality, no matter how limited or broadly conceived, has become redefined. No longer is it seen as linked to past *group* oppression and disadvantagement. It is simply now a case of guaranteeing *individual choice* under the conditions of a 'free market'.[16] Thus, the current emphasis on 'excellence' (a word with multiple meanings and social uses) has shifted educational discourse so that underachievement is once again increasingly seen as largely the fault of the student. Student failure, which was at least partly interpreted as the fault of severely deficient educational policies and practices, is now being seen as the result of what might be called the biological and economic marketplace. This is evidenced in the growth of forms of Social Darwinist thinking in education and in public policy in general.[17] In a similar way, behind a good deal of the rhetorical artifice of concern about the achievement levels in, say, inner-city schools, notions of choice have begun to evolve in which deep-seated school problems will be solved by establishing free competition over students. These assume that by expanding the capitalist marketplace to schools, we will somehow compensate for the decades of economic and educational neglect experienced by the communities in which these schools are found.[18] Finally, there are concerted attacks on teachers (and curricula) based on a profound mistrust of their quality and commitments.

All of this has led to an array of educational conflicts that have been instrumental in shifting the debates over education profoundly to the right.

The effects of this shift can be seen in a number of educational policies and proposals now gaining momentum throughout capitalist countries:

1. Proposals for voucher plans and tax credits to make schools more like the idealized free market economy.
2. The movement by the government to 'raise standards' and mandate basic curricular goals and knowledge, thereby centralizing further at a governmental level the control of teaching and curricula.
3. The increasingly effective assaults on the school curriculum for its supposedly anti-family and anti-free enterprise bias, its 'secular humanism' and its lack of patriotism.
4. The growing pressure to make the needs of business and industry into the primary goals of the educational system.[19]

These are major alterations, ones that have taken years to show their effects. Though I shall paint in rather broad strokes here, an outline of the social and ideological dynamics of how this has occurred should be visible.

The restoration politics of authoritarian populism

The first thing to ask about an ideology is not what is false about it, but what is true. What are its connections to lived experience? Ideologies, properly conceived, do not dupe people. To be effective they must connect to real problems, real experiences.[20] As I shall document, the movement away from social democratic principles and an acceptance of more right-wing positions in social and educational policy occur precisely because conservative groups have been able to work on popular sentiments, to reorganize genuine feelings, and in the process to win adherents.

Important ideological shifts take place not only by powerful groups 'substituting one, whole, new conception of the world for another'. Often, these shifts occur through the presentation of novel combinations of old and new elements.[21] Let us take the positions of the Reagan and Thatcher administrations as a case in point, for as Clark and Astuto have demonstrated in education and Piven and Cloward, and Raskin have shown in the larger areas of social policy, significant and enduring alterations have occurred in the ways policies are carried out and in the content of those policies.[22]

The success of the policies of the Reagan administration, like that of Thatcherism in Britain, should not simply be evaluated in electoral terms. They need to be judged by their success as well in disorganizing other more progressive groups, in shifting the terms of political, economic and cultural debate onto the terrain favoured by capital and the right.[23] In these terms, there can be no doubt that the current right-wing resurgence has accomplished no small amount in its attempt to construct the conditions that will put it in a hegemonic position.

The right in the United States and Britain has thoroughly renovated and reformed itself. It has developed strategies based upon what might best be called an *authoritarian populism*.[24] As Hall has defined this, such a policy is based on an increasingly close relationship between government and the capitalist economy, a radical decline in the institutions and power of political democracy, and attempts at curtailing 'liberties' that have been gained in the past. This is coupled with attempts to build a consensus, one that is widespread, in support of these actions.[25] The new right's 'authoritarian populism'[26] has exceptionally long roots in the history of the United States, for example. The political culture there has always been influenced by the values of the dissenting Protestantism of the seventeenth century. Such roots become even more evident in periods of intense social change and crises.[27] As Burnham has put it:

> Whenever and wherever the pressures of 'modernization' – secularity, urbanization, the growing importance of science – have become unusually intense, episodes of revivalism and culture-issue policies have swept over the social landscape. In all such cases since at least the end of the Civil War, such movements have been more or less explicitly reactionary, and have frequently been linked with other kinds of reaction in explicitly political ways.[28]

The new right works on these roots in creative ways, modernizing them and creating a new synthesis of their varied elements by linking them to current fears. In so doing, the right has been able to rearticulate traditional political and cultural themes and because of this has effectively mobilized a large amount of mass support.

As I noted, part of the strategy has been the attempted dismantling of the Welfare State and of the benefits that working people, people of colour, and women (these categories are obviously not mutually exclusive) have won over decades of hard work. This has been done under the guise of anti-statism, of keeping government 'off the backs of the people', and of 'free enterprise'. Yet, at the same time, in many valuative, political and economic areas the current government is extremely state-centrist both in its outlook, and very importantly in its day-to-day operations.[29]

One of the major aims of a rightist restoration politics is to struggle in not one but many different arenas at the same time, not only in the economic sphere but also in education and elsewhere. This aim is grounded in the realization that economic dominance must be coupled to 'political, moral and intellectual leadership' if a group is to be truly dominant and if it wants to genuinely restructure a social formation. Thus, as both Reaganism and Thatcherism recognize so clearly, to win in the State you must also win in civil society.[30] As the noted Italian political theorist Antonio Gramsci would put it, what we are seeing is a war of position: 'It takes place where the whole relation of the state to civil society, to "the people" and to popular struggles, to the individual and to the economic life of society has been thoroughly reorganized, where "all the elements change".'[31]

The right then has set itself an immense task, to create a truly 'organic ideology', one that seeks to spread throughout society and to create a new form of 'national popular will'. It seeks to intervene 'on the terrain of ordinary, contradictory common-sense', to 'interrupt, renovate, and transform in a more systematic direction' people's practical consciousness. It is this restructuring of common sense which is itself the already complex and contradictory result of previous struggles and accords, which becomes the object of the cultural battles now being waged.[32]

In this restructuring, Reaganism and Thatcherism did not create some sort of false consciousness, creating ways of seeing that had little connection with reality. Rather, they 'operated directly on the real and manifestly contradictory experiences' of a large portion of the population. They did connect with the perceived needs, fears and hopes of groups of people who felt threatened by the range of problems associated with the crises in authority relations, in the economy and in politics.[33]

What has been accomplished has been a successful translation of an economic doctrine into the language of experience, moral imperative and common sense. The free market ethic has been combined with a populist politics. This has meant the blending together of a 'rich mix' of themes that have had a long history – nation, family, duty, authority, standards and traditionalism – with other thematic elements that have also struck a resonant chord during a time of crisis. These latter themes include self-interest, competitive individualism (what I have elsewhere called the possessive individual),[34] and anti-statism. In this way, a reactionary common sense is partly created.[35]

The sphere of education has been one of the most successful areas in which the right has been ascendant. The social democratic goal of expanding equality of opportunity (itself a rather limited reform) has lost much of its political potency and its ability to mobilize people. The 'panic' over falling standards and illiteracy, the fears of violence in schools, and the concern with the destruction of family values and religiosity, have all had an effect. These fears are exacerbated, and used, by dominant groups within politics and the economy who have been able to move the debate on education (and all things social) onto their own terrain, the terrain of standardization, productivity and industrial needs.[36] Since so many parents *are* justifiably concerned about the economic futures of their children – in an economy that is increasingly conditioned by lowered wages, unemployment, capital flight and insecurity [37] – rightist discourse connects with the experiences of many working–class and lower-middle-class people.

Behind the conservative restoration is a clear sense of loss: of control, of economic and personal security, of the knowledge and values that should be passed on to children, of visions of what counts as sacred texts and authority. The binary opposition of we/they becomes very important here. 'We' are law abiding, 'hard working, decent, virtuous, and homogeneous.' The 'theys' are very different. They are 'lazy, immoral, permissive, heterogenous'.[38] These binary oppositions distance most people of colour, women, gays, and others from the community of worthy individuals. The subjects of discrimination are now no longer those groups who have been historically oppressed, but are instead the 'real Americans' and the 'real Britons' who embody the idealized virtues of a romanticized past. The 'theys' are undeserving. They are getting something for nothing. Policies supporting them are 'sapping our way of life', most of our economic resources, and creating government control of our lives.[39]

These processes of ideological distancing makes it possible for, say, anti-black and anti-feminist sentiments to seem no longer racist and sexist because they link so closely with other issues. Allen Hunter is helpful here:

> Racial rhetoric links with anti-welfare state sentiments, fits with the push for economic individualism; thus many voters who say they are not prejudiced (and may not be by some accounts) oppose welfare spending as unjust. Anti-feminist rhetoric . . . is articulated around defense of the family, traditional morality, and religious fundamentalism.[40]

All of these elements can be integrated through the formation of ideological coalitions that enable many people in Britain and America who themselves feel under threat to turn against groups of people who are even less powerful than themselves. At the very same time, it enables them to 'attack domination by liberal, statist elites'.[41]

This ability to identify a range of 'others' as enemies, as the source of the problems, is very significant. In the United States, for example, one of the major elements in this ideological formation has indeed been a belief that liberal élites within the State 'were intruding themselves into home life, trying to impose their values'. This was having serious negative effects on moral values and on traditional families. Much of the conservative criticism of textbooks and curricula rests on these feelings, for example. While this position certainly exaggerated the impact of the 'liberal élite', and while it certainly misrecognized the power of capital and of other dominant classes,[42] there was enough of an element of truth in it for the right to use it in its attempts to dismantle the previous accord and build its own.

A new hegemonic accord is reached, then. Though Roger Dale will add other actors, it combines dominant economic and political élites intent on 'modernizing' the economy, white working-class and middle-class groups concerned with security, the family, and traditional knowledge and values, and economic conservatives.[43] It also includes a fraction of the new middle class whose own advancement depends on the expanded use of accountability, efficiency and management procedures which are their own cultural capital.[44] This coalition has partly succeeded in altering the very meaning of what it means to have a social goal of equality. The citizen as 'free' consumer has replaced the previously emerging citizen as situated in structurally generated relations of domination. Thus, the common good is now to be regulated exclusively by the laws of the market, free competition, private ownership and profitability. In essence, the definitions of freedom and equality are no longer democratic, but *commercial.*[45] This is particularly evident in the proposal for voucher plans as 'solutions' to massive and historically rooted relations of economic and cultural inequality.

In sum, then, the right in both the United States and Britain has succeeded in reversing a number of the historic post-Second World War trends:

> It has begun to dismantle and erode the terms of the unwritten social contract on which the social forces settled after the war. It has changed the currency of political thought and argument. Where previously social need had begun to establish its own imperatives against the laws of market forces, now questions of 'value for money', the private right to dispose of one's own wealth, the equation between freedom and the free market, have become the terms of trade, not just of political debate . . . but in the thought and language of everyday calculation. There has been a striking reversal of values: the aura that used to attach to the value of the public welfare [that is, the value of the common good], now adheres to anything that is private − or can be privatized. A major ideological reversal is in progress in society at large; and the fact that it has not swept everything before it, and that there are many significant points . . . of resistance, does not contradict the fact that, conceived not in terms of outright victory but more in terms of the mastery of an unstable equilibrium, [the right] has . . . begun to reconstruct the social order.[46]

This reconstruction is not imposed on unthinking subjects. It is not done through the use of some right-wing attempt at what Freire has called 'banking', where knowledge and ideologies become common sense simply by pouring them into the heads of people. The ruling or dominant conceptions of the world and of everyday life 'do not directly prescribe the mental content of the illusions that supposedly fill the heads of the dominated classes'.[47] However, the meanings, interests and languages we construct are bound up in the unequal relations of power that do exist. To speak theoretically, the sphere of symbolic production is a contested terrain just as other spheres of social life are. 'The circle of dominant ideas does accumulate the symbolic power to map or classify the world for others', to set limits on what appears rational and reasonable, indeed on what appears sayable and thinkable.[48] This occurs *not* through imposition, but through creatively working on existing themes, desires and fears, and reworking them. Since the beliefs of people *are* contradictory and have tensions because they are what some have called polyvocal,[49] it is then possible to move people in directions where one would least expect given their position in society.

Thus, popular consciousness can be articulated to the right precisely because the feelings of hope and despair and the logic and language used to express these can be attached to a variety of discourses. Hence, a male worker who has lost his job can be antagonistic to the corporations who engaged in capital flight or can blame unions, people of colour or women 'who are taking men's jobs'. The response is *constructed*, not preordained, by the play of ideological forces in society at large.[50] And, though this construction occurs on a contradictory and contested terrain, it is the right that seems to have been more than a little successful in providing the discourse that organizes that terrain.

The politics of education

This emphasis on ideological construction, on the *politics* of culture and on the complicated relationship between the State and civil society during times of crises in accumulation and legitimation, provides the context of Roger Dale's analyses. For in order to understand the right's reconstruction of the role of the State, of the value of public *vs* private, and of what schools are for, we cannot simply say 'It's the natural working out of capitalism, isn't it? And once we understand the economic crisis, all else follows logically.'

This is an important point. Dale's work arises out of a movement that builds upon and yet rigorously criticizes classical Marxism, a movement that wishes to overcome the economism and reductionism that has played so strong a part in significant segments of Marxist approaches. Stuart Hall describes these economistic and reductive tendencies in the following way:

> By 'economism' I do not mean . . . to neglect the powerful role which the economic foundations of a social order or the dominant economic relations of a society play in shaping and structuring the whole edifice of social life. I mean, rather, a specific theoretical approach which tends to read the economic foundations of society as the *only* determining structure. This approach tends to see all other dimensions of the social formation as simply mirroring 'the economic' on another level of articulation, and as having no other determining or structuring force in their own right. The approach, to put it simply, reduces everything in the social formation to the economic level, and conceptualizes all other types of social relations as directly and immediately 'corresponding' to the economic. . . . It simplifies the structure of social formations, reducing their complexity of articulation, vertical and horizontal, to a single line of determination. It simplifies the very concept of 'determination' (which in Marx is actually a very complex idea) to that of a mechanical function. It flattens all·the mediations between the different levels of society. It presents social formations – in Althusser's words – as a 'simple expressive totality,' in which every level of articulation corresponds to every other, and which is from end to end, structurally transparent.[51]

In Gramsci's words, economism 'comes very cheap'. Not only is it theoretically problematic, but its political and practical utility is minimal,[52] especially when one is interested in the complicated politics involved in educational policy.

In traditional Marxist theory, by and large all important struggles are ultimately reduced to an industrial struggle. The difference between this and the one followed in Dale's and others' analysis of Thatcherism and the growth of the right is startling. Instead of a 'war of manoeuvre', we have a 'war of position' (if you will forgive the militaristic and masculinist metaphors) in which the various fronts of politics are multiplied. 'New institutions and new arenas of struggles [are brought] into the traditional conceptualization of the state and politics.' The objects of modern politics are now multi faceted – schooling, sexuality, race and ethnicity, the family, cultural institutions – and are no longer marginalized but brought to the fore in our attempt to understand how active consent is gained, how hegemony is won or lost in particular historical periods.[53]

Political and ideological struggles do not become pale reflections of the 'real' economic conflicts. They become constitutive in their own right and have real material effects. This realization becomes increasingly clear as one works through Dale's materials both here and elsewhere on education and the State.

There is a seemingly simple question that guides his initial inquiries. What differences does it make that schooling is largely provided by the State? Yet this is a deceptively simple question. Answering it requires that we also raise an entire array of prior issues. What is the State in the first place? What does the State itself do? Who controls it? Does the State stand alone, independently, or is it connected in some important ways to other aspects of the society, in particular the capitalist economy? Given all this, what is it that schooling itself does? Notice that, like the issue of 'Who benefits?', what started out as a relatively uncomplicated question – Does it make a difference that the provision of formal education is officially under the aegis of the State? – opens up a set of complications involving the nature of the economy, power relations within the State and between it and other aspects of the larger social formation, and an understanding of the social functions of the educational system.

These questions are rooted in a set of prior understandings and commitments, ones centred around the continuing struggle to democratize our institutions. While the answers of them are not and should not be preordained, what gives the questions their special significance here is Dale's very evident recognition of the constitutive conflicts and unequal power relations that are so much a part of this society.

In the earlier 'instrumentalist' theories that Dale wishes to go beyond, the State's primary role is to act as an agent of capital. In these theories, because of its connections to the structure of class relations and the economy, the State is, by its very nature, *necessarily* simply a reproducer of the conditions necessary for continued class domination. This occurs not only because of the interest of those groups of people who hold positions within the State. It occurs largely due to the fact that, structurally, the State has no other choice. The State is an 'arm of capital', one that is bound to do capital's bidding given the structuring of its resources, its interests and its place in the capitalist economy.[54]

For Dale, this is simply too limited; the State is seen as active, as having a multitude of 'functions' that are not reducible to economic 'necessities', and as being inherently contradictory.

The State here is no longer seen as only an administrative and coercive apparatus. It is seen as well as 'educative and formative'. It exercises moral and educative leadership and, in the process, attempts to justify the leadership of a new hegemonic bloc by gaining 'the *active consent* over those whom it rules',[55] something that is very visible in the current conservative restoration. Much of Dale's work is situated directly within the State's attempt both to provide such 'leadership' and to gain such 'active consent'.

One of the major elements in his work is his consistent ability to take these relatively abstract concerns about the role of the State and to apply them to unpack the causes and effects of educational policies on the ground, so to speak, during the conservative restoration. His analyses of TVEI, for example, or of the Tyndale affair, demonstrate how crucial aspects of the State actually operate. In this way, we are able to recognize how the varied functions of the State, in all their internal contradictions and complexities, work themselves out in practice. What makes such analyses so interesting is their joint focus – their contribution both at the level of theory and at the level of policy.

Dale is constantly using theory 'to illuminate concrete historical cases or political questions; or thinking large concepts in terms of their application to concrete and specific situations'.[56] Here, he follows a path clearly recognized by Antonio Gramsci, upon whose shoulders so much of the recent work on culture and the State in education stands. Like Gramsci, he realizes that the general framework of a Marxist theory is just that, a general theory. It is pitched at a level of abstraction in which the concepts give us insights into 'the broad processes which organize and structure the capitalist mode of production'. Yet, because of this, as soon as we move from the general to the specific, to a 'lower, more concrete, level of application', we need to apply new concepts and recognize the multiple sources of determination in each conjuncture. To think the concrete, we must understand that it consists 'in reality . . . of many determinations'.[57]

For Dale, in his earlier work on the State, the State's role was negative selection. That is, it was not necessarily geared towards winning approval for the status quo; rather, preventing rejection, 'checking the excesses', was what was needed to preserve hegemony. Now, however, it is clear that the right has altered this. The battle over ideology, the politics of common sense and the politics of acceptance, play a significant part in the maintenance of hegemonic control and the building of alliances to support it.

I have stressed the role of the State here because, as Dale so clearly documents in this volume, the key to understanding education as a state function is a recognition of the contradictory demands placed upon it. While not reducing all of the functions the State performs to those of supporting the capital accumulation process, guaranteeing a context for its continued expansion, and legitimizing the capitalist mode of production, including the role the State plays in it, Dale is clear that these three 'functions' provide the core problems the State must solve. Yet this will be very difficult. First, the core functions are contradictory. Often, responding to one set of demands makes it harder to respond to the others. Secondly, and just as importantly, the State itself is an arena of conflict. It is a site in which groups with decidedly different interests struggle over policies, goals, procedures, and personnel. Thus, state policy is always the result of multiple levels of conflicts and compromises that stem from and lead to contradictory outcomes.[58] It is no simple matter then to understand the genesis and effects of educational policy and practice.

His definition of and approach to the State, then, is much more subtle than what had existed prior to his work. This is best summarized in his own words:

> The state . . . is not a monolith, or the same as government, or merely the government's (or anybody else's) executive committee. It is a set of publicly financed institutions, neither separately nor collectively necessarily in harmony, confronted by certain basic problems deriving from its relationship with capitalism . . . , with one branch, the government, having responsibility for ensuring the continuing prominence of these problems on its agenda.

Thus, what goes even further to give Dale's work its distinctive flavour is his recognition that what occurs in schools – even as aspects of the state apparatus – is not simply the result of imposition, nor is it the 'natural' working out of capitalism's will on the educational system. The educational system may contribute to the 'achievement of those aims/needs/purposes of capitalism', but this is done 'through the medium of the solutions it constructs to deal with its various problems of internal order and control'. The results of this will as often be contradictory and unintended as they will be the straightforward reproduction of capitalism's economic and ideological 'needs'. 'Control of schools has proved remarkably difficult for any group to achieve' and the educational system has developed ways of mediating, 'in deliberate and unintended ways, the aspirations, policies, interventions, pressure, and so on of any and all groups'.

Dale then goes on to say that obviously:

> Control in schools is a necessary condition for the achievement of any purpose in education, but the attainment of that control is shaped not by the conscious reflection of any of these purposes but by the strategic and tactical responses of those employed in schools to the organizational problems confronting them. This is not to say that the aims and purposes of education are neglected in this process; rather they are part of the problem facing [us] and, in the course of their fulfillment in daily school life, they may be transformed.

All of this is correct it seems to me and its implications are more than a little telling on the claims of some of the more mechanistic theories of the political economy of schooling. For, rather than there being a simple correspondence between economic needs and what happens inside the school, 'the educational state apparatus (educational administration and schools) . . . has an independent effect on the pattern, process, and practice of education, an effect not irreducible to the demands of capital accumulation'.

This means that we must focus on the *relationship* between wider state policy and educational policy and practice as it is worked out on different levels within the educational apparatus and in the school itself. It also means we must focus not only on the economic, but on the *political* and on its own specificities and effectiveness. What are these changing relationships? How and why have they succeeded or failed? What have been their contradictory effects at multiple levels? These are the questions that Dale helps us answer.

His essay on 'Thatcherism and education' is a classic in this regard. By identifying the various groups that have been brought together into the uneasy and shifting alliance that forms the basis of Thatcherism – the 'industrial trainers', the 'old tories', the 'populists', the 'moral entrepreneurs' and the 'privatisers' – and showing how Mrs Thatcher herself is able to integrate these diverse elements under one umbrella, Dale highlights much of what has and will come to pass in education given the rightist agenda. His analysis parallels and expands the more general discussion I engaged in earlier in this chapter by demonstrating how legitimacy is actually won by changing the very terrain on which, and vocabularly in which, arguments about education are carried out.

For example, as he demonstrates, in the shift from a 'value-based' educational politics to a 'sense-based' politics, one sees a profound change in what education is for and who it serves. Rather than an educational policy that satisfies demands that have been won by the majority of people (demands that can no longer be easily met given the economic crisis in capitalist economies), we must 'shape and channel' demands 'so as to make them satisfiable'. That this new politics has been more than a little successful is documented in what Dale elsewhere (1988b) calls the change in the 'dominant vocabularies of motives' that have been institutionalized within the educational system. This vocabulary stresses 'the vocational rather than the academic, the instrumental rather than the expressive, the extrinsic rather than the intrinsic'. Rather than having to justify making our teaching and curricula vocationally relevant, we must justify *not* doing this. And 'this tends to be done not apologetically, as a regretful refusal of an invitation', as was often the case in the previous era of educational politics, 'but rather defiantly, as a principled refusal to comply with a requirement'.

These changes in the vocabularly of motives that dominate the debates over educational policies have had a significant impact on the daily life of education. By focusing on the State and then applying this focus to the concrete forming and working out of educational policies, Dale enables a clearer understanding of the effects of these policies on the lives of teachers, for example.

His analysis of teachers as state employees points out what is happening to teaching as it becomes more tightly controlled. The distinction he makes between *licensed autonomy* and *regulated autonomy* demonstrates the shift towards greater governmental scrutiny. As he puts it:

Currently, we are witnessing strenuous efforts to impose greater central control on the educational system, to impose some kind of bureaucratic/ technology form(s) on teachers as state employees. Exactly what form(s) are put forward will be dependent on the outcomes of the struggles between 'the bureaucrats' and 'the technocrats' within the state apparatus . . . and of the nature and effectiveness of the teaching profession's resistance to them. . . .

[Teachers have had] relative autonomy in respect only of the execution of the work of education systems. Teacher autonomy does not extend to deciding the goals of education systems, nor their level of funding; though it had undoubted (but fluctuating) influence in such matters, the teaching profession has no control over them. This is clearly exemplified in the case of spending cuts. These are always resisted by the teaching profession, but scarcely ever successfully. So, while he who pays the piper always in the end calls the tune, he can specify more or less broadly what kind of tune he wants, but only with far greater difficulty exactly how it should be played. Under 'licensed autonomy' the teaching profession was given what amounted to a negative programme by the paymaster – 'play anything you like but Russian music and folk songs.' Under 'regulated autonomy' the requirement is much more positive – 'play only modern German music, as far as possible just like the Germans do it – and we'll be listening to make sure you do.'

Thus, the fiscal crisis of the State, conflicts *within* the State, and the relative strength of organized bodies of teachers are constitutive of what educational policies are actually produced and how they are implemented. This is not a simple story and it cannot be told in all its complexity through old economistic formula that ignore the complicated dynamics involved in authoritarian populism.

While his discussion of changes in how the State operates in legitimating both itself and its new policies and in dramatically altering the conditions of teachers' work are very insightful, Dale does not stop here, however.

Too often, those who have been interested in the nature of the political, in how power works (in this case state policy), have employed a top down perspective, in essence saying 'Here is how the State imposes its will on others.' For Dale, this is simply insufficient not only on the conceptual grounds I noted earlier, but on empirical grounds as well. He refuses to see either schools or the teachers who work in them as passive followers of policies laid down from above. Conflict, compromise, mediation, the uses of state policies for one's own interests that may be different from those envisioned by state policy makers; all signify anything but passive acquiescence.

In his discussion of the Technical and Vocational Education Initiative (TVEI), this point of view is clear. TVEI was not simply accepted as is, but was negotiated in complicated ways, its negative affects minimized, its positive possibilities heightened, at a local level. As Dale puts it in Chapter 9:

> The main point is that whatever the orientation toward TVEI, however significant the various conditions of negotiation may be, TVEI is never merely imposed on schools. It is always accepted on certain implicit or explicit conditions based largely on the existing history, ideology, structure and location of the school, to produce a TVEI effect unique to that school.

Dale is not a romantic here, though. He recognizes, in much the same way as he did in his discussion of the changes in teachers' autonomy, that such 'uniqueness' is indeed limited: it is 'constrained'. This is clear in his conclusion to the same chapter:

> I have argued here that although TVEI varies immensely across authorities and schools, it does not vary infinitely. The variations are constrained by the origins of the initiative, the problems it was created to solve. These led to it taking on a particular broad structure and ideology, both of which allowed a very wide range of local variation. The nature and extent of that variation are shaped in the schools into their unique TVEI effect by their own history and the conditions under which TVEI was accepted into the schools. In the end, although it was changed or even transformed by TVEI, the surest guide to understanding TVEI in a school is what the school was like before.

Even though Dale's remarks are tied to one specific initiative, they are not inconsequential at the more general level of theory and politics. They point to a much more interactive approach, one that is considerably less functionalist than most approaches. By opening a space for specificity and for the agency of local schools and teachers, Dale restores history and contingency to the analysis of state policy. And by demonstrating the multiple interests at work and the conflicts that might ensue because of this, he provides new insights into the micro- as well as macro-politics of education.

One further example, taken from material not included in this volume, shows how the restoration of agency can yield insights that can transform our usual ways of understanding how the state functions. Here he applies this perspective to teachers and bureaucratic structures, demonstrating the impoverishment of those Marxist theories of the State in education that see teachers simply as automatons who passively follow the needs of the State under capitalism:

> Teachers are not merely 'state functionaries' but do have some degree of autonomy, and [this] autonomy will not necessarily be used to further

the proclaimed ends of the state apparatus. Rather than those who work there fitting themselves to the requirements of the institution, there are a number of very important ways in which the institution has to take account of the interests of the employees and fit itself to them. It is here, for instance, that we may begin to look for the sources of the alleged inertia of educational systems and schools, that is to say what appears as inertia is not some immutable characteristic of bureaucracies but is due to various groups within them having more immediate interests than the pursuit of the organization's goals.[59]

Thus, on the ground, the state policy that is actually enacted may be strikingly different than that originally envisioned, not because teachers and others are 'conservative' by nature or some other simple explanation, but precisely because they do have historically specific interests that construct the local situation. Results, hence, are never preordained, are always constructed, are not easily imposed, even given the changing conditions of teacher's autonomy and an increasingly interventionist and rightist policy when it comes to curricula and the goals of education.

These arguments become very important in my own work, published in *Teachers and Texts* (1986), on the relationship between gender and class in teaching and curriculum control. Dale's claim that we should look to the interests of teachers – not look at them as 'state functionaries' but as agents who have real and material historical effects – was one of the arguments that led me to think more carefully about the fact that elementary school teaching has historically been constructed as largely 'women's work'. Most commentators on curriculum reform had argued that elementary teachers were, by their very nature, conservative. Teachers often simply rejected 'suggestions' or mandates from above, even when these new curriculum programmes were massively funded and pressure to employ them was intense. This, for the commentators, was not a good thing. Teachers were standing in the way of 'reform', 'more effective and efficient curricula', and 'progress'. As numerous studies had shown in the United States, for instance, when the disciplinary oriented 'new' maths and 'new' science material was introduced into schools – much of it in the form of prepackaged kits – it was not unusual for it to be taught in much the same manner as the 'old' maths and science. It was altered so that it fitted into the existing regularities of the school and into the prior practices that had often proven successful in teaching.

Using the general approach urged on us by Dale, it is wiser to see this not merely as the result of a bureaucracy that is slow to change or a group of consistently conservative teachers; rather, it is perhaps more helpful to think of it more structurally in terms of labour process and gender. The supposed immobility of the institution, its lack of significant change in the face of the onslaught of such curriculum material, is tied in important ways to the interests and resistances of a female workforce against external incursions into the practices they had evolved over years of labour and over years of struggle to gain recognition of, and respect for, their skills. It is in fact more than a little similar to the history of ways in which other women employees in the State and industry have acted during other attempts to take control of their labour and daily lives.[60]

While Dale does not himself highlight these questions of gender and labour, it would have been much more difficult for those of us interested in the critically important conflicts between teachers and a State that is increasingly interventionist at the level of their practice without having benefited from his analyses of possible contradictory interests within the State itself.

In fact, on a more general level, our understanding of all of these themes – contradictory interests, conflicts, the actual formation and effects of state policies, and the responses of living, breathing actors to these initiatives – would not have been nearly as advanced had Roger Dale not helped us to see more clearly how significant they are. In a time when the rightist reconstruction has such damaging effects on the lives and futures of so many people inside and outside of education, such understanding is of even greater consequence. While struggles over state educational policies and over their effects in schools will not by themselves make the latest initiatives 'melt away', we can be certain that the politics of education at all levels provides one crucial arena in which the struggle for a democratized economy, a democratized culture and a democratized polity, will be carried out. A close reading of the chapters which follow provides ample evidence of the power of the political. We ignore it at our risk.

Notes

1. Quoted in Lash, S. and Urry, J. (1987). *The End of Organized Capitalism*, p. 1. Madison: University of Wisconsin Press.
2. See, for example, Bowles, S. and Gintis, H. (1976). *Schooling in Capitalist America*. New York: Basic Books.
3. Apple, M.W. (1979). *Ideology and Curriculum*. London: Routledge and Kegan Paul; and Bourdieu, P. and Passeron, J.C. (1977). *Reproduction in Education, Society and Culture*. London: Sage.
4. See, for example, Hogan, D. (1982). Education and class formation. In Apple, M.W. (ed.), *Cultural and Economic Reproduction in Education*. London: Routledge and Kegan Paul; Bernstein, B. (1977). *Class, Codes and Control*, Vol. 3. London: Routledge and Kegan Paul; and Willis, P. (1977). *Learning to Labour*. Westmead: Saxon House.
5. The work of Madeleine Arnot is essential here. See also Apple, M.W. (1986). *Teachers and Texts*. London: Routledge and Kegan Paul; Omi, M. and Winant, H. (1986). *Racial Formation in the United States*. London: Routledge and Kegan Paul; and McCarthy, C. and Apple, M.W. (1988). Class, race and gender in American educational research. In Weis, L. (ed.), *Class, Race and Gender in American Education*. Albany: State University of New York Press.
6. See Apple, M.W. (1982). *Education and Power*. London: Routledge and Kegan Paul; and Apple, M.W. and Weis, L. (eds) (1983). *Ideology and Practice in Schooling*. Philadelphia: Temple University Press.
7. See Carnoy, M. and Levin, H. (1985). *Schooling and Work in the Democratic State*.

Stanford: Stanford University Press; and my reply to them in Apple, M.W. (1986). Bringing the economy back in to educational theory. *Educational Theory*, **36** 403–415.

8. Shor, I. (1986). *Culture Wars*. London: Routledge and Kegan Paul.
9. Horne, D. (1986). *The Public Culture*. London: Pluto Press.
10. Hall, S. (1988). The toad in the garden: Thatcherism among the theorists. In Nelson, C. and Grossberg, L. (eds), *Marxism and the Intepretation of Culture*, p. 42. Urbana; Ill.: University of Illinois Press.
11. Ibid.
12. Apple, M.W. (1982). *Education and Power*; and Apple, M.W. (1986). *Teachers and Texts*.
13. Gintis, H. (1980). Communication and politics. *Socialist Review*, **10**, 193.
14. Ibid., p. 194. See also Bowles, S. and Gintis, H. (1986). *Democracy and Capitalism*. New York: Basic Books.
15. Apple, M.W. (1986). *Teachers and Texts*.
16. Anderson, M. (1985). *Teachers Unions and Industrial Politics* (unpublished doctoral thesis), pp. 6–8. School of Behavioral Sciences, Macquarie University, Sydney.
17. Bastian, A., Fruchter, N., Gittell, M., Greer, C. and Haskins, K. (1986). *Choosing Equality: The Case for Democratic Schooling*, p. 14. Philadelphia: Temple University Press.
18. I wish to thank my colleague Walter Secada for his comments on this point.
19. Apple, M.W. (1986). National reports and the construction of inequality. *British Journal of Sociology of Education*, **7**(2), 171–90.
20. Apple, M.W. (1979). *Ideology and Curriculum*; and Larrain, J. (1983). *Marxism and Ideology*. Atlantic Highlands, N.J.: Humanities Press.
21. Hall, S. (1985). Authoritarian populism: A reply. *New Left Review*, **15**, 122.
22. See Clark, D. and Astuto, T. (1985). The significance and permanence of changes in federal educational policy. *Educational Researcher*, **15**, 4–13; Piven, F. and Cloward, R. (1982). *The New Class War*. New York: Pantheon; and Raskin, M. (1986). *The Common Good*. London: Routledge and Kegan Paul.

   Clark and Astuto point out that during the current Reagan term, the following initiatives have characterized its educational policies: reducing the federal role in education, stimulating competition among schools with the aim of 'breaking the monopoly of the public school', fostering individual competition so that 'excellence' is gained, increasing the reliance on performance standards for students and teachers, an emphasis on the 'basics' in content, increasing parental choice 'over what, where, and how their children learn', strengthening the teaching of 'traditional values' in schools, and expanding the policy of transferring educational authority to the state and local levels (p. 8). There will be, of course, some differences here between the U.S. and Britain, but the overall tendencies remain the same.

23. Hall, S. and Jacques, M. (1983). Introduction. In Hall, S. and Jacques, M. (eds), *The Politics of Thatcherism*, p. 13. London: Lawrence and Wishart.
24. Hall, S. (1980). Popular democratic vs. authoritarian populism: Two ways of taking democracy seriously. In Hunt, A. (ed.), *Marxism and Democracy*, pp. 160–161. London: Lawrence and Wishart.
25. Ibid., p. 161.
26. I realize that there is a debate about the adequacy of this term. See Hall, S. (1985). *New Left Review*, **151**; and Jessop, B., Bonnett, K., Bromley, S. and Ling, T. (1984). Authoritarian populism, two nations, and Thatcherism. *New Left Review*, **147**, 33–60.
27. Omi, M. and Winant, H. (1986). *Racial Formation in the United States*, p. 214.
28. Burnham, W.D. (1983). Post-conservative America. *Socialist Review*, **13**, 125.

29. Hall, S. (1985). *New Left Review*, **151**, 117.
30. Ibid., p. 119.
31. Hall, S. (1980). In Hunt, A. (ed.), *Marxism and Democracy*, p. 166.
32. Hall, S. (1988). In Nelson, C. and Grossberg, L. (eds), *Marxism and the Interpretation of Culture*, p. 55.
33. Hall, S. (1983). The great moving right show. In Hall, S. and Jacques, M. (eds), *The Politics of Thatcherism*, pp. 19–39.
34. Apple, M.W. (1982). *Education and Power*.
35. Hall, S. (1983). In Hall, S. and Jacques, M. (eds), *The Politics of Thatcherism*, pp. 29–30.
36. Ibid., pp. 36–37. For an illuminating picture of how these issues are manipulated by powerful groups, see Hunter, A. (1984). *Virtue with a Vengeance: The Pro-family Politics of the New Right* (unpublished doctoral thesis). Department of Sociology, Brandeis University, Waltham.
37. Apple, M.W. (1986). *Teachers and Texts*.
38. Hunter, A. (1987). The politics of resentment and the construction of middle America (unpublished paper), p. 23. American Institutions Program, University of Wisconsin, Madison.
39. Ibid., p. 30.
40. Ibid., p. 33.
41. Ibid., p. 34.
42. Ibid., p. 21.
43. Ibid., p. 17.
44. See Apple, M.W. (1986). *British Journal of Sociology of Education*, **7**(2); and Apple, M.W. (1986). *Teachers and Texts*.
45. Hall, S. (1986). Popular culture and the state. In Bennett, T., Mercer, C. and Woollacott, J. (eds), *Popular Culture and Social Relations*, pp. 35–6. Milton Keynes: The Open University Press.
46. Hall, S. (1988). The toad in the garden. In Nelson, P. and Grossberg, L. (eds), *Marxism and the Interpretation of Culture*, p. 40. Urbana; Ill.: University of Illinois Press.
47. Ibid., p. 45.
48. Ibid.
49. Mouffe, C. (1988). Hegemony and new political subjects: Toward a new concept of democracy. In Nelson, C. and Grossberg, L. (eds), *Marxism and the Interpretation of Culture*, p. 96.
50. Ibid.
51. Hall, S. (1986). Gramsci's relevance for the study of race and ethnicity. *Journal of Communication Inquiry*, **10**, 10.
52. Ibid., p. 11.
53. Ibid., pp. 19–20.
54. For a review of theories of the state, see Carnoy, M. (1984). *The State and Political Theory*. Princeton: Princeton University Press.
55. Hall, S. (1986). *Journal of Communication Inquiry*, **10**, 19.
56. Ibid., p. 7.
57. Ibid.
58. See Apple, M.W. (1988). Social crisis and curriculum accords. *Educational Theory*, **38**, 191–201.
59. See Chapter 3.
60. This is argued in considerably more detail in Apple, M.W. (1986). *Teachers and Texts*.

PART 1

The State and Education

1 Education and the Capitalist State: Contributions and Contradictions

The State in the sociology of education

Given all that sociologists, economists and political scientists have had to say about the meanings and assumptions, the processes and practices, the functions and outcomes, of education systems in recent years, it is really very surprising to find almost no analysis of the implications of State provision, irrespective of the particular approach adopted. It seems that both for sociologists and economists of education who effectively ignore, and for those political scientists who study, the inner workings of the 'education sub government', the State is regarded as an effectively neutral means of delivery of intended outcomes decided elsewhere; the sociologists and economists have concentrated on revealing the intended outcomes, while the political scientists have looked for organizational obstructions to the achievements of those outcomes. The State is, then, put in the position that teachers were put in in much early curriculum reform work – it is assumed to be unable to contribute anything of its own (and it is undesirable that it should do so) to the achievement of desired outcomes, but it may unwittingly interfere with it; the best that can be hoped for of the State (or of the teacher) is that it will remain as neutral a conduit as possible for the achievement of outcomes decided elsewhere.

Consider, briefly, the three major approaches to the sociology of education over the last decade or so, broadly the structural–functionalist approach, the 'new' sociology of education and the political economy of education. In none of them is the fact of state provision taken as anything more than marginal and in most work they have generated it is ignored. The first, with its assumptions of consensus and integration and its focus (post-Sputnik) on the technological contributions of education to the economy, implicitly relegated everything that happened between input to and output from the education system to 'black box' status. This omission was partly repaired by the 'new' sociology of education, with its concentration on the content of schooling and on how particular conceptions of reality were constructed and sustained in schools and classrooms. The State, though, still remained in the black box, and so it did, more surprisingly, in the political economy critique of the new sociology. This stressed the neglect of conceptions of power and structure in the 'new' sociology of education, but leap-frogged the fact of state provision and went directly to the needs of the capitalist system, again implicitly marginalizing and neutralizing the importance of state provision, even though it is never clear quite how the needs of the capitalist system are conveyed to and met in each school and classroom.

On the other hand, writers who do make the State the focus of their interest have normally paid little attention to education. This applies as much to the contributors to the recent resurgence of interest in Marxist theories of the State (though I shall be attempting to extract implications for education from some of them below) as it does to mainstream political science. There are, though, exceptions in both approaches which it will be instructive to consider. One Marxist exception is Althusser's ISA (Ideological State Apparatuses) essay (Althusser, 1971). In this, education is seen as the key ideological state apparatus in the reproduction of the capitalist mode of production. The particular conception of a state apparatus which Althusser holds, however, is not one which permits increased understanding of the implications of state provision of education. For, as Laclau (1977: 68–9) has pointed out, 'implicit in the conception of ideological state apparatuses there lies a conception of the State which entirely ceases to consider it as an institution . . .' (for Althusser) '*everything* which serves to maintain the cohesion of a social formation forms part of the State. In that case . . . the State must simply be a *quality* which pervades all the levels of a social formation' [emphasis in original]. Trying to explain education systems through analysing them as Althusserian ISAs, then, is not much different from explaining education solely or pre-eminently as a form of social control, in both its question-begging and its negativity.

Those political scientists who have focused on education have confined their studies very much to education politics rather than the politics of education.[1] By this I mean that they have concentrated much more on studying the effectiveness of education systems and forms of education government in achieving goals presented to them, rather than on the relationship between the production of goals and the form of their achievement. To put it another way, political questions are bracketed out and replaced by questions about processes of decision making; politics are reduced to administration. The focus is on the machinery, rather than on what powers it, or how and where it is directed.

The approach I intend to adopt to the analysis of the relationship of the State and education may perhaps be inferred broadly from the two preceding paragraphs. What is not clear is why such an analysis is worthwhile. After all, may it not be the case that there are very good reasons for the relative neglect of the State in analyses of education? Could it be that it really does not make any difference?

There are two broad justifications. First, I hope to demonstrate below that the approach I am advocating can *explain* patterns, policies and processes of education in capitalist societies more adequately than existing approaches. As has been suggested many times before, macro and micro approaches are mutually blind. One attempts to explain all education systems on the basis of a single principle – system integration, or the capitalist mode of production, or whatever – and the other seeks to achieve understanding through the continuing assembly of detailed studies of schools or classrooms. The one can explain everything in general, but nothing in particular, the other can explain everything in particular, but nothing in general. Just as importantly, their explanations are neither complementary nor overlapping. There are areas of problems to which neither speaks effectively. Among these areas is one of the most important tasks for the sociology of education, that of understanding the source and nature of educational stability and change.

The second justification for an approach concentrated on the role of the State, then, is that it permits questioning in this area. The political economy approach of Bowles and Gintis (1976), for instance, is able to produce few strategies for bringing about change, short of (working towards) a revolutionary overthrow of capitalism, largely because it has little place for politics. Crudely, the schools are regarded, implicitly, as being directly controlled by the needs of capitalist accumulation, and hence it is only by changing that that we can change what goes on in schools. Why the needs of capitalist accumulation are expressed in such different forms in different social formations, and the implications of this for a politics of education that could reveal some levers of educational change, are never made clear. On the other side, micro studies which insulate schools from society are equally unable to indicate the source and nature of the control over even the schools they study, and which it would be crucial to establish before bringing about any change in them. Focusing on the source and nature of control over education and schools entails focusing on the immediate provider of education, the State, and it is in the analysis of the State that we may begin to understand the assumptions, intentions and outcomes of various strategies of educational change.

The nature of the capitalist State

It will be my argument in this section that the most important consequence of focusing on state provision of education is that it enables us to see that the basic problems facing education systems in capitalist countries derive from the problems of the capitalist State. Before attempting to indicate what those problems might be and how they might contribute to an agenda for education, however, I should make clear two limitations on this discussion. First, in arguing that the problems of the capitalist State derive from its relationship to the maintenance and reproduction of the capitalist mode of production, I do not make the assumption that all state activity derives from this relationship. Rather, I take here Gramsci's point that 'The democratic–bureaucratic system has given rise to a great mass of functions which are not at all necessitated by the social necessities of production, though they are justified by the political necessities of the dominant fundamental group' (Gramsci, 1971:13). Secondly, I do not intend to suggest that everything that goes on in schools is explained by, or related to, the problems of the capitalist State. The questions raised by both of these areas are very important and they are discussed as refinements to the central thesis in later sections.

It is probably true to say that the dominant conception of the State in political sociology sees it as a neutral means of distributing social goods among competing groups or élites on the basis of their relative strength and effectiveness. This approach has been subjected to increasing criticism in recent years from resurgent Marxist work on the theory of the State.[2] The first line of criticism came through the instrumentalist approach chiefly associated with the name of Ralph Miliband. As he puts it (Miliband, 1968: 31):

> What is wrong with pluralist-democratic theory is not its insistence on the fact of competition but its claim (very often its implicit assumption) that the major organized 'interests' in (advanced capitalist) societies, and notably capital and labour, compete on more or less equal terms, and that none of them is therefore able to achieve a decisive and permanent advantage in the process of competition. This is where ideology enters and turns observation into myth . . . business, particularly large scale business (enjoys) such an advantage *inside* the state system, by virtue of the composition and ideological inclinations of the state elite . . . [and] enjoys a massive superiority outside the state system as well, in terms of the immensely stronger pressures which, as compared with labour and any other interest, it is able to exercise in the pursuit of its purposes.

State activity then, is not neutral, but is the result of the state apparatus being taken over by, and used, as the instrument of the ruling class. However, Miliband does not move beyond the democratic élite theorists except by showing that they make the wrong assumptions about who controls the State and how. The State is still conceived as a neutral instrument, with the nature of the policies it follows decided by the desires of those who control it. Moreover, as David Hogan (1979) pointed out, the functions of institutions cannot be 'read off' from an analysis of who controls them. This is basic to the critique which suggests that the functions of the State in capitalist societies are given not by the direct control of capitalists or capitalist sympathizers within the state apparatus, but are in fact objectively given by the imperatives of the maintenance and reproduction of the conditions of existence of the capitalist mode of production.

It is important to examine this approach in a little greater depth, since its implications for an analysis of education which starts from the view that the dominant problematic for education systems derives from their states' problematic, are of clear and central importance. It is necessary initially to try to settle difficulties associated with the term 'function'. It is not clear, for instance, when the functions of the education system are referred to, whether 'function' is being used teleologically, in the sense of the *purposes* of the education system, or descriptively, in setting out what the education system does. The approach I wish to adopt excludes both those uses of the term, the former use because that way of asking questions about education systems prespecifies one set of answers and precludes others *a priori*, the latter because understanding and explaining education systems (or anything else) entails more than merely cataloguing what they do. The procedure I intend to adopt is to identify what I will call 'core problems' of the capitalist State as a whole and of education systems in capitalist States. This does not involve any prejudgement about their relative prominence on the agenda of any particular state apparatus, nor of how, or how effectively, they will be dealt with. It does involve a conception of the capitalist mode of production, and the positing of a particular kind of relationship between the State and the capitalist mode of production in those social formations where the capitalist mode of production is dominant, such that those core problems are permanently insoluble and permanently on the agenda of the state apparatus (without, again, specifying their relative importance, or claiming that they exhaust the activity of state apparatus). The point of this approach is to lay down non-arbitrary priorities and guidelines for the analysis of education systems.

Briefly, then, all modes of production have a number of basic conditions of existence, but in the capitalist mode of production, capital cannot by its own efforts provide or secure the conditions of its existence or reproduction. At one level, the nature of the necessary 'rules of the game', the whole legal framework of contract and property, the guarantee of money, can be neither provided nor guaranteed by capital, since those rules have to be specified by a disinterested party with the power to enforce them. At another level, the existence and reproduction of the mode of production which generates both competitors and antagonists has to be protected from attacks both internal and external to the social formation in which it is (assumed) dominant. And thirdly, individual capitals are not only highly mutually competitive, but also largely confined within particular economic sectors whose separate conditions of optimum existence may conflict with those of others. As Offe puts it, drawing on Rosa Luxemburg, 'Simply stated, the irrational limitation of individual capitals concerning their particularized and short-term realization interests prevents "long-term planning of the conditions for the survival and expansion of the capitalist mode of production".' Hence there has become established within the framework of the state apparatus:

> the logic of the compensatory plugging of functional holes which, in the capitalist accumulation process, are the result of the irrational limitation of individual capitals and the pressure to compete. Individual capitals

thus endanger the unbroken continuity of this process, whose 'anarchic' character precludes correction by genuinely capitalist mechanisms (accumulation and competition). It is inevitable, therefore, that eventually a 'high authority' has to step in (i.e. through the use of public power). (Offe, 1975a: 103–104)

It is possible, then, to derive from this analysis a list of 'core problems for the capitalist State' which it can then be assumed will be on the agenda of all state apparatus and institutions including the education system. However, (a) drawing up a list of the core problems of the capitalist State does not exhaust the contribution of the kind of political sociological analysis of the State I am suggesting, as I hope to demonstrate in the following sections, and (b) there are a number of qualifications to be made before the value of isolating 'core problems for education systems' can be realized and, indeed, to prevent such an approach becoming sterile, mechanical and counterproductive.

It will be useful to outline what seem to be the core problems for the capitalist State and then to see the ways in which these raw concepts have to be refined for effective use to be made of them. I would suggest that three broad core problems can be isolated:

- support of the capital accumulation process;
- guaranteeing a context for its continued expansion;
- the legitimation of the capitalist mode of production, including the State's own part in it.

The isolation of these three problems is relatively arbitrary, and relatively unimportant in that the analytic approach being put forward is not dependent on their close and unambiguous definition.

What qualifications and refinements have to be made? First, *specifications* of the problems facing the State in any particular social formation cannot be laid down theoretically in advance; they do not always appear in the same form. They have to be extracted through an analysis of each separate social formation. Therborn (1978: 163) outlines a useful approach to this when he notes:

The ability of a particular bourgeoisie (or fraction thereof) to hold state power is . . . structurally determined by: (1) the state reached by capitalism in the society in which it functions; (2) the central or peripheral position, and the advanced or retarded stage of the capital it represents, as well as the expansion, crisis or contraction of international capitalism as a whole; (3) the manner in which its relations to feudalism and petty commodity production, as well as its own internal cleavages, have historically evolved and currently manifest themselves in the given constellation of forces; and (4) the international conjuncture facing the ·social formation – the peculiar strengths and weaknesses of the latter within the international configuration of harmonious or conflicting forces.

Thus, for instance, the common problem of supporting the process of capital accumulation will present itself in very different forms, not only between social formations but within them as well. The range of assumptions made about whether, how and why education should contribute to 'economic growth' illustrates this in one narrow area.

Secondly, identifying the core problems of the capitalist State does not entail identifying the particular means by which they will be tackled. Neither does such identification imply that the state apparatus as a whole is well attuned to overcoming the problems, nor that the machinery available in any given social formation is especially relevant to tackling them in the form they manifest in a particular conjuncture. We should note, too, that the State is not a monolith; there are differences within and between its various apparatuses in their prioritizing of demands made on them and in their ability to meet those demands.

Thirdly, the state policy makers do not possess perfect knowledge of the State's needs or of how to meet them, through education or any other means at their disposal. Even if the need to 'plug' a particular 'functional hole' were rather obvious, the implications for any particular state apparatus are by no means necessarily equally obvious, nor is it necessarily obvious that any particular state apparatus can contribute to their 'plugging'. This again will be dependent in part on the historical evolution of particular state apparatuses, and what it is supposed they can achieve.

Fourthly, even where a particular programme may be designed to meet a particular demand, there is no guarantee that it will be possible to implement it. Offe (1973, 1975b) points to two reasons for this. First, he argues, there is no adequate model of internal structure of the organizational form for meeting the demands made of the capitalist state. The three possible models he discusses each contain a specific contradiction: the bureaucratic is 'wasteful at best and ineffective at worst and thus *insufficient* as a model for productive state activity; the purposive-rational may be both efficient and effective in itself, but its application requires interference with the prerogatives of the private accumulation process, the resistance to which on the part of the accumulating units makes its application impossible', while participating models 'tend to crystallize conflict and protest and can thus easily become *subversive* of the balance between the state and the accumulation process' (Offe, 1975b:143). More generally, there is a 'structural discrepancy' between abstract, surplus-value related functions of state support of the capitalist order and the concrete use-value related forms such support takes; the introduction of this alien, parasitic, yet crucial element potentially threatens the whole accumulation process at the same time as it preserves and defends it. For, as Offe puts it:

> No 'higher insight' can *a priori* guarantee that recourse to the state as a steering mechanism will not simultaneously reinforce the state's capa-

city of acting as a relatively self-autonomous 'alien element'. The question that remains unanswered, left solely open to contingencies, is whether the intervention of any 'separate' sector of the State to counteract the functional gaps arising in the market-controlled capital accumulation process will, in the long term, serve to stabilize or jeopardize this process. (Offe, 1973: 111)

Fifthly, as has been repeatedly stated, the core problems do not account for everything either the State or the education system does. This may in part be linked to the difficulties of specification and execution just mentioned. In this situation, Offe argues:

> there is a very real possibility that in order to retain their capacity of control (derived from political power and legitimacy) the state agencies will feel compelled to block the purpose of use value production strictly complementary to capital accumulation by giving in to the claims which emerge merely from party competition and political conflict, but in no way directly result from the actual requirements of capital accumulation itself. (Offe, 1973: 115)

Those views bring us back a little closer to earth and introduce a sixth and perhaps the most important qualification about a core problems approach. This is that there is no place in it for any opposition or resistance. It implies not only a smooth identification of problems based on omniscience of state functionaries but also a conflict-free implementation of solutions through the thorough confidence in them of everyone involved. Just as we have seen that identification is exceptionally difficult, so we should recall that the State we are discussing is a class State, that the problems identified for it are to be settled in pursuance of the maintenance of class rule and that in a class society this has necessary repercussions for the subject class, which it is likely to resist. Indeed, the continuing subjection of that class is one of the problems of the capitalist State. Opposition, then, not support, must be expected and a major part of state policy is concerned with dealing with that opposition in one way or another.

Finally, and equally importantly, is the assumption that because all the problems are related to the same overall purpose, their solutions must be complementary with each other; they are, in fact, mutually contradictory. The central contradiction is, of course, that while the capitalist mode of production is driven by the creation (through the universalization of the commodity form) and realization of surplus value, the conditions for its success and reproduction can only be guaranteed through the extraction of some part of that surplus value by the State and its diversion into non-commodity forms. This creates a central tension between State and capital. Beyond this, we have seen that the provision of the conditions of capital accumulation are not monolithic, but varied. However, the most important point is that they are not merely varied but mutually contradictory. The contradictions involved in tackling the core problems of the State are seen as intrinsic and incapable of permanent solution. Developments in one area inevitably require changes in the other areas, but cannot provide or sustain the means of such changes. At one level this leads to a 'fiscal crisis of the State' (O'Connor, 1973) where the ever-increasing level of state expenditure in absolute terms becomes ever less tolerable to capital, but also where the proportion of occupational activity involved in surplus value creation (from which state spending is financed) is failing to a point where it will be impossible to maintain existing levels of state expenditure. So, while capital is increasingly dependent on the State for maintaining and improving the conditions for capital accumulation – Keynesian remedies are the obvious example – those very remedies themselves set up not only fiscal, but also wider political and legitimatory requirements. For instance, such state intervention has the effect of making unemployment not a 'natural' phenomenon, but one which is infinitely adjustable by state intervention and hence a crucial political matter, whereby levels of employment are decided as much on political as economic criteria. Such strains are not avoidable but are intrinsic to the system; and this creates obvious legitimation problems.

Rather similar is the whole Welfare State apparatus, which gave capitalism a much more human face, and by demonstrating that it (capitalism) could care for all its dependants, enabled the State to preserve a context amenable to capital accumulation. However, the maintenance and increase of the benefits of the Welfare State became major political matters, throwing immense strain on the process of surplus value creation to provide the means for it to continue delivering the goods, and on the legitimation mechanisms to make up for any shortfall of such delivery. The point is that the State does not have at its disposal the means of quickly and cleanly cauterizing these contradictions. They can only be solved in ways that lay the seeds of further contradictions. Thus 'buying loyalty' in various ways is fine but the price keeps going up as privileges become rights; creating mechanisms to disguise the nature of the state activity is fine, but there is the danger that they will come to be taken at their word. ('Education for personal development' is one of the best examples of this.)

The problems faced by the State overall are writ small in the education system. It may be required to find solutions in all three core problem areas simultaneously and it is unable to do so. In education as elsewhere, these solutions are often mutually contradictory.

For instance, the basic question of whether the *process* or the *context* of accumulation is to receive priority treatment, reverberates through education policy. The process argument calls for an élitist system of education, devoted to the early recognition and fostering of 'ability' and its processing through a largely 'instrumental' curriculum. Such a policy clearly has enormous implications for several of the 'basic myths' which comprise the legitimating function of the State and of the education system in particular. But legitimation is achieved not only through the rhetoric, but through the practice of the education system, and the fundamental changes which such an élitist policy would entail would represent a major threat to education continuing to legitimate the system successfully.

It is hardly necessary in order to make the point about contradiction to spell out the consequences of a policy which took an opposite line, i.e. one which sought to strengthen the *context* of accumulation by, for instance, adding more substance to the rhetoric of, say, educational equality, by applying itself to achieving equality of educational outcomes rather than equality of educational opportunity.

Such contradictions are to be found at all levels of the education system, not just at the policy-making level. Controversies over such issues as streaming represent in part a reflection of the existence and mutual contradictoriness of the various demands made on education. So too, do arguments over the optimum content of education. In so far as they define the shifting parameters of the structural context within which schools operate, their mutual contradictoriness even becomes evident, and important, at the level of the classroom (Dale, 1977). It is particularly at times of major crisis of accumulation, which set up reverberations throughout the whole state apparatus, that the intrinsic mutual contradictoriness of the various demands of education becomes clear; at other times it may remain muted, seem non-existent. However, all the time, the existence of these contradictions, reflecting contradictions in the capitalist State, provides a major dynamic in education systems. Moves to meet one demand inhibit moves to meet another, not just because of limited budgets, but because the three core problems identified above are intrinsically mutually contradictory (as well as being, as Offe argues, jointly contradictory with surplus value production and realization).

This recognition of the contradictory nature of the demands on education is quite crucial to any adequate explanation of it. Isolating a single dominant requirement not only impoverishes the study of education systems by failing to provide a comprehensive account of their work, but the account it does provide of the particular highlighted feature cannot be adequate even of that feature in isolation if we recognize that the various demands on the education system take their character at least in part from their relationships to other demands on it. But not only are 'single dominant function' explanations of education systems separately inadequate, it is not sufficient either merely to aggregate them, to establish that education does have a number of, albeit overlapping, different functions. In order to understand why education systems are as they are, we have to understand the *relationship* between the ways they tackle the various problems confronting them, and that I have argued, is a relationship of contradiction.

Education as a state apparatus

A major emphasis in the foregoing section was on the relative autonomy of the education state apparatus. While it was suggested that certain core problems were permanent features of its agenda, it was also stressed that this did not either guarantee their prominence on that agenda, or stipulate the means by which they would be tackled. Though recognizing the existence of the core problems and their mutual contradictions is a necessary condition of an adequate understanding of educational policy and practice, it is by no means sufficient. As a further step in that direction, we have to consider the effect of the form of the state apparatus on educational policy and practice.

Examining education as a state apparatus enables us to raise a number of questions that usually go unasked and to clarify some of the ambiguities and confusion that frequently seem to attend discussions of the State. For instance, the distinction between the State and the Government often goes unremarked either because no such distinction is recognized or because it is considered irrelevant. One consequence of this confusion is the assumption that the study of the effect of state provision on education systems is exhausted by, or identical with, the study of educational policy making; this is another defect of the tendency to reduce the politics of education to education politics, which I mentioned above.

Government is clearly a most important part of the State. It is the most active and the most visible part of it, but it is not the whole of it. This is demonstrated, for instance, in the ability of states to carry on functioning in the absence of governments. So, while government action constitutes a key part of the work of any state apparatus, it does not account for all of it. It is essential, therefore, to try to identify the limits of governmental and other aspects of state apparatus bearing in mind that these limits are not common to all social formations (compare, for instance, centralized and decentralized education systems), and that they are not fixed; they are fluctuating counters in the political game.

There are two kinds of limit to government control over state apparatuses. The first is directly practical. It is quite impossible for the whole range of activities of a state apparatus to be regarded permanently as politically problematic, for everything that is at any one time *administered* to become a subject for government. What aspects are the focus of government activities at any time is a valuable and interesting topic of study, but it does not exhaust the possibilities for a political sociology of education.

The second kind of limit is what I will call the organic; I will concentrate on it in the remainder of this section. 'Organic' in this case refers to the relative autonomy of state apparatus from government control which derives from their own particular history. Partly because of the inability of government to effectively institute day-to-day control over every aspect of an apparatus's activities, they (the apparatuses) develop in directions, and take on a broad overall character, within the constraints of the basic demands made of them, which does not merely *not* follow the design of any one government, but can render them ineffective or inadequate vehicles for the execution and imple-mentation of particular kinds of policy. State apparatuses are not directable at will. As Therborn (1978: 35) puts it:

In the historical course of the class struggle, the state apparatuses came to crystallize determinate social relations and thus assume a material existence, efficiency and inertia which are to a certain extent independent of current state policies and class relations. It follows that, although the variance between state power and the state apparatus is limited by the fact that they express the class relations of the same society, at any given moment significant disjunctures appear between the two. The possibilities of variance are substantially increased by the co-existence within a particular state system of several apparatuses, in which different sets of class relations may have crystallized.[3]

What can be achieved through education, then, is constrained not only by the basic problems confronting it, but also by the nature of the apparatus for tackling them – and everything else it does. If we want to understand the similarities as well as the differences between education systems in capitalist countries, and their implications, one crucial area of investigation is the similarities as well as the differences in their state apparatuses – Archer's (1979) very detailed analysis of the origins and consequences of centralized and decentralized systems contributes usefully here. Let us then examine the education state apparatus in more detail. This is clearly much more difficult than establishing the core problems, for while capitalism as a mode of production dominates many social formations, the capitalist mode of production alone does not determine the form that education state apparatuses will take.

We are dealing here with two levels of the selectiveness of state institutions. At the one level, their selectiveness in terms of policy options, may be seen to be broadly guided by the 'needs' of the capitalist mode of production; it is at this level that the arguments in the previous section were cast. The other level at which they operate selectively concerns how their particular form of operation facilitates the putting of certain kinds of relevant questions, and inhibits others. What is at issue here is much more a matter of the histories of the individual state apparatuses; within particular social formations, education systems as different as the American and the French are possible.

One generalization we can make is that state apparatuses everywhere tend to be organized in the form of bureaucracy. The immense scope of the questions opened up by a consideration of bureaucracy makes it necessary to limit the discussion here rather brutally. Thus we shall not be considering the purpose for which the bureaucratic mode was introduced (whether, for instance, rationality or repression was dominant – though they are not necessarily exclusive alternatives), or the extent of its penetration into all kinds of institutions. Rather, the focus will be very narrowly on one area of the consequences of its dominance, that of what kinds of questions and answers it facilitates in respect of the problems confronting it.

As is very well known, Weber's ideal type bureaucracy was characterized by the maximization of rationality, specialization, impersonality, hierarchy and accountability, all in the interests of efficiency. (A further characteristic of fundamental importance to education systems is that bureaucracies recruit on the basis of objective educational qualifications and credentials; the almost universal spread of the bureaucratic form of organization has placed a major requirement of credentialling on education systems.) This ideal type of organization has been supplemented (or supplanted) by what Therborn calls managerial technology. We may leave aside the question of whether this development represents a quantitative or a qualitative change, but we need to address its consequences. This change results from the changing role of the capitalist State. In Offe's (1975b) terms this has involved a change from 'allocative' state policies, where resources and powers that intrinsically belong to, and are at the disposal of, the State, are allocated, to 'productive' state policies, where the State acts to remedy actual or anticipated disturbances in the accumulation process or to avoid or eliminate perceived threats to accumulation. In Offe's view, the ideal type bureaucracy is appropriate to the former type of state activity, while the 'application of predetermined rules through a hierarchical structure of "neutral" officials is simply insufficient to absorb the decision load that is implied by productive state activities'. What is involved is a different set of evaluation criteria. Under bureaucracy the most successful action is that which conforms most closely to established rules and procedures; under managerial technology the effectiveness of the product is the criterion of success.

Naturally, in any particular state apparatus, these two forms of organization will co-exist in various, and shifting, combinations. While there is an apparent effort to subsume an ever wider range of activities under technological criteria, i.e. to cast an ever wider range of problems in a form susceptible to technical solutions, what technological processes are incorporated where and how are not decided solely on the basis of technological rationality. As we shall see below, there is a great deal of what often presents itself as inertia within organizations, that prevents this coming about. It is clear, though, that the nature of the problems confronting the contemporary capitalist State is such as to push it in the direction of increasing 'productive' intervention, and thus away from the purely Weberian model of bureaucratic organization.

What, then, does this very basic knowledge of the organization of state apparatuses tell us about their 'selectiveness'. I want to consider just two contributions. First, it helps us to recognize more clearly how the way the apparatus is organized constrains what it does. Policy options are selected on the basis of solutions available, and often it seems, questions are framed with available answers in mind. What appear as the available answers will result from the particular combination of bureaucracy/technology dominant in a state apparatus at a given time, which is obviously a matter for empirical investigation in any particular case. What we have here is something similar to the celebrated notion of 'the politics of non-decision making', except that the agenda is not assumed to be directly manipulated in favour of a particular individual or group; rather the process of agenda formation itself affects the agenda.

The second point concerns the direction in which this selection process operates. We cannot infer from the absence of direct manipulation involved that the effects of the organization of the apparatus are in the end neutral, with one balancing out the other, as it were. Both forms, the purely bureaucratic and the technological, contain built-in biases, and both tend in the same direction. Both, for instance, emphasize the importance of expertise and specialization; only the areas favoured differ. Both then are not only predisposed towards expert-devised and administered solutions, rather than 'popular' ones, but both have an in-built tendency to undervalue 'popular' reactions to and appraisals of, policies. Further, as Erik Wright (1977: 218) puts it: 'Effectiveness and responsibility are not "neutral" dimensions of technical, formal rationality; they intrinsically embody certain broad political orientations.' At the same time, as has been frequently pointed out, attempts to reduce complex political problems to technical problems tend to have conservative implications. Thus the problem of rationality or repression as the purpose of bureaucracy may be an illusory one. Rationality entails social control; repression is a necessary concomitant of an organization based on impersonality and conformity. It hardly needs saying that it cannot be inferred from the foregoing sketch of the changing form of state apparatuses that they are effective in discharging the tasks laid upon them. This is far from the case, and this topic is the centre of one of the most important 'sub-debates' about the nature of the capitalist State, namely whether state apparatuses can ever have the capacity to do what is required of them.

We must turn now from considering the form of the state apparatus in general, to an examination of the substance of education state apparatuses. This examination will focus chiefly on the nature of the teaching profession. Just as it is difficult to generalize about the nature of state apparatuses, so it is about teachers. They are not all paid, or everywhere licensed, by the State; in any particular case, the character of the teaching profession will be the product of the relationship between the conditions available at different levels of the education system, and between the public and private sectors. However, in this area, there is a good deal more consistency and we would be justified in assuming that most teachers in all capitalist States are publicly trained, certified and paid. It is also important to note the different social positions of teachers at different levels of the education system. While it seems that in all societies greater prestige and autonomy attaches to tertiary rather than to secondary teachers, and to secondary rather than to primary teachers, there is no similar consistency with respect to the absolute and relative extent of such differences.

The key point to be made, however, is that while teachers are typically state employees, they are not typically state officials. That is to say, their role performance does not conform to that of the ideal type bureaucratic official. They are not mere rule followers; they do not have access to a set of correct answers on procedures, or to a means of ensuring that problems will be posed in ways appropriate to such correct answers and procedures. Teaching in a mass education system is intrinsically inimical (though not necessarily impervious, or successfully resistant) to attempts at bureaucratic routinization and it is this that is the basic source of whatever classroom autonomy teachers have.

It is similarly difficult to make technicians of teachers. If bureaucracy is essentially characterized by rule following, technology is essentially characterized by the achievement of successful outcomes.

Here, the problem has to do with defining successful educational outcomes. We have already laid considerable emphasis on the mutually contradictory nature of the demands of education, and their closer specification in terms of immediate, technically realizable, objectives seems likely to do little more than make such contradictions more salient. None of this is to say that attempts have not been made to counter this intrinsic resistance to routinization.

Teachers, then, enjoy a certain autonomy from direct control – the very nature of the circumstances which inhibit routinization also makes it difficult for any but 'insiders' to evaluate teachers' work. The extension and defence of this intrinsic autonomy by organized teachers' organizations is basic to our understanding of what is typically regarded as the 'inertia' of education systems, their lack of responsiveness to new requirements. Very broadly, the autonomy has been extended through (not always successful) attempts to adapt new demands to existing structures and practices, rather than vice versa, to an extent where education systems might almost be said to be self-reproducing. This applies both to curriculum and pedagogy, both of which currently display similarities to the practice of 50 years ago which are truly remarkable given the nature and pace of technological and social change in that period, and the supposed close relationship of education systems to such changes. What is typically characterized as the 'inertia' of education systems, then, as if it were somehow inherent to their nature, is better seen as an extension and defence by teachers of the autonomy intrinsic to their practice, which has as its target the protection of what they see as their own interests (and such perceptions will obviously differ across time and space), rather than the fulfilment of any broader or narrower appeal, especially one which might substantially damage those perceived interests.

Credence in the 'inertia' thesis is strengthened by the fact that the kind of resistance just mentioned has traditionally been, and been able to be, passive. This was possible due to the comparatively restricted, allocative, role played by the State; and also, associatedly, to a period of apparently permanently and regularly increasing economic prosperity. In such circumstances, where the need for the State (and education system) to meet all the demands on it was not so pressing, and where, hence, their mutually contradictory nature was not so apparent, the kind of control over the education system ceded by the State to the teachers under what I have called 'licensed autonomy' (see Chapter 8) was not inappropriate or ineffective. Economic slump, however, totally wipes out such preconditions. It effects all state apparatuses, both directly and indirectly, in two ways.

The direct effects appear in the form of cutbacks in financing and resources of all kinds. These are, in fact, comparatively easily dealt with without major changes in the relative autonomy of the education system or of the teaching profession within it. Booms, like slumps, do not develop at an even pace, and even within the era of continuing expansion there were hiccups which caused temporary cutbacks, with the result that the education system and the teaching profession had become used to administering them in ways which did not affect the basic balance of forces. Cuts, up to a certain point, and never willingly, can, like other external pressures on education systems, be interpreted within, and made to fit, the existing pattern of control over the education system.

What is proving much less easy to incorporate, and is, indeed, in England certainly, threatening to bring about a qualitative change in the nature of control over the education system, is the form of the indirect effects of economic decline. This has major effects on the nature, as well as the extent of state activity. Not only is the State compelled to take on new activities, which necessarily has implications for its existing activities of all kinds, but it is compelled to review and redirect those existing activities. That is to say, there is a change in the core problems of the State, bringing about a tighter – and quite possibly different – specification of the requirements of each of the state apparatuses, and the necessity, following this respecification, of attempting to curtail all state activity which now appears to be irrelevant or non-effective. What this entails for education systems, then (and we should note that it is not just education systems which are affected – the widespread militancy among state employees in many countries can be seen as evidence of this), is not just cutbacks in resources, or intensified external pressure for redirection of the system, but a partial restructuring of the whole state apparatus.

It is at this point that the two halves of the state apparatus identified in this section come together. As has been implied, there is a permanent tension between the bureaucratic form of the state apparatus and the substance of its practice. The outcome of this tension at any given time frames the kinds of questions that can be answered, and the kind of answers that can be given, through education as a state apparatus. Currently, we are witnessing strenuous efforts to impose greater central control on the education system, to impose some kind of bureaucratic/technology form(s) on teachers as state employees. Exactly what form(s) are put forward will be dependent on the outcome of the struggles between 'the bureaucrats' and 'the technocrats' within the state apparatus which we briefly discussed above, and of the nature and effectiveness of the teaching profession's resistance to them.

Three points need to be made in brief conclusion to this section. First, the existence of a degree of autonomy does not, of course, determine how it will be exploited, or in what ways it will be expanded, or what parts of it will be most strenuously defended, or how they will be defended. Such uses will be affected by the nature of the relationship between the levels of education, the relationship of education to other state apparatuses, the relationship between the organized teaching profession and major political groupings, power blocs and trade unions, and the nature and extent of state penetration of educational provision, all in the historical context of a particular social formation.

Secondly, and associated with the previous point, it is essential to recognize the limited nature of this autonomy. It is a relative autonomy in respect only of the *execution* of the work of education systems. Teachers' autonomy does not extend to deciding the goals of education systems, nor their level of funding; though it has undoubted (but fluctuating) influence in such matters, the teaching profession has no control over them. This is clearly exemplified in the case of spending cuts. These are always resisted by the teaching profession, but scarcely ever successfully. So, while he who pays the piper always in the end calls the tune, he can specify more or less broadly what kind of tune he wants, but only with far greater difficulty exactly how it should be played. Under 'licensed autonomy' the teaching profession was given what amounted to a negative programme by the paymaster – 'play anything you like but Russian music and folk songs'. Under regulated autonomy the requirement is much more positive – 'play only modern German music, as far as possible just like the Germans do it – and we'll be listening to make sure you do'.

This argument is directly relevant to the problem of prominence and priority. While applying itself to the core problems may not be an objective necessity for an education system, there are significant pressures keeping them out of the 'any other business' place on the agenda, and ensuring that typically the core problems are among the most prominent targets of its activity. This does not mean that they are all equally prominent all the time, or at all levels of education. But while the State is dependent for its revenue on successful capital accumulation, guaranteeing the conditions for its continuation must come high on the list of priorities of all state apparatuses.

Thirdly, a major intention behind this brief consideration of the nature of education as a state apparatus has been to point to ways of locating key points of tension within it, and to try to identify the ways in which different patterns of control over the education system create different spaces and opportunities for initiating or resisting change in education. Only by understanding not only the tasks confronting education systems, but the ways they are set up to carry out such tasks and the problems they have in arriving at and implementing programmes of action, can we effectively determine how programmes might be made to serve the needs of those for whom they are the only source of enlightenment and understanding of the world.

Let us very briefly look at some of the ways that education systems are controlled. First of all, they are legally constituted. What can and should be done through them, and how, is broadly defined in legal terms. Apparent breaches of this legal framework can only be challenged through the courts, always a costly and lengthy process, which is thereby limited in its availability as a form of bringing about change. The courts though, have been used successfully to bring about educational change; it is very interesting to note that in the United States legal action has been employed successfully to bring about broadly 'progressive' changes (in the desegregation of schools, etc.), whereas in England the opposite has been the case. Here, the courts have most notably been used to thwart attempts by Labour governments to introduce comprehensive secondary schooling (e.g. the Enfield and Tameside cases).

Education systems are also run as bureaucracies, emphasizing rule following, objectivity and, of particular importance in this discussion, universalism, the view that all the rules and provisions apply equally to everyone. These characteristics imply that to change any particular situation it is necessary to change the rules pertaining to all similar situations. This is, of course, to accept the 'ideal type'. In the 'real world', no system of rules is sufficiently comprehensive or unambiguous to ensure that interpretation and negotiation are not only possible but unnecessary. This produces grounds for contestation between the various affected parties at three separate levels – that of the rules themselves, that of the area(s) it is appropriate to apply rules to, and that of their implementation and interpretation. In all state education systems contestation over the implementation and interpretation of rules goes on throughout the system, including individual schools; its intensity in any particular sector will be partly a function of the established mode of educational administration, with the centralized/decentralized distinction of particular importance. Disputes over the nature and appropriateness of rules are typically fought out in the 'higher echelons' of the system, though not in total isolation from the practitioners and clients. A good example is the current discussion over the introduction of a 'core curriculum' in English schools. Any decisions on its desirability or content will be made by government: it becomes, therefore, a party political contest, though not exclusively so, for it is obvious that no government or opposition can afford wilfully to neglect or reject out of hand the views of practitioners. Those views, though, have to be put in a form in which they can be assumed to have an impact on party political deliberation. (On this latter point see Nigel Wright's (1976) discussion of the different strategies and policies of the National Union of Teachers and the Rank and File group within the NUT.)

The other characteristic of state apparatuses highlighted above was their tendency towards technocratic management, their increasing eagerness to replace politics with technical solutions. Examples of this tendency can be seen in the introduction of corporate management techniques to local government in England (see Cockburn, 1977) and in the seemingly permanent attempts to 'technicize teaching' (of which teaching machines are only the most visible form). Part of the intention behind these attempts appears to be increasing 'teacher accountability' (though more rarely the accountability of other functionaries within the system or indeed of the system as a whole).

Major moves in this direction have recently been, and are still being, made, especially in the United States, but with considerable British interest and imitation. Two broad forms of opposition suggest themselves here – the demonstration of the ineffectiveness of the techniques/instruments in achieving their ends, and the demonstration that the ends themselves are seriously flawed. Both these strategies were, of course, employed in the eventually successful campaign against selection at 11+ in England. In considering forms of control and resistance at the level of the school it is necessary to specify the chief relevant implications of state provision. What difference, if any, does state provision make? First, we should remember that state schools are part of a bureaucratic state apparatus. Headteachers or principals are bureaucratically accountable to their superiors for what goes on in their schools. This may be contrasted with the recent experiments with voucher systems in education which involve almost commercial notions of account-ability with the introduction of market principles and consumer sovereignty to education. State schools have very little, if any, control over the amount of funds and resources they receive, and frequently this applies to the disburse-ment of those funds too. They have no way of getting emergency or immediate increases in funds – Parent Teacher Association jumble sales and social events may provide some schools with a few extras but they cannot ordinarily pay the salary of an extra teacher. On the other hand, its clients have no financial sanctions they can use directly against a state school – in fact they have very few sanctions of any kind.

The State has an obligation to educate all children between certain ages and the power to enforce compulsory attendance. Disaffected pupils may under certain circumstances be expelled from particular schools but they cannot be expelled from the system as a whole; the State retains the responsibility of providing them with education until the minimum school-leaving age. State schools have little control over whom they will educate: most of their pupils are allocated to them on the basis, usually, of age and residence, sometimes together with gender and/or measured ability. Such formulae effectively restrict parental choice of school very closely, even where there are possible alternatives. Parents can have very little official influence over what goes on in schools generally; schools are formally controlled by boards or authorities made up of representatives elected by the whole community and not only by those with a demonstrable interest in the schools (but see Chapter 7 for the position in 1989).

State schools cannot, then, choose whom they will teach or, except within certain broad limits, what they will teach (the English headteacher's much vaunted seignorial authority over his/her domain had its real limits rather sharply exposed in the William Tyndale case; see Chapter 8). They are only indirectly accountable to their clients; what they offer is not determined by their clients' perceived needs. They do not exist, in other words, primarily to serve the needs of any particular cohort of clients but of the community as a whole. State schools are, then, an imposition on all their clients; just how much of an imposition they are varies with the degree of coincidence between what they want from schools and how what the community wants from them is interpreted. It varies, that is to say, with the continuity between the values and aims of the school – as expressed in its rituals, for instance – and those of the home.

What this kind of legal bureaucratic framework of schools produces is what Corrigan and Frith (1975) call 'institutional incorporation'. It ensures the attendance of all children between certain ages and their exposure to certain forms of educational experiences. This institutional incorporation is policed at the school level through the medium of school rules, a quasi-legal framework of operation with sanctions to ensure compliance (at least theoretically). However, as Corrigan and Frith argue, 'institutional incorporation' is not *necessarily* ideological incorporation: ' . . . to take account of an institution is not necessarily to accept it'. They go on:

> [Working class children] *do* go to bourgeois schools: their ideas about what education is and what it is for and how it should be organised are the ideas embodied in their schools; there are no alternative, working class, 'educational' institutions; no notion of resisting education *as* education. And yet the evidence is that working class kids do, to a greater or lesser extent, resist something in the school system – how else explain the overwhelming evidence (that any teacher would confirm) that a school is a battleground, the pupils' weapons ranging from apathy through indiscipline to straight absence. And in this battle the school always is (precisely in terms of ideology) the loser. Every use of formal, repressive power reinforces working class experience of education as *imposition* (and not as a good-thing-that-will-extend-my-horizons-and-make-me-a-good-person); every (regular) experience of failure confirms the reality that 'this place has *nuthin'* for me'.
>
> The irony of this situation is that the kids' ideological resistance to bourgeois education (i.e. their rejection of a set of norms and values) takes place in the context of and as *a result of* their incorporation in bourgeois institutions. The point is actually an obvious one: working class *experience*, even of bourgeois institutions, is not bourgeois experience; the working class situation, even within bourgeois institutions, is not a bourgeois situation.

This line of argument has been extended most notably by Paul Willis (1977), and by Corrigan himself (Corrigan, 1979), while the essential continuity between the values of the school and the bourgeoisie's requirements of the school have been described by Bourdieu and Passeron (1977). It is important to note, however, that if we are correct in stating that the central problem facing state education systems is the maintenance of an hegemony not inimical to the capital accumulation – presenting and having accepted as valid and appropriate a version of the world and the way it works which is in conformity with continuing capital accumulation – this does not mean that hegemony is static or unchanging. On the contrary, it is constantly changing under pressure of events, constantly forced to assimilate potential alternatives to its forms. So, and this is very important, incorporation does not entail subjugation; it can involve the hegemonic form being changed as well as, or even rather than, the alternative form. Neither is hegemony monolithic. Its various components (whose own boundaries and classifications are permanently shifting) develop and incorporate unevenly, so that alternative forms incompatible within one sector of hegemony are not so within others; again the various forms of hegemonic gender relations are the best example. It also seems to follow from this that hegemony is not so much about winning approval for the status quo, winning consent for it or even acceptance of it. Rather, what seems to be involved is the prevention of rejection, opposition or alternatives to the status quo through denying the use of the school for such purposes. It seems to me that if we seek a positive and active role for the schools in the maintenance of hegemony, we rapidly find ourselves in deep theoretical and empirical waters (How is it laid down and by whom? How do the teachers react?, etc.). On the other hand, if we see the status quo being maintained by the 'normal process' of a relatively autonomous state apparatus with the occasional checking of excesses, we may be nearer terra firma.

Finally, it is important to recognize that the economic and political reproduction that goes on in school goes on in a particular political context, the main parameters of which have been outlined above. Different kinds of resistance, with both different targets and different forms, are called forth from different groups. The state apparatus is by no means monolithic in either its aims or its modes of operation; the forms of control implemented through educational institutions will not themselves be entirely consistent or free of contradictions. Thus, not only do the basic forms of control – bureaucracy and technocratic management – in their 'pure' forms themselves call forth particular kinds of resistance, but so do the various common combinations of them.

And, furthermore, the nature of their combination will itself be affected by the forms of resistance experienced. What we are faced with then is not either preparations for, or the early (or late) stages of, a set piece battle, but a continuing series of rarely conclusive skirmishes on shifting terrain, between shifting alliances, in an overall context of a system attempting to carry out contradictory functions through means that may conflict with its objectives. It is in the spaces and interstices created by these and other contradictions that we must look for resistance to coalesce.

Notes

1. I have in mind here the work of, for instance, Robert Manzer and Maurice Kogan. See Boyle and Crosland (1971), Kogan (1971, 1975), Kogan and Packwood (1974), Kogan and van der Eyken (1973) and Manzer (1970). Interesting and partial exceptions to this tendency are Kogan (1978) and Tapper and Salter (1978).
2. I cannot go into an adequate discussion of that work, but will rather put forward a particular position which owes most to the work of Claus Offe. Valuable summaries of, and contributions to, that debate on the nature of the capitalist State are to be found in Frankel (1979), Gold *et al.* (1975), Holloway and Picciotto (1978), Jessop (1977) and Esping-Anderson *et al.* (1976).

3. The effects of this heterogeneity of state apparatuses are particularly visible in the different definitions of women and children they separately use. For an analysis of definitions of childhood used in different legal discourses, see Fitz (1980).

2 Implications for Education

We are now in a position to draw out some of the implications of the analysis of the State for the study of education, and beyond that for the education system. Neither studying education in isolation, nor studying it with an explicit, but vague, appreciation of its relationship with society, is adequate. While very many social forces affect education in very important ways, the major motor of educational change in capitalist societies is the changing nature of the capitalist State. Thus, while I would, for instance, agree very largely with Margaret Archer's (1979) view of the influence of the organized teaching profession on educational change since the war and especially over the last 20 years, neither the profession's rise to the peak of its influence, nor its recent fall from that peak can be explained by examination of its composition, its policies, its leadership, its size, its level of expertise or anything else internal to it. All these factors are necessary to explain the *form* that the rise and fall took, but cannot explain *why* it took place. To do that, we have to examine the changing demands on the State in carrying out its basic functions and the way that these affect the structure and process of the education system. As Claus Offe (1976) suggests, crises should be 'conceptualized not at the level of events, but rather at the superordinate level of mechanism that generate events'.

We are, indeed, fortunate that the relevance and value of the approach suggested here is so apparent in the early 1980s. The process marked by James Callaghan's Ruskin College speech, the Great Debate and Shirley Williams's Green Paper, is as clear an illustration as one could wish for of changes in the requirements of the State leading to major changes in the structure and direction of the education system. I do not want to go into that specific case now, however, for the reason that tying the approach too closely to the analysis of one particular case could tend to lead to an assumption that it was only associated with, or particularly valuable for, that case. The crucial danger of this is that it could lead to an association of *forms* of intervention with *functions* of intervention, and perhaps the most important point I want to make is that the nature of the functions of the State does not imply the forms in which these functions will be carried out. The same broad functions can be met in very many different ways, and the study of these ways is not only valid but essential for a comprehensive understanding of the education system. Similarly, I would not want it to be thought that everything that goes on in schools can be related back to one of the functions of the State. To oversimplify it, the selection mechanism implied by the functions the State must perform operates on a basis of *exclusion* rather than of *inclusion*; that is to say, it is much more difficult to explain the content and form of schooling as positively designed to support capitalism than it is to see it as excluding elements considered potentially or actually threatening to capitalism. For instance, the only compulsory element of the curriculum of English schools (at least in 1980) is religious education – and it is not easy to see in what way many elements of the curriculum make a greater contribution to the support of capitalism than potential alternatives which are not as commonly found.

A better explanation of what is included is to be found in the history of the particular society and its education system. Naturally, this will have been reinforced by changing conceptions of the contribution of education to the national interest, particularly as expressed in education acts and reports. Yet it has been a feature of the English education system that such acts and reports have tended not to prescribe in any detail what should be taught in schools, nor have the provision of these acts or reports all been implemented or closely monitored. Of course, the reality differs somewhat from the formal picture; while there may be no formal compulsion on headteachers to provide mathematics teaching in their schools, for instance, there is no doubt that there is effective pressure on them to do so. But to understand why this is so we need to look at the working of the education state apparatus, at how it is administered, at the interests and aims of the teaching profession, and so on.

While there is very little evidence to support the idea that the content and form of schooling are positively selected to support capitalism, there is evidence that apparent threats to capitalism in schooling are excluded. Frith and Corrigan (1975), for instance, argue that in the nineteenth century state schooling was used deliberately to exclude all alternatives. In more recent times, there have been a number of well publicized cases of allegedly socialist or anarchist forms of schooling being heavily criticized and excluded from the state education system. Names such as Duane (Berg, 1968) and Mackenzie (Mackenzie, 1970) are obvious examples. The most recent case, and perhaps the most widely publicized of all, was that of William Tyndale (see Part 4). The nature of the reactions to these cases provides a better basis for understanding the contents of the education system than does its direct support of capitalism. In explaining the relationship between the 'needs' of capitalism and curriculum selection, then, it is a case of 'those who are not against us are for us', rather than one of 'those who are not for us are against us'. I would like to draw out some of the implications of making an analysis of the capitalist State central to an analysis of education, and to consider just how they enable us to make sense of those recent developments in the British education systems (but not only of those).

The following list is not meant to exhaust the implications that could be drawn from the analysis of the State, but rather to suggest some ways it can be put to use.

1. The basic problems facing the capitalist State are the preservation of the process, context and legitimacy of the capital accumulation process. In doing this, it *must* act to eliminate anything that appears to threaten the long-term success of that process; it *may* act to strengthen and develop it. Hence, as I have already said, the principle of selection is exclusionary, rather than inclusionary. This is another way in which this approach parts company with the 'correspondence theory', which is implicitly inclusionary, i.e. the education system is seen as being designed to achieve certain particular ends, rather than, as is argued here, eliminating possible threats to a broadly conceived process. Implicit in what has been said in this paragraph is the view that passive acceptance of, rather than active consent to, state policies and the activities of state apparatuses, is sufficient to 'preserve' the capital accumulation process.

2. The correspondence theory also tends to use one section of capital – industrial manufacture – as the model of what the education system is to support. However, the argument here is that the State does not act on behalf of any particular capital, or any broad section of capital, but in the long-term interests of the preservation of capital accumulation. For Offe and Ronge (1975) this entails the State not even acting on behalf of capital, however broadly conceived, alone, but on behalf of the whole population. There are other implications here. First, the demands made by individual capitals on the education system vary considerably; the requirements of car manufacturers are different from those of supermarket operators, those of local government different from those research establishments, or the armed forces, and it is impossible for the education system to provide its products with *qualifications* for all employment possibilities at once, as Hussain (1976) argues. What it must do, following Offe and Ronge, is to make sure that its products are *employable*, which in the present situation of very high levels of youth unemployment has more implications for maintaining their motivation than for ensuring that they are adequately scholastically prepared.

3. The education system cannot be expected to stay immune from the increasing politicization of all areas of life entailed in greater state intervention. I have tried to indicate how economic changes and the need for the State to take a more decisive part in the management and direction of the education system led to the breakdown of the post-1944 'supra-political consensus' which had managed the education system, and to the consequently greater politicization of it. It was not that parents suddenly discovered a voice and hence found the Taylor committee recommending they play a more prominent part in school management. It was rather that, though parents had always been vocally interested in their children's education, never had their

concerns, which were essentially (if not in a partisan sense) political, been voiced in a context which so clearly recognized the political nature of education. In the same way, the authority and influence of the teaching profession depended largely on education being seen as 'above politics'; once it ceased to be above politics, that authority and influence was converted into a requirement to be accountable. The seat and extent of control over education, then, is also affected by changes in the State.

4. Habermas (1976) claims that the State has two resources to deal with political and legitimation crises: value and sense. The education system, like other state apparatuses, can forestall problems by providing value; that is to say, it can continue to meet the promises it implicitly or explicitly makes to the public, and to cope with the rising expectations it generates. This has very much been the pattern which state apparatuses have been able to follow since 1944. However, unless the economy continues to grow faster than the social wage, there will either be a major fiscal crisis of the State, or social spending will have to be curtailed (or possibly both). In a situation such as that in Britain in recent years, where social spending has been growing much faster than the economy, it becomes increasingly difficult for state apparatuses such as education to maintain their existing level of provision and hence to legitimate themselves through the value they provide. The likely subsequent problem is that what can no longer be bought with value must be purchased with sense. It is in this kind of crisis that the basis of state intervention in the education system changes from exclusionary to inclusionary. There is an attempt to find a new means of legitimation for both the education system itself and for state policy as a whole, following the undermining of 'value-based' legitimation. At the present, this includes a shift in the rationale for education, from an implicit rationale that education is for the development of the individual to the explicit rationale based on the contribution of education to national survival; this is to be achieved through the preparation of an appropriately skilled and motivated workforce (see Offe and Ronge on possessive individualism); it is almost as though someone had read, and accepted, and seen the value of, the correspondence principle!

5. This redefinition of what education is about is not confined to the promulgation of official statements; it sets up reverberations throughout the education system and affects every level of it. And this brings me to my final point. This is that the three basic problems confronting the State are paralleled throughout the education system, and do not exist only at the level of overall education policy; many of the problems facing individual teachers in classrooms can be traced back to contradictions engendered by the attempt to solve two or more of the problems simultaneously. The education system is expected to contribute to the meeting of the economic, political and legitimatory needs of the State and, at any and every level of education, just as in the State as a whole, the simultaneous solution of these problems is impossible. Further, it is quite crucial to recognize that their mutually contradictory implications are the dynamic forces of the education system. The conflict between these solutions is permanent, and they all have their

supporters within the education system. I would want to argue very broadly, for instance, that the individual and professional commitment of teachers is largely to the legitimatory function of education, i.e. to education as a good in itself; this may be the basic source of their influence on the very uneven implementation of education policy. For, to repeat, the contradictions involved in tackling simultaneously basic problems facing education in the capitalist State are played out at, and give their broad character to, every level of the education system, from national policy making to PTA meetings, and no explanation of education and schooling that does not recognize this can be complete.

PART 2

Education as a State Apparatus

3 What is the State?

One of the most difficult problems in discussing the effect of the State on education, or anything else, is defining just what is meant by 'the State'. At one level we know pretty well broadly what we mean by it. In one sense, for instance, it's 'them', whether 'they' are protecting us or controlling us, taxing us or paying us benefits. But we need to be rather more precise in our understanding when the nature of the State is as central as it is in this book, and I want to set out briefly and broadly what I will mean when I use the word.

The best way to begin may be to distinguish the State from the government. Often, no such distinction is made; a number of those quoted in this book do not make it. This may be because they do not see the value of any such distinction or because they do not see the relevance of it. Government is the most visible, and arguably the most important and the most active, part of the State, but it is not the whole of the State. If it were, states would cease to function when governments fell; quite clearly states are able to operate perfectly well (cynics say far better!) in the absence of governments. What are the boundaries between the government and the State, then? While no unambiguous answer can be given to that question, because the boundaries are not fixed but shifting, some basic distinctions can be drawn.

Very broadly, we might say that governments attempt to represent the short-term interests of the temporarily dominant coalition of forces within a social formation; these coalitions are represented in political parties, and party policy reflects, on the one hand, the shifts of interest and influence between the groups making up the coalition and, on the other, its conceptions of what is required to secure majority electoral support. In one sense, then, the government acts to mediate the State and its subjects to each other. It is the activity generated by such intragovernmental problems which creates what Gramsci (1971: 13) referred to as the 'great mass of functions which are not all necessitated by the social necessities of production', or what Offe (1973: 115) called 'the claims which emerge merely from party competition and political conflict, but in no way directly result from the actual requirements of capital accumulation itself'. One consequence of this is that it helps to confirm parliamentarism as the key mode of state rule and thus disguises the nature of the basic functions of the State. The prominence accorded to Parliament tends to attract attempts to change the type and direction of state activities to itself. However, parliamentary channels, while they are far from negligible, are intrinsically incapacitated as sole means of bringing about such changes. Not all changes in the type and direction of state activities are, or could be, the results of parliamentary activity; indeed, it is frequently argued that Parliament is becoming ever less significant as a source of educational change (see, e.g. Kogan, 1978).

If government does not account for the whole of the State, what does the remainder consist of? I want to suggest that it consists of 'state apparatuses' – specifiable publicly financed institutions. Most of these are accountable officially to government. A list would include government departments (departments of state), the military, the police, and so on, all of which are officially accountable to government; but it would also include the judiciary and the legal system which are not accountable to government in the same way. There are a number of points to be noted about this list. First, it applies to both national and local states – a local education authority is as much a state apparatus as the Department of Education and Science (DES). Secondly, it excludes institutions which, while they might be performing similar functions to state apparatuses, are not publicly financed (even though they may be in part publicly accountable). Thus the BBC is a state apparatus but not Yorkshire Television; public schools are not state apparatuses, but church schools are (because they are predominantly publicly funded). There are, then, obvious difficulties attached to confining the label to publicly financed institutions, but I want to retain that distinction largely because the alternatives appear to generate even more difficulties. It might be argued, for instance, that it is very difficult to distinguish between the effects of the BBC and Yorkshire Television, or between, say, former direct grant schools in the public and private sectors, and that hence what distinguishes state apparatuses is their effects and not their status. However, as Laclau (1977) has argued in response to Althusser's notion of state apparatuses, such an approach has the effect of making 'the State' a *quality* which becomes extremely difficult to isolate and analyse. 'State' becomes an adjective applicable to anything which brings about, however incidentally, a particular range of effects. So churches, trade unions, underground newspapers may be at times state apparatuses. It is in the light of the difficulties inherent in this conception that it is preferable to confine the definition to a set of publicly financed institutions, even given the difficulties that raises.

It is essential to be aware that labelling a particular set of institutions state apparatuses cannot be taken to imply that they all have a common purpose in that they all operate in the same way. The reality is very far from this and an assumption of major divergences in the interests and methods of state apparatuses would be more justified. A number of illustrations can be drawn from the sphere of education. Perhaps the most obvious is the national/local tension. An example of this is the case of the comprehensive school policy where central government and the DES were unable to impose the comprehensive policy on all local authorities. This situation was further complicated by the invoking of legal procedures in (successful) attempts to prevent the imposition of the policy. Recourse to the law was initiated by groups of private citizens – the Enfield parents' case is the best known – but the Tameside case, where a local authority successfully took a government department to law over the implementation of the comprehensive policy, is the outstanding demonstration of the possibility of different interests and methods among different state apparatuses. It is particularly telling in that the arguments take place within a particular sector of state apparatuses.

When we move outside a particular sector, differences of interest between state apparatuses become greater, with the broad aims of the education sector as a whole coming into conflict with those of other sectors of state apparatuses. There are obvious tensions between the Treasury and all major spending departments, for instance. More subtle tensions may be discerned between education and other areas of state activity; one interesting version of the relationship between education and a number of other agencies, for instance, is contained in this extract from a lecture given to the education section of the British Association by the (then) Chief Constable of Devon and Cornwall, Mr John Alderson:

> It was the educators who taught our children to challenge the statements of their elders, to expose the ignorance of their parents, to demand the source of the policeman's authority, to question the control of the employer, and even to show pupils how to go on strike. They let the genie out of the bottle as they have always done. Now we ask for the same energy and dedication towards new social control and containment of excessive and unacceptable criminal behaviour. (Quoted in the *Guardian*, 7 September 1978)

Finally, just as different sectors of educational apparatuses sometimes have conflicting objectives, so they also have different impacts on particular areas of the social world. The most important example of this is the way that the family is constituted differently by different state apparatuses in terms of the assumptions and expectations they actively or tacitly hold of it. 'The family' is differently conceived by the law – and by different discourses within the law, as John Fitz (1981) makes clear – by social security regulations, by schools, by local social services departments, by children's homes and old people's homes, by the State as employer, in factory acts and employment legislation and so on. This point is introduced here to indicate how important it is not to think of the State as some kind of monolithic social actor.

Partly because of the inability of governments to institute effective day-to-day control over every aspect of an apparatus's activities, the apparatuses take on a broad overall character, within the constraints of the basic demands made them, which does not merely not follow the design of any one government, but can render them ineffective or inadequate vehicles for the execution and implementation of particular kinds of policy. As Renate Mayntz (1979: 633–4) puts it:

> To say the public bureaucracies are agents of policy implementation does not mean that they are lifeless instruments. Public agencies have significant margins for discretionary action in the fulfilment of their tasks. How wide these margins are depends, first, on the nature of the task and, secondly, on the extent of central (hierarchical) control to which a given agency is subject. Planning functions and the provision of technical or personal services which require a strong professional element, as for instance in the fields of health and teaching, imply much larger margins for discretionary action than the enforcement of exactly defined norms or the payment of financial transfers to applicants who meet stipulated criteria. As for central control, the public sector is never a fully integrated hierarchy but must rather be seen as a highly differentiated macro-system of organizations, a network which is more or less hierarchized by virtue of existing vertical lines of communication, but which is basically made up of relatively autonomous elements.

This is reflected, for instance, in contemporary discussions of the power and accountability of the Civil Service and its alleged ability both to block policies it dislikes and promote those it favours (see, e.g. Kellner and Crowther-Hunt, 1980). At least part of the difficulty here may be traced to the fluctuating emphases on bureaucracy and technology within major state apparatuses. This is not the place to go into a rather abstract development of this argument. It is possible, though, to see how tensions are generated and how different possibilities for, and new directions of, the activity of state apparatuses are opened up from a very brief consideration of the changing role of the Ministry of Education/DES over the past 20 years. Throughout that period it has been under almost permanent pressure (though this pressure has been of varying strength) to manage rather than administer the education system and to provide it with more decisive direction. A major consequence of this has been an increasing emphasis on planning, and an associated shift in criteria of success from the faithful following and application of rules to the transformation of the situation under review; a shift, that is to say, broadly from rationality to effectiveness. In a sense, with the central government department taking a much more central role, planning is replacing politics. The original strategy for the introduction of comprehensive education, for instance, may be seen as a political rather than a planning strategy. It relied largely on changing the rules gradually and on political persuasion. It did not involve the identification of a necessary series of steps towards the desired outcome, or evaluation in terms of the achievement of those steps and the cost of doing so. Over this period, moves were made to make the DES more 'business-like' with the introduction of planning and evaluation techniques intended to improve the Department's effectiveness as well as its efficiency (though an OECD report on the DES in 1975 found it wanting in its ability and facilities for planning). How far technical effectiveness has replaced efficient administration, however, is not the point of this brief excursion into the innards of the DES. What it is intended to show is that different forms of organization, different methods and different criteria of success employed by state apparatuses have a major impact on what that apparatus is considered able to achieve, and how successfully, and how it can achieve those objectives.

One further very brief point should be made about the education state apparatuses. This is that the largest category of staff in them is teachers, and that therefore no account of how education state apparatuses operate and what they can achieve is complete without some reference to the teaching profession. I do not want to go into this in any great detail, but I do want to suggest that teachers are not merely 'state functionaries' but do have some degree of autonomy, and that this autonomy will not necessarily be used to further the proclaimed ends of the state apparatus. Rather than those who work there fitting themselves to the requirements of the institutions, there are a number of very important ways in which the institution has to take account of the interests of the employees and fit itself to them. It is here, for instance, that we may begin to look for the sources of the alleged inertia of education systems and schools; that is to say that what appears as inertia is not some immutable characteristic of bureaucracies, but is due to various groups within them having more immediate interests than the pursuit of the organization's goals.

The State, then, is not a monolith, or the same as government, or merely the government's (or anybody else's) executive committee. It is a set of publicly financed institutions, neither separately nor collectively necessarily in harmony, confronted by certain basic problems deriving from its relationship with capitalism, with one branch, the government, having responsibility for ensuring the continuing prominence of those problems on its agenda.

4 From Expectations to Outcomes in Education Systems

This chapter will exploit the space opened up by reservations about what correspondence theories can tell us about the process and practice of schooling. I will argue that the importance of the maintenance of order within schools and within the wider education systems leads to the creation of particular institutional forms which are indifferent to the pursuit of capital accumulation, though sharing some kind of elective affinity with forms of internal control of other kinds of institutions in capitalist society. I do not want to argue that the aims/needs/purposes of capitalism are not structurally, rather than contingently, on the agenda of the education systems of capitalist states (see Chapter 1). Indeed, Offe and Wiesenthal (1980) have demonstrated that there are good reasons to assume that capitalist interests are both better articulated than those of any other 'pressure group' and more compatibly organized with respect to decision-making channels. I would contend, though, that the education system's contribution to the achievement of those aims/needs/purposes of capitalism are made through the medium of the solutions it constructs to deal with its various problems of internal order and control; and the nature of these solutions, if not to subvert, is not necessarily, automatically, or unambiguously, to facilitate the achievement of those aims/needs/purposes. Institutionalization and bureaucratization have had contradictory, not straightforward, consequences for education and for its relationships with not only the economy and the labour process, but also a whole range of other social institutions. In brief, in order for any group to achieve its purposes through schools, it is necessary for the group to achieve control of schools and control within schools. Control of schools has proved remarkably difficult for any group to achieve – not because of any balancing out of interest groups but because, as it has developed, the education system has come to mediate, in deliberate and in unintended ways, the aspirations, policies, interventions, pressure, and so on, of any and all groups. Control in schools is a necessary condition for the achievement of any purpose through education, but the attainment of that control is shaped not by the conscious reflection of any of those purposes but by the strategic and tactical responses of those employed in schools to the organizational problems confronting them. This is not to say that the aims and purposes of education are neglected in this process; rather they are part of the problem facing teachers and, in the course of their fulfilment in daily school life, they may be transformed.

The educational state apparatus (educational administration and schools), it will then be argued, has an independent effect on the pattern, process and practice of education, an effect not reducible to the demands of capital accumulation. Nor is the nature of this independent effect solely determined by or restricted to the 'resistance' of the students. It is evident, then, that this independent effect is very complex and, in the next part of this chapter, I will attempt to clarify it.

It is most crucial to define accurately the nature of the involvement of the education state apparatus (at all levels) in the execution of policy. It has been argued above that the effects of that involvement are varied and important and that they cannot be accounted for by the state apparatus acting as the unambiguous agent of any outside interest. However, to say that they are independent of outside interests only makes it the more important to isolate what is the dynamic of their involvement.

What I want to argue here is that the dynamic comes not so much from the pursuit by state personnel at either level of their own independent political interests as from their efforts to control as far as possible their work situation – to preserve convenient, acceptable, and tested ways of doing things, even in the face of changing demands. Let me simplify a little. Negatively, it is difficult to conceive of an interest common to the whole of the state apparatus and sufficiently well articulated to promote policies based on such a sectional interest. This is not to say, however, that there are not 'elective affinities' between the interests of certain groups within the state apparatus and other group interests outside it. And in education, for instance, we might expect greater affinity between the teaching profession and external groups keen to expand the education system than with those bent on contracting it. These sectional interests are, of course, pursued chiefly outside the State through orthodox pressure group demands; but they can also be pursued through selective implementation of policy, the best examples of which occur where practitioners have a wide range of discretion in implementing policy and which, perhaps, is most clearly demonstrated in the area of law enforcement.

Associated with the pursuit of sectional interest, but not wholly reducible to it, is the attempt to control the work situation. This may be done formally through trade union action, such as (in the case of education) attempting to achieve limits on class size. Less formally, it is pursued through the medium of occupational and workplace cultures.

Implementation and facilitation

It is possible to divide the education service roughly into two levels – schools themselves and the educational administration. It is also possible to distinguish among the procedures and rules within schools and the educational administration, those which contribute directly to the implementation of the goals of the education system and those which indirectly facilitate that implementation. Curriculum matters fall into the implementation category, whereas compulsory attendance and streaming fall into the facilitating category. (I am assuming here that even if daily attendance at school or becoming accustomed to a society stratified by ability are considered sufficiently 'good' to be rated as aims of education, they were not originally conceived as such, being essentially means of making mass schooling work.)

There are a number of things to be noted about this rough and ready distinction. First, not all aims of education can be implemented through the overt curriculum. Some of them – for example, respect for democratic values – are much better taught through the form rather than the content of schooling; one implication of this is that the distinction between implementation and facilitation does not really parallel that between the overt and the hidden curriculum (a concept whose increasing imprecision and flexibility make its continued use of questionable value).

Secondly, the aims and expectations of education are far from homogeneous and are, in fact, frequently contradictory. (I have developed this argument at length in Chapter 1; for example, the goal of realizing every individual's potential lies very uneasily with the goal of fitting in with national manpower planning and with that of producing well-behaved, socially conforming citizens.)

Thirdly, 'implementation' is essentially to do with the making of policy and with policy's transformation into specific programmes – and hence with practice. In all this, implementation is in a dialectical relationship with facilitation; policy is the solution of problems with available methods and resources, and existing facilitating arrangements comprise the most important category of available methods and resources. The creation of new educational policies and programmes (e.g. more natural science and less social science in the curriculum) has to proceed in the context of arrangements originally set up to facilitate quite different policies – and now, possibly, far from ideal for the proposed new policies.

In the transformation of programmes into practice, the tension between implementation and facilitation is especially acute. In the pedagogic structure typical of mass schooling systems, 'learning' is both dependent on, and hobbled by, the need to establish and maintain order, and here the boundaries between implementation and facilitation are in constant flux. However, this tension tends to be relieved by the 'facilitation' category absorbing the 'implementation' category, because the structural context of teaching (Dale, 1977) contains an inbuilt bias toward facilitation rather than implementation on the part of teachers (which can create conflict between their occupational

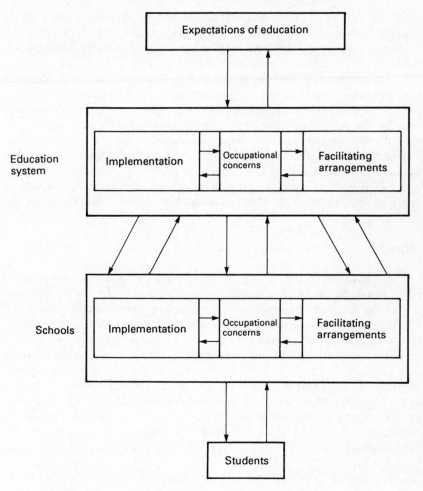

Figure 1 From expectations to outcomes in education systems

interest and their occupational ideology). The mediation of the tension between implementation and facilitation occurs in schools term by term, day by day and lesson by lesson. While this has to be achieved by each individual teacher, it is accomplished through tacit sharing of an occupational culture which necessarily emphasizes the need for survival above the need for success – and survival, of course, is grounded in the maintenance of classroom order rather than the efficient transmission of specified bodies of knowledge. This, of course, generates problems not only for the students but also for those higher up the educational hierarchy (where similar tensions exist).

It is clear, then, that the teachers (at the level of schools) and the educational bureaucrats and experts (at the level of educational administration) effectively perform a 'filtering' function related to, but not wholly determined by, what are called here implementation and facilitation procedures. Indeed, more than that – it is the occupational personnel at the two levels who mediate the tensions between the two. The structure just outlined is set out diagrammatically in Fig. 1.

It is worth noting that this figure differs from the orthodox diagrams which provide for no horizontal differentiation within levels and in which all control and influence pass in one direction only. This figure is intended to indicate that the pattern of schooling is the outcome not only of a successively filtered implementation of the aims of education but also of the rules set up to facilitate that implementation and of the reaction of the teachers and other education employees to the occupational problems that implementation under such rules generates for them. Furthermore, this pattern is not wholly imposed 'top-down' – rather, it is contested both within and between levels.

Expectations of education

So far, I have talked rather vaguely about the aims, goals and purposes of education. Here I want to suggest that what education systems are required to implement are not raw abstract aims, goals or purposes, but particular sets of expectations deriving from them. The list of aims, goals and purposes rhetorically accepted for education is, if not endless, far longer than could ever be contemplated for implementation by any education system. So the first problem to tackle is how particular aims become transformed into expectations by being included on the 'official agenda' of an education system. It is important to note that this is not a purely calculative process. The process of transformation of aims to expectations is shaped not just by 'immediate demands' but also by 'tradition'. Raymond Williams puts this very well:

> It is not only that the way in which education is organized can be seen to express, consciously and unconsciously, the wider organizations of a culture and a society, so that what has been thought of as simple distribution is in fact an active shaping to particular social ends. It is also the fact that the content of education, which is subject to great historical variation, again expresses, again both consciously, certain basic elements in the culture, what is thought of as 'an education' being in fact a particular selection, a particular set of emphases and omissions. Further, when this selection of content is examined more closely it will be seen to be one of the decisive factors affecting its distribution: *The cultural choices involved in the selection of content have an organic relation to the social choices involved in the practical Organization.* (1965: 145 – emphasis added)

Williams here emphasizes the importance of the cultural tradition in which education is located: the aims of education in any society can neither be plucked from the air nor developed in hermetically sealed units. Furthermore, assumptions about what education is *capable* of achieving, what we might call the feasible expectations of education, are not wholly the product of deliberate rational calculation but are rooted in existing ways of doing things in a society. Hence we might expect the feasible as well as the normative expectations of education to vary culturally – to be affected, for instance, by the degree of centralization of state activity, by the proportion and strength of various religious groups within the society, and by the existing development of educational provision within the society.

However vague and well hidden (and both those features have historically characterized the aims of much of English twentieth-century education), there is always an official agenda for education. I indicated briefly above (following Offe and Wiesenthal, 1980) that there are good reasons to expect aims generated by the capitalist class to find their way more readily on to the official agenda and hence to become expectations of the education system. This has remained true over the past few years, a period in which the official agenda for education has become both more explicit and more precise, as the range of expectations of education and the extent of educational provision have both increased. Two (compatible) reasons, both of which affect the nature of the expectations of education and the prospects of their fulfilment, might be put forward very briefly to account for this. The first, which will be alluded to frequently below, is based on the recognition that the very growth of educational provision creates a group of education workers with a central interest not only in maintaining that growth but in ensuring that it takes a form favourable to them. Secondly, and as important, changes in the demands on the capitalist State have produced extra and different kinds of pressure on education systems. Very briefly, the 'human capital revolution' provided education with a new set of more precise, and apparently more vital, tasks to perform than ever before. At the same time, state intervention in an increasing range of areas of life generated a greater need for legitimation, which, it was assumed, education systems could help meet. This process has been closely analysed by Jurgen Habermas (1976: 71), who argues that:

> The expansion of state activity produces the side effect of a disproportionate increase in the need for legitimation not only because the expansion of administratively processed matters makes necessary mass loyalty for new functions of state activity but because the boundaries of the political system vis-a-vis the cultural system shift as a result of this expansion. In this situation, cultural affairs that were taken for granted and that were previously boundary conditions for the political system, fall into the administrative planning area. Thus, traditions withheld from the public problematic, and all the more from practical discourses, are thematized. An example of such direct administrative planning of cultural tradition is educational planning, especially curriculum planning. Whereas school administrators formerly merely had to codify a canon that had taken shape in an unplanned, nature-like manner, present

curriculum planning is based on the premise that traditional patterns could as well be otherwise.

However, this is not a straightforward process, for as Habermas argues earlier in the same book, 'while organizational rationality spreads, cultural traditions are undermined and weakened. The residue of tradition must, however, escape the administrative grasp, for traditions important for legitimation cannot be regenerated administratively' (p. 47). What is taught in schools cannot then be entirely subject to curriculum planning. Education cannot be wholly rationalized and routinized, while the relative freedom of educational personnel over implementation enables 'tradition for legitimation' to be retained.

What constitutes an 'expectation of education', then, is not a static thing; it is limited in a number of ways related to national, cultural and administrative traditions and to changing demands on the education system. It is clear, too, that the process of creating an official agenda out of the whole range of possible aims of education itself has an effect on how likely it is that the expectations contained in the agenda will be fulfilled. As the discussion of legitimation demonstrates, it is not that the expectations contained in the official agenda will be inevitably changed in the process of their fulfilment; they will be modified owing to a range of competing, 'unofficial' aims seeping onto the agenda in the course of their implementation. And, finally, we should be aware of the criticism and pressure permanently directed at all levels of the education system because of its failure to meet all expectations. Such pressure is inevitable for the simple reason that it is impossible for the education system to fulfil all expectations (see Katz, 1980). For example, schools alone cannot bring about equality or even equality of opportunity. Some expectations cannot be met because they contradict other expectations, e.g. the identification and cultivation of the brightest talent and the boosting of all children's self-esteem. This inevitable and predictable failure of education systems has a range of consequences for the practice and process of schooling.

5 The Scope of Education: Mandate and Capacity in TVEI

There are two major linked problems – both more or less well recognized – in talking about the Technical and Vocational Education Initiative (TVEI): the vagueness of its definition and the very wide diversity of its practice. In the press, for instance, TVEI has been variously described as a scheme where 'children receive a technological or business-based instruction as part of their curriculum and what they learn is placed in the context of the world of work' as 'making schools and colleges more technically and vocationally oriented', as 'providing resources for job related training for 14- to 18-year-olds in which industrialists work with teachers in this development of courses' as a 'learn and earn' scheme, and as 'aimed at steering youngsters to the boom spheres of business and industry'.

The problems associated with this range of definitions are compounded by the diversity of TVEI practice. This very diversity means that it would be possible to find evidence to justify almost any argument about TVEI. On the basis of particular TVEI schemes, it is as easy to refute criticisms of the Initiative as it is to expose its pretensions.

In view of these difficulties, this chapter intends to take one of the undeniable 'facts' about TVEI – that it is funded and ultimately controlled by the Manpower Services Commission (MSC) – and examine some of its implications. We shall do this by asking rather different questions about the effects of TVEI, from those which have so far proved rather sterile and inconclusive. Most discussions about TVEI, for instance, have been about its effect on the curriculum – is it narrowing the curriculum, as many educators contend, or 'one of the most significant broadenings of the curriculum this century', as Lord Young argues? Again, the diversity of TVEI practice makes it extremely difficult to resolve such questions empirically. What is needed, then, is some progress towards *conceptualizing* TVEI more adequately.

One step towards this is the development of sensitizing concepts which present the possibility of going beyond the mere aggregation of descriptive accounts of different schemes based on different, and frequently tacit, purposes, methods and theories. Such sensitizing concepts would be an attempt at an initial focusing of enquiry, a medium for the possible grounding of theory. What we are proposing here, then, is delaying consideration of TVEI's impact on the *content* of schooling until we have considered the changes it signals in the *scope* of education policy. And we shall be examining in particular the effect of the hybridization of education and employment policy which TVEI represents.

In this chapter, then, we expand on the idea of TVEI as a hybrid, comparing the two traditions which make it up in terms of their assumptions about the mandate and the capacity of the education system.

Of course, there is a long history of attempts to bring education more closely into line with the apparent requirements of the economy. The roots of the efforts to reconcile 'secondary' and 'technical' education, and the consequences of the failure to do so, have been very well charted by McCulloch (1986; McCulloch *et al.*, 1985). As he puts it:

> TVEI might be interpreted as in the tradition of the Bryce Report of 1895, the Spens Report of 1938, and the Crowther Report of 1959. All sought to reconcile technical with secondary education by stimulating a distinct kind of 'secondary technical education'. (McCulloch, 1986: 40)

However, 'reconciliation' of these two strands of education has rather more limited connotations than those we wish to suggest are associated with potential changes in the scope of education policy created by the kind of hybrid TVEI represents. It is not so much a question of the reconciliation of these two unfortunately – and indefensibly – separate strands of secondary education. Rather, central to our concern are the outcome of that larger hybridization, and the different assumptions held in the two contributing traditions about the scope of education policy. By the scope of education policy I mean broadly what it is assumed a public education service should be, and is capable of, doing. That is to say, the scope of education policy is concerned with assumptions about the *mandate* for the education system and about its *capacity* to fulfil that mandate. This chapter tentatively compares MSC and DES assumptions about the scope of education policy and the consequences of their hybridization in TVEI.

Educational mandates

Mandates for the education system are made up of conceptions of what it is desirable and legitimate for the education system to seek to bring about. At any one time there exist myriad mandates, giving different priority to the three major categories of targets to be achieved by the education system. These are succinctly set out in the White Paper *Working Together – Education and Training*: 'children go to schools so that they can develop their talents, become responsible citizens and be prepared for work' (para. 2.1). The co-existence of strong mandates separately (and often contradictorily) stressing each of the three main targets of education is a common, if not permanent, feature of education in this country, and an essential part of its dynamic. Over the past 10 years, though, one of these mandates has been dominant, that contained in the 1976 Green Paper, *Education in Schools*. This document both prefigured and required the kind of hybridization of education-training for employment whose culmination is TVEI. Essentially, that mandate called for a much greater emphasis on the preparation of workers and citizens than on the development of individual talents.

This was a mandate for the education service prepared within the education service, albeit with unprecedentedly extensive and unprecedentedly welcome input from outside the education service. The MSC, then a relatively small organization, was not a significant factor in drawing up the mandate nor in the plans for its fulfilment. However, MSC was at that time beginning to work in adjacent areas, and there is considerable overlap between the *Education in Schools* mandate for education and MSC's developing approaches to the problems of training and youth employment. The Holland Committee, for instance, recommended the creation of the Youth Opportunities Programme to guarantee some form of work experience to all unemployed school leavers. It is significant that:

> it was authoritatively rumoured at the time that a battle raged in Cabinet before the decision was made between the DES and the Department of Employment about which of them should be given the money to provide for the young unemployed. We are told that DE won because it could guarantee to produce places very quickly on the ground. The DES could provide much less because it would have to make grants to local education authorities and simply exhort them to deliver. (Short, 1986: 42)

Thus, there is clear overlap in the mandates of the two organizations in respect of the education and training of young people. There are, though, distinct differences in their capacity to fulfil this mandate. This applies not just to the broad, overall conception of 'vocational education', but also to such issues within it as gender equality, the management of the curriculum, and teachers' careers too, which will be discussed below.

What I am suggesting, in effect, is that there are crucial differences between (and within) the political and administrative discourses of DES and MSC. The nature and consequences of these differences can be clarified by examining the two bodies' respective conceptualizations of the scope of a public education service.

Interpreting the mandate

I have already pointed to some overlap in the education and training mandates of the DES and MSC. There are though, very important differences of interpretation and emphasis between the DES and MSC. These differences have two, linked bases. The first lies in the different traditions of which they are part. In giving reasons why the MSC's work 'is still largely separate from that of the DES and the local authorities that maintain schools and employ teachers', William Taylor (1985: 109) lists the following:

Administratively, training has been linked with employment rather than education. Politically, governments have been somewhat less than satisfied with the way secondary schools have dealt with their older age groups. Financially, it has been difficult to earmark for particular purposes the funds made available to local authorities. But more fundamentally, the separation reflects the way in which history, economic circumstances and social structure have given us a heritage of values, attitudes and assumptions that constitute education and training as two separate metaphors, a heritage which continues to influence our thought and our practice.

It is not difficult to identify the values conventionally associated with these two metaphors. Education is often depicted as soft, person-centred, moralized, academic, critical, contemplative, radical in attitude but traditional in form, theoretical, norm-referenced, enclosed, a consumption good rather than an investment. In contrast, training is represented as hard, task-centred, materialistic, practical, oriented towards action, criterion-referenced, pragmatic, innovative in structure but conservative in substance, unselective, open, a valuable national investment.

The second basis of the difference of interpretation and emphasis is the 'policy obligations' of the DES and MSC. These are perhaps best set out in the lists of objectives of the Department of Employment and of the DES which appear, symbolically, on the inside front and back covers, respectively, of the *Working Together* White Paper

Objectives of the Department of Employment
The prime aim of the Department of Employment is to encourage the development of an enterprise economy. The way to reduce unemployment is through more businesses, more self-employment and greater wealth-creation, all leading to more jobs.
The key aspects of the Department's work are to:

1. Promote enterprise and job creation in growth areas such as small firms, self-employment and tourism.
2. Help business to grow and jobs multiply by cutting 'red tape'; improving industrial relations by ensuring a fair balance under the law and encouraging employee involvement.
3. Improve training arrangements so that young people get a better preparation for work, and adults obtain the skills they need to compete in the world.

4. Help the young and those out of work for some time find work, training or opportunities likely to lead to a job.

In addition to the nationwide network of High Street Jobcentres, there are over 30 training, employment and business help schemes. Among them are schemes for people employed, unemployed, skilled, unskilled, young or old.

The Department's many other activities include:

● helping unemployed people by the prompt payment of the benefit and allowances to which they are entitled
● helping protect the employment of individuals, including those disadvantaged on grounds of race, sex or disability
● helping maintain and improve health and safety at work.

The Department of Employment Group also comprises the Manpower Services Commission, the Health and Safety Executive and the Advisory Conciliation and Arbitration Service.

Objectives of the Department of Education and Science
The principal aim of the Department of Education and Science is to improve standards throughout the education service and to increase the value obtained for the substantial resources allocated to it by the taxpayer and the ratepayer.

In *schools*, the Department aims

● to promote agreement on the curriculum and ensure that it is broad and balanced for all pupils;
● to foster the application of what is learnt to real problems and situations;
● to stretch pupils of all abilities;
● to give parents more influence; and
● to enhance the powers of governing bodies.

In *non-advanced further education*, the Department aims

● to increase the responsiveness of the service to the needs of employers;
● to provide a sound education for young people and adults; and
● to secure an improved use of resources – and in particular a significant tightening of student : staff ratios.

In *higher education*, the Department aims

● to raise quality and standards while preserving the full breadth of educational provision;
● to make the system more responsive to the needs of the economy;
● to improve management systems in universities, polytechnics and colleges, and
● generally to increase value for money by rationalization.

The Department is also responsible for

● *adult and continuing education*. The principal aim is to update the skills of the national workforce at all levels.
● the *civil science base* financed by the University Grants Committee and the Research Councils. The principal aims are to promote excellence by greater concentration and selectivity of research activities and to stimulate commercial applications of new ideas.
● *teachers*. The aim is to secure the supply of sufficient teachers of the quality needed to teach the agreed curricula and to update the skills of the existing teacher force.

Throughout the education system – at all levels – the output of citizens competent in mathematics, science and technology must be increased. The DES – in cooperation with the other Government Departments concerned – is developing a range of policies to that end.

What is meant by policy obligations can be derived from these lists. For instance, while the DES is *obliged* to 'ensure a broad and balanced curriculum for all pupils', the DE(MSC) is not – though that is not to say that in its forays into education it will not seek to do so, as it claims to have done with TVEI. Similarly, it is not an obligation, let alone a prime aim, for the DES to encourage the development of an enterprise economy – though again it *may* choose to meet its aims in part by doing so. The main relevant difference between the two departments for our present purpose is that while the DES is obliged to pursue all three broad targets for education, the MSC is not; while education is an end in itself for the DES, for the MSC it can only be a means to achieving its (MSC's) own objectives. We are not suggesting either that every action of MSC and DES can be directly related to their policy obligations, or that either of them are entirely monolithic (we know that neither is), merely that they are subject to different fundamental pressures.

To return to the mandate contained in the 1976 Green Paper: its fulfilment provided two major problems for the education system. The first was that the system itself was identified in the Green Paper as one of the obstacles to the mandate's fulfilment. The degree of autonomy of the education system, schools and teachers, and the ways that autonomy was alleged to have been used, made the system as much part of the problem the new mandate addressed, as the key means of fulfilling it. The mandate indeed implied not only changes in the orientation of education policy, but changes in the way it was formulated and implemented too – not only changes in the content and purpose of education but also in the way those changes were devised and introduced into the system.

The formulation and implementation of policy – in particular, the inability of the DES to institute system-wide change – comprised the second major problem. The DES was not able to compel compliance, only to persuade and pressure in various ways (Ranson, 1985). It was this inability to fulfil the 1976 Green Paper mandate – together with massive rises in youth unemployment

– which brought MSC, via Prime Ministerial initiative, into the educational system at school level for the first time in 1983.

The different policy obligations of the DES and MSC emerge clearly in their respective assumptions about the scope of education policy. Two such assumptions are especially important. The first concerns whether education policy is predominantly *strategic*, i.e. aimed at effecting the world outside education as much as directly affecting those in the system, or largely confined to bringing about changes within the education system for its own sake. The policy obligations of the MSC and DES clearly differ in this respect. The MSC's policy obligation has little to do with an 'intrinsic' education policy. It must seek to use education to bring about changes in the world outside education. This orientation is nicely caught in the very first paragraph of the *Working Together* White Paper:

> We live in a world of determined, educated, trained and strongly motivated competitors. The competition they offer has taken more and more of our markets – both overseas and here at home.

This sets the tone for an education policy that is almost entirely strategic. The DES, on the other hand, can only look to such strategic considerations when they are congruent with its obligations – and, of course, a great deal of the debate about meeting the *Education in Schools* mandate has been precisely about the degree of congruency that can, or should, be achieved between tactical and strategic considerations.

The second difference in DES and MSC assumptions about the scope of education policy is whether education policy is typically involved with structural (system-wide) *reform* or with more restricted local *innovations* (Papagiannis *et al.*, 1982). We would suggest that both tradition and policy obligation push MSC to the former and DES to the latter of these positions. As Taylor suggests, training has been regarded as requiring central direction and control, while there is a very strong tradition of decentralization – and variation – in the education system. Within the education system, even the most far reaching attempt at structural reform – the introduction of comprehensive education – offered alternative models (based on existing local practice) to local authorities, rather than imposing one system nationwide. The most interesting tensions at the birth of TVEI were concerned with this very issue of whether the scheme was to be administered through LEAs or through a separate set of institutions. As we know, it was decided to administer it through LEAs and that decision was the origin of the peculiar administrative and ideological hybridity which now characterizes TVEI.

Capacity to implement the mandate

There are perhaps even greater potential differences between DES and MSC in terms of their capacity and *modus operandi* than there are in their traditions and policy obligations. In understanding TVEI, differences between DES and MSC in this area – and the way they are hybridized – are at least as important as differences in interpretation of the mandate. The capacity and *modus operandi* of the DES and MSC differ significantly in a number of ways.

1. The DES is a Department of State headed by a Cabinet Minister politically accountable through Parliament to the *electorate*. It operates according to a structured, bureaucratic rule-following model. The MSC, on the other hand, is a corporate body, made up of people representing particular *interests*, particularly the two sides of industry. This means both that MSC is a coalition of potentially competing interests, and that any decisions and actions it takes can be assumed already to have the approval of those they affect (in so far as they are represented on the Commission); those actions and decisions do not have to go through further consultative, participative discussion stages – which is one of the reasons that the MSC is able to act much more quickly than the DES. As the Director of the MSC puts it:

   > MSC . . . is no advisory body, but a public board charged with executive responsibilities. . . . When a commissioner commits himself/herself to a particular programme, policy, or line of action, he/she is also committing many more people and organizations in the world outside. This commitment . . . is the key reason why so many far-reaching developments have taken place so quickly under the Commission's auspices. (Holland, 1986: 88)

2. The MSC's operating model differs from the DES's. Rather than being bureaucratic and process-orientated, it is technocratic or even commercial. For the MSC, achieving results is the criterion of action, while the DES is bound by the need for accurate rule-following. The DES can only bring about major change by changing the rules, i.e. by introducing legislation; for the MSC it is a much more straightforward matter of changing the substance in the most immediately effective way.
3. Until relatively recently, it had been assumed that DES could only operate through the local education authorities, whom it could not in any case compel to follow a particular path; perhaps the best known example of this is the failure of Shirley Williams as Secretary of State at the DES to get local authorities to spend, for the State's purposes, the £7 million she had earmarked for in-service training. The implications of this are clear from Clare Short's comment quoted above, and in the introduction of TVEI itself.
4. Certainly, in the education area, MSC has operated more like a fire-brigade than a police force. It is essentially a crisis-management organization. It could withdraw altogether from education and has no built-in continuing commitment to the area. Thus not only is it able to introduce different kinds of programmes, it is also able to do so less hampered by the ramifications they may have for the rest of the service or by the need to continue supporting them if they appear initially to be unsuccessful.

5. Associated with this is the different pattern of funding available to the two bodies. The MSC's funds are for particular programmes, typically contracted for by providing agencies on terms laid down by the MSC. Its budget is not immutably tied up in continuing financial obligations which take up almost all its resources, unlike the DES, with its major commitments in the area of school building and higher education, for instance. The DES has, then, been financially as well as constitutionally restricted in the kind of intervention it could make in the education service.

6. A further financial difference is that the DES needs (from the Secretary of State) approval *before* committing expenditure, whereas the MSC is accountable only *after* spending the money. The corollary of this, however, is that the MSC has to do far more monitoring, auditing, etc., of projects *after* they are set up (and this has been a major source of irritation to teachers and schools in TVEI).

7. The MSC is much more likely to intervene from the supply-side, whereas the DES's tradition has been much more demand-led funding. The MSC provides funds whose levels are known beforehand for specified programmes aimed at identified objectives, and subject to monitoring. The DES has traditionally been much more reactive (within its constitutional limits), responding to pressures and suggestions within the education system, rather than using fully what powers it had to steer the system.

8. Another difference in the mode of intervention lies in the source of the resources used. Though this is beginning to break down, certainly informally (as other chapters in this book demonstrate), DES assumptions have traditionally been that state education will be wholly state-funded. MSC assumptions are quite different, and deliberately so. Efficiency of performance and cost-cutting through competition are much more important in determining which bodies will carry out the work than a commitment to state provision.

9. These various constitutional and financial differences combine in the different types of activity and intervention the two bodies make. This difference can be summarized as the difference between what Claus Offe calls 'allocative' and 'productive' types of state activity, and it is worth expanding on the distinction a little. Offe's distinction is usefully summarized by Jessop (1982: 110–11):

> Allocation involves the use of state resources to secure the general framework of economic activity and/or to provide general public services in accordance with general constitutional or legislative codes which effect the prevailing balance of political forces. Production involves direct state-sponsored provision of material resources as a precondition of crisis-avoidance or crisis management where there is no general code that can be applied and decision rules must therefore be developed in order to determine more effective action by case. Offe then argues that, although rational-legal bureaucratic administration may be appropriate to the allocative activities of the

state, it is inadequate to the demands of state productive activities insofar as they are oriented to the attainment of particular objectives rather than the general application of pregiven rules.

This distinction encapsulates much of the difference between the DES and the MSC, and the ramifications of MSC sponsorship, in terms of substance, style, purpose and method, that mark TVEI as a form of education policy at least as effectively as the funds it provides.

TVEI as a hybrid

The hybrid that is TVEI is far from being sufficiently settled or organized to specify anything more than a range of broad patterns of practice. Indeed, it may never emerge as a clearly identifiable separate strain of education policy. The two sets of factors making up the hybrid combine in different ways in different circumstances, where existing patterns of practice (themselves largely in the education rather than employment tradition) appear to have been frequently influential. In this situation of flux, as many opportunities as constraints are likely to be found, with the combination of traditions providing greater freedom for teachers and schools in some areas, greater control over them in others.

TVEI does not, of course, represent a new issue as much as a new solution to a recurrent problem (see Reeder, 1979). What essentially distinguishes TVEI from previous attempts to bring education and employment closer together is not so much its influence on the mandate addressed by education policy makers – which, with greater or lesser variations, has characterized all phases of the recurrent debate – as its influence on the *capacity* of the education system to meet that of the mandate. Rather than relying on exhortation, persuasion or even pressure – all of which connote action from *outside* – on the education system, in TVEI the employment interest has become a *partner* with the educational interest in *achieving* as well as devising a broadly agreed mandate. It is its operation in the spheres of both the mandate and the capacity of the education system that makes TVEI unique.

PART 3

Politics and Education

6 Thatcherism and Education

In a relatively brief period, 'Thatcherism' has become an essential part of the vocabulary of British politics. It is used on both the left and the right of the political spectrum. However, its exact meaning, and what it implies in any given context, remains rather imprecise; it is connotative rather than denotative. It is, though, clearly distinguishable from other forms of conservatism, if only in its relative readiness to own up to being 'ideological', while it is possible to identify intellectual guiding lights in Friedman and Hayek, though neither of these is followed slavishly. It is further characterized by what Stuart Hall (1979, 1980) has very aptly called 'authoritarian populism', which both draws on selectively, and recombines, existing strands of conservatism (particularly those which appeal to the grass roots rather than the hierarchy of the Conservative Party); and it loosely knits these together with opportunistic reactions to contemporary problems.

In examining the impact of Thatcherism on education policy, I shall be seeking both to define it rather more precisely and to question the assumption of its unequivocal dominance in all areas of Mrs Thatcher's government policy. Education policy is, in fact, a particularly useful area to carry out this kind of examination given its control for the second part of Mrs Thatcher's 1979–84 government by the chief ideologue of Thatcherism, Sir Keith Joseph, backed up by its chief propagandist, Dr Rhodes Boyson. The opportunity and the desire to implement key precepts of Thatcherism can rarely have combined more favourably than they did in education at the beginning of the 1980s.

The opportunity was provided by the education-political situation that was crystallizing towards the end of the 1970s, whose chief characteristics may be very broadly listed as:

- the withering of the Welfare State consensus;
- growing unemployment, especially of youth;
- the failure of social democratic policies, not only in not producing greater equality and social justice, but in the production of casualties in the form of

the neglected and those who felt themselves 'levelled down' (a key constituency of Thatcherism); and
● associated with these things, the decline of faith in the state education system.

This situation was one to which the educational traditions of Conservatism, especially as felt at the grass roots and under Mrs Thatcher, were far better able to react than those of the Labour Party. However, before moving on to discuss Tory education policy under Mrs Thatcher, it will be necessary to make a very brief diversion to consider the kinds of education policies which previous post-war Tory governments had followed. Certainly from 1955, when Sir David Eccles was appointed Minister of Education, until the 1964 election, Tory education policy was essentially non-partisan and even, when Sir Edward Boyle was Minister of Education, almost bipartisan; following the precepts of R.A. Butler's 1944 Act, the education service expanded greatly, in the number of schools, teachers, students in higher education, and so on. Under Boyle, commitment to selection for secondary education and automatic opposition to comprehensive education ceased to be central parts of official Tory education policy, while the value of education in producing the kinds of people and skills necessary to ensure continued economic growth was very much taken for granted.

This approach was not, however, without its critics, particularly after the election defeats of 1964 and 1966. It was in this period that the first Black Papers were published, with their emphasis on standards, excellence, authority and the other traditional virtues held to be at the core of the grammar school. In this period, too, suggestions based in anti-statist, economic liberal thought, and the airing of ideas for educational voucher schemes began to appear (see Corbett, 1969). Most of this opposition came from the grass roots of the Conservative Party, rather than from its parliamentary representatives or from those with responsibilities for the party's education policy. For instance, an analysis of motions on education submitted between 1965 and 1970 to the Conservative Party Conference shows that around 55% of them emanated from what the author calls the libertarian right and which has a number of features in common with Thatcherism (Wilson, 1977). The two most common topics were tax relief on private education fees, and opposition to comprehensive schools. The strength of this opposition is clear from the fact that at the 1968 party conference the official motion on education was defeated, with Sir Edward Boyle stating that he would not fight Socialist dogma with Conservative dogma.

So, by the time Margaret Thatcher was appointed Minister of Education in 1970, to the delight of the Party's right wing (Russell, 1978), there were clear cracks under the surface of the non-partisan approach of Eccles and Boyle. There is insufficient space to go into Mrs Thatcher's period as Education Minister in any detail, but it is certainly important to try to draw out some general impression of it (see Woods, 1981).

Such a task is not, in fact, very easy. True, within 3 days of taking office she issued circular 10/70, which removed the obligation on LEA's to submit plans for comprehensive reorganization and before much longer, she was, notoriously, 'snatching milk', but at the same time she did implement the Raising of the School Leaving Age (which the previous Labour Government has postponed) and she did increase spending on primary education. The powerful advice from a number of quarters of her party to smother the new-born Open University was rejected. And while 'she wasn't disposed to listen to the unalloyed liberalism of the education service' (Kogan, 1975: 44), she did not, at a time when the belief in the value of education was beginning to be seriously questioned, and when sceptical eyes were being cast on human capital theories, cut back overall spending on education or introduce policies which very obviously prefigured Thatcherism. However, if the contents of her policies were pre-Thatcherite, it is possible to read more proto-Thatcherite leanings in her style. On comprehensive schools, for instance, she not only legislated against their compulsory spread, but she also deliberately slowed down even those schemes for comprehensive reorganization submitted by Conservative local authorities, often by going out of her way to encourage pro-grammar school groups of parents (Woods, 1981).

In fact, many of the roots of Thatcherism were contained within the so-called Selsdon philosophy, which the Party adopted under Edward Heath and to which it was committed when it won the 1970 general election. This philosophy represented an attempt to break the neo-social democratic, state interventionist consensus through which the country had been governed for almost two decades. State intervention in industry was to be severely curtailed, lame ducks were (in a mixed metaphor) to be allowed to go to the wall, market forces were to be unshackled. The reversal of this policy and a return to Keynesian strategies, and in spite of that, the defeat in the 1974 election held on the issue 'Who Governs Britain', restoked the fires of ideological conflict within the Conservative Party and forged the alliance within the Party which brought Mrs Thatcher to the leadership. The hope was that she would both demonstrate who governed Britain and, with her greater personal commitment to Selsdon-type policies than her predecessor, refuse to be deflected from that course when the going got tough. The mood was certainly right for radical change within the Tory Party. Objectively, the oil price rises of the early 1970s had accelerated and highlighted Britain's long-term economic decline. Subjectively, the 1974 defeat was the more humiliating not just because it showed a loss of national confidence in the Party and because it had been received at the hands of militant trade unionism, but also because it could be seen to be in an important sense self-inflicted, the result of the desertion of some basic principles of conservatism. The neo-social democratic Welfare State policies for which they had abandoned those principles had been a mistake – the price that had been paid was too high, the pay-off too low. Not only was such a level of state intervention against their deepest instincts, it proved what they had always felt about its ineffectiveness. The Welfare State had provided not so much security as featherbedding, weakening the moral fibre and the incentive to work and be responsible for self, without succeeding in eliminating anti-social behaviour, for instance, or even illiteracy. This is most graphically illustrated in Sir Keith Joseph's initial embrace, and subsequent rejection of, the idea of a cycle of deprivation (Joseph, 1979).

Quite crucially, however, this reaction, which formed the basis of Thatcherism, was not homogeneous, but brought together a number of strands of old as well as new conservative thought into a far from easy, and frequently shifting, alliance. And in order to understand Thatcherism we have to begin to separate out some of these contributing strands, and to locate their history and the nature of their support.

The industrial trainers

This strand of thought is part of the 'pragmatic' (as opposed to 'principled') reaction to the Welfare State. The label comes from Raymond Williams's (1965) well-known tripartite division of educational ideologies (though I am no more happy with its exact appropriateness than I am with that of the labels I will suggest for other groups).

Though the ideology of the bipartisan policy may come largely from those I will call the Old Tories, what might very loosely be called its 'material base' was located in those sections of (large) industry which had a great deal to gain from an expanded and improved state provision of qualified manpower. Their interest was in maximizing the benefit they could draw from the education system, through exercising direct and indirect pressure to deflect it in directions amenable to them. Ralph Miliband (1978: 406) defined this group's position very neatly:

> the people who run the most important and powerful sectors of British capitalist enterprise are by no means unequivocally in favour of 'free enterprise'. On the contrary, they very much want the state to help them, in a permanent and extensive system of intervention which would yet leave them free from state control; and the same people have long found that this could be got from a Labour Government, as well as from a Conservative one. . . . They may, on the whole, prefer a Conservative Government, to a Labour one; but unlike many Conservatives at the grassroots and in the political leadership, they are not at this point bent on 'counter revolution'.

It is from this position that arguments about education, like those put forward by Arnold Weinstock (1976) of GEC and John Methven (1976), then Director-General of the CBI, emerge. There is a clear, if implicit, acceptance that the State is the appropriate provider and controller of education. It must, though, recognize how those who provide its revenue and the country's wealth, generate that wealth, and attempt to make sure that the education system is at the very least not counterproductive – which is what Weinstock claims many teachers are – and at best productive – which is what Methven's programme is designed to ensure.

Industry does though suffer from policies designed to cut public spending and state intervention in industry. Especially in periods of economic slump, large-scale industry has become more dependent on Keynesian counter-cyclical, state-initiated projects for support. Thatcherism was resolutely opposed to these, with consequent complaints and requests for better treatment from the CBI. As I shall detail below, this shift from neo–Keynesian to. neo–Friedmanite strategies on public spending seriously affects both the place and the funding of state education, having little appeal for those who have until now received major benefits from the state education system, in both the provision of variously skilled labour, and of research and development. However, as will again be elaborated below, one thrust of Thatcherite education policy may welcome the administrative separation of 'training' from 'education'. This is already beginning to happen, with the increasing scope and responsibility, especially in the 16+ age range of such para-educational institutions as the Manpower Services Commission. The MSC has already had a tremendous effect on the structure and practice of further education and training, putting in question the effectiveness of the formal control of these institutions. At the government level, the DES's relatively slow and 'educationist' response to problems posed by widespread youth unemployment has led to its losing ground in the provision for this group to the relatively more open and pragmatically attuned MSC/DoI/DoE. And while the MSC was originally inspired by a human capital rationale, it seems clear that the purposes of current programmes are becoming less to fit young people for jobs, and more, because the jobs are not there, to perform a kind of social holding operation.

The industrial trainers do, though, continue to be one of the legs propping up the key themes of accountability and standards. Though the precise meaning to be attached to these terms is elusive, the need for education to be broadly responsive to the demands of the economy remains a central component of Conservative (and, it should be said, Labour) education policy. The question of whether that accountability and those standards are best brought about through market mechanisms or by the State appears not to be a crucial issue for this group.

The Old Tories

It is in this group that traditional conservative values are still dominant. Their essence is that kind of benevolent paternalism which Robert Eccleshall takes to characterize English conservatism. As he puts it:

> During the nineteenth century, the idea of paternal guardianship was deployed by many Tories in order to condemn the effects of growing industrialization upon traditional bonds of social dependence. More significantly in a period when the working class was becoming

enfranchised, the persistent appeal of a stable, intimate social hierarchy enabled Disraeli to devise a formula for the leadership of propertied groups around the theme of one nation. The effect, by furnishing a set of potent cultural symbols around which to marshal attitudes of social deference was to bequeath the legacy of protective élitism to the twentieth century (Eccleshall, 1980: 4).

The relative decline of influence of this strand of conservatism thought can be recognized in the use of Disraeli's name and authority as a 'code' to attack Thatcherite policies; at one point Edward Heath hardly seemed to make a speech which did not contain Disraeli's famous statement that 'it is upon the education of the people of this country that the future of this country depends'. And as a member of the Tory Reform Group, Trevor Russell, points out, the social order which Disraeli is said to have brought to Victorian England, and which Mrs Thatcher and Dr Boyson like to recall as a 'golden age', was, in fact, based not on Thatcherite policies, but on a considerable level of state intervention (Russell, 1978).

Another of the principles of 'Old Toryism' is the belief that political wisdom resides in a dominant minority. This was perhaps most clearly expressed by the then Quintin Hogg, in the aftermath of the 1944 Education Act:

> Precisely because it arouses fierce religious differences and social resentments education is a matter which must be handled by statesmen on pragmatical and objective lines in a country of many religious differences and social distinctions, [while] not the least valuable feature of (Mr. Butler's Act) is that it has placed the general framework of our educational system beyond the range of party politics. (Hogg, 1947: 143–4)

This contrasts rather with the kind of populism and the emphasis on parental choice in education, which is much more characteristic of Thatcherism.

A further contrast is found in the interpretation of the idea of self-help. Eccleshall brings this out well. He contrasts the 'paternal guardianship' and 'one nation' themes of Disraeli, with what we would see as a much more Thatcherite, bourgeois rhetoric in which:

> society appears . . . as a collection of independent individuals each intent on pursuing self-interest . . . [it is] a fluid structure in which individuals rise to the social level concomitant with their natural abilities. Riches are seen as the due reward of those who have expanded maximum energy, intelligence and agility in making material provision for themselves. Conversely, poverty is taken as a sign of some innate deficiency, the failure of individuals to exercise sufficient skill to secure comfortable existence; those who prove themselves incapable of seizing opportunities that are equally available to everyone must expect to pay the penalty of a lower standard of living. (Eccleshall, 1980: 4)

The distinction between these very different notions of self-interest, individualism and a kind of commonality, albeit one which 'contrives a cosy image of an affective community where all may be brothers but never equals' (Eccleshall, 1977: 68), emerged very clearly in the House of Lords' rejection of that part of the 1980 Education Act dealing with the proposed introduction of the possibility of charging for school transport, where a coalition of Old Tories, Roman Catholics and Socialists successfully fought against the measure (see Bull, 1980). This was then denounced by Ralph Harris, writing in the *Spectator*, as:

> a triumph for false compassion, sectarian interest, timidity, nostalgia, political paternalism and economic irresponsibility [as] . . . complacency, conformity, old fashioned conservatism and cheap compassion – at other people's expense. (Harris, 1980: 12–13)

The continuing strength, but novel defensiveness, of this traditionally dominant strand of conservative educational ideology (best epitomized in Butler's Act and above all in Sir Edward Boyle's tenure of the DES), is seen in the frequency and tone of the objections to its supersession by a much more abrasive and divisive approach. Not only conservative politicians like Mr Heath and Sir William van Strabenzee (see the *Times Educational Supplement*, 16 October 1981), but other such bulwarks of Old Toryism as the chairman of the Headmasters' conference (Thorn, 1981), spoke out against the nature and the extent of the cuts imposed on education by the Thatcher government. There is a consistent theme running through all of them – that of betrayal of the duty to succour the less well off, and of the failure to mitigate the price the many have to pay for the success of the few.

The differences between this previously dominant approach and key strands of Thatcherism may be best gleaned from a consideration of the differences between two views of educational vouchers, published in the *Times Educational Supplement* in 1975. The one, in a paper prepared for the Conservative Political Centre by Vernon Bogdanor, may be taken as broadly representative of what is called here 'Old Toryism'. The other is a response to it by Rhodes Boyson, a major power in Thatcherite education policy. For Bogdanor, 'there is a necessary tension between the freedom of the market and the demand for equal rights in a democracy', and believers in parental rights must strike the balance between these. 'What is at issue' Bogdanor concludes, 'is whether the commercial principle should be brought into the state sector of education so as to override the equal rights established by modern legislation and in particular by the Butler Education Act of 1944'. Boyson's response focuses very much on individual parents' freedom. He claims that educational voucher schemes are weapons against socialist excess since they 'move power from the state to the family'. He argues, too, that the Government 'can never maximize the potential of each individual child. . . . Only the parent can know his own child sufficiently well to fit his individual talents' (Boyson, 1975a). There is much more to this significant and interesting debate than space permits me to include here; it not only catches very well the distinction between 'Old Tories' and 'Populists', but also indicates something of the nature and the extent of the departure from traditional thought which Thatcherism represents.

The populists

So far, populism has been examined as it contrasts with 'Old Toryism', but I want now to consider it in slightly more detail. Populism in the broad sense of appeal to the 'national instincts' of the people and to unifying factors like nationality above 'divisive' factors like class, race and gender has been identified by a number of writers (e.g. Hall, 1979, 1980) as a key strand of Thatcherism. One of its most explicit adherents and propagators, generally, and particularly with respect to education, is Rhodes Boyson. I wish here merely to identify what seems to me some salient points of Boyson's educational philosophy, which contribute powerfully to the structure of Thatcherism (see, e.g. Boyson, 1975b, and numerous speeches reported in the educational press; see also Wright, 1977). Basically, Boyson is set upon promoting common sense above theory, and the people (together with 'natural' social units, like the family) above the experts. His attacks are aimed at the betrayal of the people by experts, social engineers who claim to know best what's good for people, but whose half-baked theories have led only to drastic decline in standards and discipline, and to a collapse of confidence in education. It is this strand of conservative educational thought to which the Black Papers have most contributed, with their revelation of the consequences of half-baked progressive ideas and of assuming that all children can be equal.

Four points need to be noted about this kind of populism to enable us to make some evaluation of its contribution to Thatcherite education policy. First, we should recognize that 'the people' appealed to and allegedly represented in this populist strand, by no means includes 'everyone'. Effectively, it means the deserving, those able and willing to make the most of opportunities offered them, and those most stifled by Welfare State nannying. It does not include the improvident or those unwilling to help themselves. The second point to bear in mind is that this kind of populism is not so much anti-statist as anti-social democratic. The objection to the social democratic State is that it tries to bring about 'unnatural' things, like social justice. This involves upsetting the natural hierarchy – or even meritocracy – which it is the legitimate task of the State to maintain, along with the family and other 'natural' social units. It may even be a part of the State's job to make sure that the natural hierarchy of talent is properly attuned to national economic needs through the education system. Indeed, it is in this way that the state education system can be most effective, both for the individual and the nation. Thirdly, we should note that it is not only through the Black Papers that this strand of thought has been publicized. It is also the educational theme, most commonly represented in the conservative popular press, especially perhaps the *Daily Mail* (see School Without Walls, 1978). This press support has proved a very potent factor and undoubtedly contributed greatly to the shifting of the whole ground of educational debate which took place in the mid-1970s and which culminated in a Labour Government donning at least some of the populists' clothes in the creation and agenda of the Great Debate on education (see Donald, 1981). This link with the popular press suggests a fourth distinguishing feature of the populist approach. It tends to replace the pragmatism of traditional Toryism with a much more abrasive opportunism; having inherited neither the feeling of a natural right to rule, nor the benevolent paternalism which the Old Tories insist should be the corollary of such an inheritance, and hence lacking, too, a stabilizing belief in the ability of the basic social hierarchy inevitably to adapt to superficial change, the populists are squeezed towards creating and seizing short-term political advantages which their 'grander' colleagues would disdain and find distasteful. Hence, a certain volatility, and unpredictable interpretation of its basic themes, might be expected from adherents to the populist approach.

The moral entrepreneurs

Once again this label is used in a rather different way here from its original use by Howard Becker. What I have in mind is in fact not too distant from what Alan Wolfe, in his analysis of Reaganism, calls 'conformist individualism'. He writes:

> There is apparently a distinction made in right wing thought between individualism and self-indulgence. Hence discipline is as vital as freedom. An inability of the nation to control its libidinal impulses – in short, sin – is responsible for *inflation* (too many people consuming instead of saving); *crime* (too many people accumulating the easy way, without working); *urban decline* (too many governments spending too carelessly); *national weakness* (too much pleasure seeking at the expense of sacrificing to meet the external challenge); and *dissent* (women wanting to avoid housework – gays having too much fun). (Wolfe, 1981: 26)

In respect of contemporary education policy, however, it does seem important to identify a crusading group rather than an orientation which would be common to several of the stands I am discussing. Those I am calling the moral entrepreneurs see education at the heart of a fight for a particular morality and against (im)moralities which would undermine it. This group is inevitably associated with the name of Mary Whitehouse, who when she was a teacher, became concerned that certain TV programmes were seducing children into sub-Christian life styles (see Tracey and Morrison, 1979). This led to the 'clean-up TV' campaigns, and thence to the Festival of Light and

other campaigns against sexual permissiveness. This kind of moral entre-
preneurship is curiously poised between authoritarianism and privatism. On
the one hand, it argues that things like sex education are essentially private
matters and are the concern of the family rather than of the State or school.
On the other hand, the whole point of the moral entrepreneurs is that social
behaviour should be controlled by a set of rules and moral imperatives, and
that it is an area which *laissez-faire* had no place. It is not state intervention but
unrestrained market forces which produce pornography. Hence, both legislation and some kind of moral lead from the State are called for by the moral
entrepreneurs – which puts them in the difficult and paradoxical position of
asking that institutions like schools must give a moral lead on matters which
are simultaneously held to be properly none of their concern.

Nevertheless, in spite of these paradoxes, and irrespective of whether such
groups as Mrs Whitehouse's have any links with the Conservative Party, the
moral entrepreneurs do seem to be an important influence on current
education policy in at least four ways. First, they have a clear influence on
some well-known Conservative politicians [e.g. Mrs (now Dame) Jill
Knight], whereby their views are both publicly amplified and inserted into
intra-Party debates. While their direct influence is more clearly evident at the
grass roots of the Party and at Party conferences, there seems little doubt that
Mrs Thatcher herself is in much greater sympathy with such sectors of the
Party than were any of her predecessors, and hence the fact that that particular
set of views is not adopted by the traditional Party hierarchy is less important
now than it has been previously.

Secondly, the moral entrepreneurs pick up and reinforce themes prominent in other strands of conservative ideology. The clearest examples here are
the need for self-discipline and a national moral regeneration. Thirdly, and
closely associated with this, is the encouragement of, and conviction of the
importance of, the traditional family as the basis of social harmony and
healthy personal development, which begins to identify working mothers,
and feminism generally, as key causes of many of the evils it sees. That
women's place is not predominantly at work has been an implicit theme of
British post-war education policy (see Wolpe, 1976; Deem, 1981).

Recently, though, Miriam David (1982) has argued that the emphasis on
preparation for sex differentiated roles in adulthood is becoming established
in official curricular advice. She argues that the DES now clearly acknow-
ledges that family life is not entirely a private matter but is circumscribed by
public laws and state policies: 'It accepts its own duty to clarify to children what
the state believes is entailed in being a parent' (p. 33). These beliefs, David
argues, draw on particular fundamental values, which are to be achieved 'both
by means of moral exhortation and special teaching or moral or religious
education'. Matters may not yet have reached this stage, but the pressure on
parents to be responsible for their children and not 'leave everything to the
state' is clearly mounting, reaching a peak with captions to front page photos of
children involved in the 1982 summer disturbances which asked boldly what
their parents were doing to allow this, and comments in the same papers that it

was not a social breakdown which produced the disturbances, but the break-down of the traditional family and parental authority.

The final form of the influence of the moral entrepreneurs may have the most immediate and effective impact upon educational practice. It results from the climate of caution and circumspection created by the tactics typically adopted by the moral entrepreneurs, of public exposure of what they classify as immorality. This can easily lead to mild self-censorship, and soft-pedalling, even avoiding, potentially contentious issues. Though it is most difficult to prove, impressionistic evidence suggests that the threat of public exposure, even when one believes totally in the rightness of what one is doing, is a very effective way of ensuring schools' conformity.

The privatizers

It is this group which provides the intellectual and economic case for the move away from the Welfare State and for the return of the services it provides to the market (the recently formed Social Affairs Unit takes up these themes: see Anderson *et al.*, 1981). There are a number of interesting similarities between this group and those dubbed the neo-conservatives in the United States, but space precludes examining those similarities in any depth. Indeed, for our immediate purposes, the appointment of the Conservative Party's chief ideologue, Sir Keith Joseph, to head the DES in 1981, makes it particularly appropriate largely to confine this analysis to a brief considera-tion of his relevant statements.

An article by Nick Bosanquet (1981) outlines Sir Keith's view of conser-vatism. It is composed, he argues, of elements of thesis and antithesis.

The thesis – the integrating force in society – is the underlying process of economic growth. The antithesis is the impact of 'Politicization' set up by the short-term stresses of 'creative destruction' and the nature of the political process itself. (Bosanquet, 1981: 326)

The elements of the thesis are briefly summarized as:

1. Society has inherent tendencies towards order and justice. This role of government should be restricted to that played by the maintenance department of a factory; citizens are able to act in their own best interest.
2. 'Inequality is the inevitable and tolerable result of social freedom and personal initiative' . . . ('it arises from the operations of innumerable individual preferences and so cannot be evil unless those preferences are themselves evil').
3. 'Capitalism is a system which has ensured growth and improved stan-dards in the long run.'
4. 'The entrepreneur is the key figure in ensuring for all the gains to be had from economic growth.'

5. 'Economic growth will first reduce, then eliminate poverty in absolute terms.'

The elements of antithesis picked out by Bosanquet are:

1. Origins of politicization – which leads to the despotism of the majority, centralization and statisms (which will almost always produce bad results, while individual action will nearly always serve the interests of the 'spontaneous order').
2. A more intense class conflict.
3. The fallacy of social cost, i.e. the market does not necessarily ignore social needs.
4. The shortcomings of the Galbraith thesis; giant corporations do not control the State.
5. Rising public expenditure; brought about by self-serving bureaucracy, and political 'vote buying'.
6. Industrial subsidies. Government intervention in industry will always find, and generate, problems of efficiency, productivity, etc., in subsidized forms.
7. The failure of the Welfare State. The wealthy benefit most from it, while strong vested interests support it in spite of its failures. The poor would generally benefit from a market-orientated system.
8. The pressure from bureaucracy. Bureaucracy also works both independently and under pressure from political democracy to raise public spending.
9. The fall of the trade unions.

Some idea of Joseph's views on education may be gained from consideration of speeches reported by, and articles written for, the *Times Educational Supplement* in late 1974. The initial Birmingham speech, which became so notorious for its apparently eugenicist arguments attacked the education system largely for its part in the decline of civilized values. Indeed, with its references to the danger of left-wing ideology both in higher education and among teachers, it has a lot in common with the moral entrepreneurs. But Sir Keith's chief concern was that the demand for absolute equality had turned into a new inequality, with the universities, he claimed, having been constrained to lower their entry standards for entrants from comprehensive schools. He summed up his beliefs as follows:

> I remain a passionate advocate of education; but blind partisanship is the worst enemy of a cause. If equality in education is sought at the expense of quality, how then can the poisons created help but filter down. (*Times Educational Supplement*, 25 October 1974)

In his reply to criticisms by the *TES* of his Birmingham speech, Sir Keith acknowledged the Tories 'had been remiss in neglecting our own instincts for those of self-styled progressives' and reiterated the need to 'stop the rot', again emphasizing the importance of the traditional family and authority, and the dangers of the few percent of radicals (in the teaching profession) 'who reject as bourgeois what we should call professional conduct and fair play' (Joseph, 1974a).

His rejection of the post-war progressive consensus, which 'has not furthered the greatest good of the greatest number' (ibid.) is fairly comprehensive. Its essence seems to be, for him, the project of social engineering and it is this which he finds both distasteful and unsuccessful. First, as we have seen, he considered its major goal – equality – inherently unattainable as well as undesirable; its pursuit has been responsible for the difficulties of the education system. Secondly, these difficulties were compounded by the increased power of the teachers entailed by the progressive consensus. This enabled a minority of them to disrupt the whole process and purpose of education. And, thirdly, Sir Keith has doubts about one of the central aims of the progressive consensus, 'human capital theory'. He does not, for instance, accept arguments for university expansion which are premised on it (though it should be noted that he does see a place – the proper place – for vocationally relevant courses, in the polytechnics). University expansion has been:

> encouraged by fallacious views of the economic benefits to be gained and by slovenly thinking regarding the moral and social justification for providing benefits on such a scale for the minority at the expense of a majority, which is not nearly such a cut and dried question as expansionists take for granted. (Joseph, 1974b)

And the earlier themes are tied in when he writes:

> the worship of vocational relevance owes everything to an overgrown and grotesquely status conscious academic profession which has argued that the quality of the work force would be improved by the fastest possible expansion of universities of the traditional type. (ibid.)

Thatcherism in education

So what distillate of these five ingredients constitutes Thatcherism in education? I want to argue that the crucial factor uniting the various strands into a coherent philosophy and policy (in so far as these exist) is Mrs Thatcher's own personal political stand. She has seen herself as representing the greatest casualties (though she might want to call them victims) of the social democratic Welfare State and the inflation that is held to be its automatic companion, who are also those least deserving to suffer as a result of its policies. This is the group whose embrace of the traditional virtues of thrift, hard work, self-restraint, responsibility and respectability has been set at nought (often literally) by the Welfare State's pursuit of the illusory goals of equality and social justice. 'Deservingness' is the inevitable victim of egalitarianism and universalism, and it is this quality which Thatcherism defines, identifies and seeks to reward above all, in education as in other sectors. It entails accepting selectivity and unequal treatment, with a full awareness of the consequences for those who show themselves undeserving. It accepts, and wittingly reinforces, social stratification and social inequality, purposely and explicitly doing more for some than for others.

This philosophy appears to be directly rooted in Mrs Thatcher's own personal experience and, we might add, in those of Rhodes Boyson and Norman Tebbitt too. There is little respect here for those Tory grandees and paternalists who preach a form of universalism without ever having to experience its dirty end. There is little readiness to dole out equal benefits to those who are going to make good use of them and those who will just squander them. There is a distinct reluctance to support those unwilling or unable to support themselves, especially if it means that there is less for the deserving. And so, Thatcherite education policy might be seen as not so much anti-statist as anti-universalist and anti-social democratic. While the State is to be rolled back – or at least cut back – that is to be done selectively. Thatcherism is very much in favour of selectiveness, of allowing the natural differences between people to grow, both as a reward to the talented and successful, the intellectually and morally deserving, and as a spur to the less well-endowed, successful or responsible, to make the most of what they have. This spur is signally absent from a universalistic, social democratic Welfare State.

This does not mean that the approach is not anti-statist. Far from it. The market is to be preferred to the State at all points because the desired stratifying power and mechanism are intrinsic to its operations. The market ensures that the best is available to those, and only those, who deserve or can afford it, and that those who neither deserve nor can afford anything else end up with the worst, or nothing, or what is left. But while there is a consequent pressure to return many state-provided services to the market, there is also a recognition of both the practical and the political difficulties associated with such a project. One further, crucial point must be made before we go on to look at the outcomes of education policy under Mrs Thatcher's government. This is that Thatcherism cannot be assumed to have been the only, or the overwhelmingly dominant, force creating that policy. It is clear from the contributions made to Thatcherism by the various strands of conservative educational thought I have briefly outlined that there are major differences of approach and emphasis, goals and assumptions between Thatcherism and especially what I called Old Toryism. It is also clear – from the House of Lords' decision on school transport finance, for instance, and from the serious reservations about the drift of education policy expressed by senior and influential figures at the 1981 Conservative Party Conference – that Thatcherism by no means has things all its own way as far as education strategy and programmes are concerned. Indeed, Mr Heath threatened that proposals for a massive shift of expenditure from the State to the private sector of education would split the Conservative Party from top to bottom, split the country, and alienate the teaching profession (*Guardian*, 15 October

1981). And so we have to recognize that the government's education programmes do not represent undiluted Thatcherism, not because of its ineffectiveness or incoherence, or because it is demonstrably unsuitable or irrelevant, but because it is not overwhelmingly pre-eminent in the Conservative Party itself.

Outcomes and effects

This is, of course, a very long way from saying that Thatcherism is an irrelevance, at least as far as education is concerned, or that it has had negligible impact. It undoubtedly has had major and perhaps lasting effects on the state education system. The most important of these is its confirmation of the gradual removal of education from the place in the public expenditure sun it had enjoyed for the previous 20 years or more. Crudely put, the replacement of Keynes by Friedman as the guiding light of the government's political economic strategy entails both quantitative and qualitative changes for education. Not only is it, along with all other items of public expenditure, to be severely cut back, but also both what is, and can reasonably be expected of it, is altered. Albeit more gradually, a shift from state to private provision is to be encouraged and implemented. So, for example, the appeal of human capital theories declines, with a concomitant pressure towards the separation of education and training, which is, of course, most visible in the debates and discussion about the appropriate eduational provision for 16- to 19-year-olds.

However, there are distinct limits to the extent and direction of any changes in education policy, to how far and how easily desired outcomes can be achieved through the formal political process – and the nature of these limitations itself deflects political activity into particular demands. It is, for instance, interesting to speculate how far it would have been possible to introduce even those changes that have been brought in without the 'slack' created by falling rolls. A former DES minister, for instance, has estimated that 98% of the budget of the education service is consumed in the execution of its basic statutory duties (Fowler, 1981). An analysis of the government's education record in its first year in office (Williams, 1981) suggests that if we are looking for education policy initiatives that are worthy of all three labels (i.e. genuine reflections of policy preference rather than tactical reactions), Mrs Thatcher's government could claim little more than the Assisted Places Schemes.

Williams's paper is confined to legislation, but we should not assume that this is either the only or the most effective way to implement party preferences in education. The cumbersomeness of legislation and its relative ineffectiveness in some areas has had a number of effects on both the strategy and the target of Tory education policy. It tends to lead to change efforts being directed at targets outside the statutory (5–16) system. At a time when pre-school provision is already rather sparse, and the further education sector under great pressure as a result of youth unemployment, this has contributed to the higher education system becoming the most prominent victim of the cuts in education spending. Such cuts also fit in well with the Thatcherite emphasis on deservingness and with Sir Keith Joseph's views of the proper roles of higher education.

However, an equally important consequence of Thatcherism's less than total dominance of the Conservative Party, and the difficulties associated with introducing education policy initiatives, has been the continuing centrality of its ideological barrage. This becomes increasingly important as it serves not just to refine ideological purity, but as the means through which its impact on actual educational practice is most direct. I have already argued that the moral entrepreneurs have a particularly direct impact through their implicit threat of exposure, and it seems likely that well-publicized aims and preferences, likes and dislikes, through letting it be known clearly which way the wind is blowing, suggest what kinds of practices, policies, etc., will be rewarded and which penalized.

One clear example of this is the continuing emphasis on the role of the school in the moral regeneration of a nation whose morale, motivation, self-respect and self-responsibility are seen as seriously damaged by prolonged exposure to a nannying and intrusive Welfare State. The Welfare State has removed the incentive to do a fair day's work for a fair day's pay and to behave in decent, upright ways. The education system, it is held, cannot escape blame for this, taken over as it has been by alien, progressive, morally relative and socialistic doctrines, and it bears a major responsibility for rectifying this state of affairs. It is difficult to see how changes of this kind could be brought about effectively through legislation, which puts added emphasis on forms of direct intervention. It is too early yet to isolate any effect of this thrust towards moral regeneration, but it is difficult to ignore its palpable targetting.

The clearest examples of the effects of this Thatcherite ideological barrage are seen in the hostility towards both social science in general and the 'progressive consensus' among educators. This hostility has certinly been expressed quite directly in the very close attention paid to the SSRC and the withdrawal of the Schools Council's life-support system (for which the legendary CIA phrase 'termination with extreme prejudice' seems not inappropriate). This hostility is able to draw on the deep-rooted opposition within many sectors of conservative ideology towards the intrusion of 'experts' into areas of social life which, if left alone, naturally achieve a kind of organic harmony. The intrusion of experts undermines the sense of community which means so much to the Old Tories. The professionalization of teaching under a progressive banner has turned children against industry and wealth production. It has led to teachers dictating to parents what can happen to their children. It has led to the questioning and undermining of Christian morality, by people who live off the State and use it to destroy society.

This hostility extends particularly to sociology. Not only is the very idea that a thing as naturally and organically self-regulating as society might be subject to analysis and deliberate change offensive to many conservatives, but it is taken as demonstrated (especially in the influential writings of the American neo-conservatives) that 'expert' tampering with social institutions only makes them worse.

Underlying much of this hostility towards both sociologists and progressive teachers is the fear that they may be politically motivated, that they are using the state education system to destroy not only (or not even preeminently) capitalism, but the sets of values on which conservative conceptions of the order of things are based. This is clear, for instance, in many of Sir Keith Joseph's speeches quoted above. It reached its apogee in a pamphlet by C.B. Cox, one of the original Black Paper authors, published by the Conservative Political Centre, which appears to see reds under, in and making the bed. Cox's theme is that education policy has been dominated since the 1960s by left-wing educationalists 'whose aim is revolution, not by armed overthrow of the government, but by transformation of institutions from within' (Cox, 1981: 5).

In a very brief summary, then, its own ideology, its strength within the Conservative Party, and the relative difficulty of directly implementing policy initiatives mean that the main consequence of Thatcherism for education are likely to be:

1. Its further displacement from its previous uncritically accepted place of honour.
2. Increasingly lower levels of funding, especially in the non-compulsory sectors.
3. A gradual separation of responsibilities for education and training.
4. Further encouragement of private education.
5. Pressure towards using the school as an agent of moral regeneration.
6. Continuing attacks on, maybe culminating in action against, radical teachers.
7. Further moves aimed at restratifying especially secondary education.

7 Political Change, Educational Change and the State in England, 1944–88

The society I want to live in is one in which government itself is limited, and therefore, political activity is decentralized to many different non-government institutions. It is not a question of seeking to keep politics out of education, but to extend the political process so that it can draw on a wider segment of society. This means more politics not less, but not necessarily more politics of the kind which fuel the party debate. It means the politics of the pressure groups described by Professor Maurice Kogan in his recent study of Educational Policy Making. It means the politics of parents' meetings and staff meetings and governors' meetings; of the Schools Council and the Arts Council and the Sports Council; the luxuriant politics of higher education and the strident politics of the pre-school movement. It means the politics of the individual teacher in his own classroom, and the politics of students at every level of sophistication.

This, one way or another, seems to be what happens and also what ought to happen. If the politics which emerge are not always sound, this is because of human frailty and malice, not because there is necessarily anything wrong with the implied relationships between education and politics. At every level, the public and the private, the political and the professional should interact to reflect a relationship which does justice to the splendidly confused, complex but organic connexion between education and society. (Maclure, 1976: 25)

This chapter has several interconnected lines of argument. In it I suggest that to be effective, responses made to changes in the problems facing education systems have to include political as well as educational changes. In making this argument I shall also suggest that current explanations of how education policy is made pay insufficient attention to the variability of institutional and constitutional forms; they assume the permanence of these forms rather than seeking to explain their relationship to wider economic, political and social conditions. The limits of some of these explanations have been made clear by recent legislation. Finally, I will attempt to demonstrate something of the relationship between the form and the content of education policy making, specifically the ways that the former limits and shapes the possibilities of the latter.

In Chapters 1 and 2 I have argued at some length that three key problems are always present on the agenda of education systems – direct support for the capital accumulation process, the provision of a wider social context not inimical to the continuing capital accumulation and the legitimation of the work of the State and the education system. I have developed this argument at some length, pointing out in particular that the 'solutions' to the three sets of problems were often mutually contradictory, but that the three sets of problems by no means exhausted the agenda of education systems, and could not even be assumed always to be the dominant issues. I want to elaborate briefly two futher points embedded in that argument. First, the nature of the problems, and their relative importance and prominence vary considerably over time. Secondly, the nature of the response to them is not laid down or determined by the nature of the problems. I briefly alluded to this above when I pointed to the non-homologous relationship between the form of the State's response to a problem and the function it performed. I want to develop that point here by arguing that the form of the machinery available to address these problems, as well as the nature of the problems themselves, the quality and relevance of the responses, and the level of resource available, is critical in determining the form of the response.

The changing agenda

Of the three items permanently on the agenda of education systems the economic is much the most familiar. It has received the most attention from writers on education, and it is hardly necessary to do more than rehearse the widely accepted broad relationship between education and the level, pace and direction of economic development. These have been outlined in earlier chapters, but in brief we can say that economic conditions have two kinds of effects on education systems. On the one hand, they affect the amount of public funding and resources available to support and develop the system. On the other, demands for education to be more economically relevant tend to be louder when the economy is doing badly than when it is doing well. Very broadly we can say that for around 20 years after 1944 the post-war and Korean War booms created conditions of continuing economic growth and very high levels of employment. Maintaining full employment was indeed the cornerstone of the post-war settlement and economic conditions made it relatively easy to sustain. As those economic conditions altered with the tapering off of the post-war boom, the first impact began to be felt in education through some diminution of funding, and as this decline acceler-ated after the first OPEC crisis in 1973, both effects of economic decline on education, on its funding and on its orientation, were intensified and have remained dominant features of the context of education policy making. Education is relatively worse funded and required to be much more vocationally relevant than it was in the years following the 1944 Act.

It is possible to detect similar changes in the second key problem area, providing a social context for capitalist growth. Though this has not been carried out as systematically as was the economic case, it is possible here also to point to factors that contribute to those changes and crucially continue to define its contemporary shape. There have been two major shifts in the nature of this problem. The first came as previously subordinated class, generational, gender and, in rather different ways, racial groups found the expanding post-war economy providing a material basis for addressing, if not overcoming, their subordination and deference. The process worked differently with each of the groups. Trade unions found themselves with greatly increased bargaining power. Young people became financially independent of their parents more completely and much earlier. The women's movement struggled for, and increasingly achieved, an environment hostile to their subordination by and to men. The 'second generation' of Asian and Afro-Caribbean immigrants have been much less tolerant of the widespread discrimination against them in all areas of life. At least the last three of these problems were seen as problems for education.

The second shift was, of course, that brought about by the rapid and dramatic increases in youth unemployment over the last 10 years. These have borne particularly on working-class and especially black young people, exacerbating the problems for an economic system which requires a basic level of social harmony, and for an education system expected to contribute in major ways to achieving that harmony.

This links to the third area of problems – legitimation. In the immediate post-war years, the education system carried a heavy burden of legitimation as it implemented such key parts of the post-war settlement as the replacement of ascription by achievement, and gave substance to equality of opportunity. With the State continuing until very recently to recognize and accept responsibility for the education system, legitimation has been a major task for the education system. It has received two major challenges since 1944. First, was the challenge based on inequality of access to grammar schools. The apparent unfairness of the distribution and access to differential life chances and social goals represented a major challenge to the legitimacy of the education system. Though the most obvious and immediate cause of this challenge to legitimacy (11+ and all that) was at least partially rectified, this has continued to be a major threat to the legitimation function of state education. It is still very much an issue today and may indeed be considered a chronic and insoluble problem though, as I shall argue below, currently a novel and radical attempt has been set in motion to overcome it. The other threat to legitimation essentially took – and again still takes – the form of attacks on the quality and relevance of education. For 20 years after the 1944 Act, education was regarded almost unequivocally as a good thing, and entirely worthy of all the support that could be mustered for it. This began to break down with the publication of the Black Papers in the late 1960s and has intensified consistently over the intervening 20 years.

Changing responses 1944–76

Just as it is necessary for the purposes of adequately understanding the nature of the fundamental problems facing the education system to look back to their changing nature over the course of the post-war settlement and its breakdown, so too we must consider briefly the history of the form through which educational policy is made. Because the central argument of this chapter stresses the importance of this form, it is particularly important to trace its origins, since they continued to lay down some of the basic assumptions on which education policy has been made until very recently.

The standard treatments of the structure and ideology of the education system following the 1944 Act will be sufficiently well known to most readers of this book to require no more than the merest outline here. The Act produced a tripartite 'partnership' between central government, local government and the organized teaching profession. There was a balance between them such that:

> power over the distribution of resources, over the organisation and context of education was to be diffused among the different elements and no one of them was to be given a controlling voice. (Bogdanor, 1979: 157)

Though there continues to be debate over the precise power given to central government in the Act, there is little disagreement that, certainly over the immediate post-war years, any such power was used sparingly and/or indirectly by central government. Indeed, it might best be seen as a reserve power, for it was the local authorities who mostly set the pace and patterns of educational development at this time, with at least the acquiescence of central government, and cooperation from the teachers. What is clear about the immediate post-war years is that education policy was made and implemented by central and local government administrators and professionals. There was very little party political input, and very few pressure groups with an interest in education.

The basis of this structure and ideology lay in the post-war settlement. This settlement, based on a high and stable level of employment, but including in the package the 1944 Education Act, created 'a framework within which political equilibrium, economic activity and social improvement would be balanced' (Middlemass, 1986: 341). Middlemass argues that the key figures in developing and sustaining this settlement were the senior civil servants; they can be seen 'not merely as guardians of a balanced post-war settlement (as in each generation they defined balance) but as guardians of the state's interest in its continued existence' (ibid.: 352). Two further things should be noted about this settlement. One is the persistence of its central assumptions. As Middlemass (1986: 342, 351) puts it:

> The settlement was not only a break with the past. Simple institutional momentum cannot explain why the great majority of policy-makers continued to defend it against accumulating criticism from left and right far beyond 1961 and why they upheld its ideals as central to the normal expectations of political life. . . . Long after 1961 they continued to view the 1944 arrangements as a political contract to which all partners, even governments, could be held. In that sense the civil service acquired a wider but legitimate, historic mission. Without in any way discounting responsibility to Ministers and parliament, and without asserting countervailing power, mandarins could continue in peacetime the essence of their wartime work. They became in effect guardians of the settlement's stability, as the Bank of England remained guardian of the currency.

The other thing to note is the principles that guided the implementation of this settlement. As Middlemass (1986: 352) puts it:

> The political elite as a whole had invested its intellectual and moral capital in the idea of a post-war settlement [and] had drafted its various documents with reference to what the public interest as well as the national interest required. Their conception of the state continued to be technocratic rather than party-political, Fabian rather than populist . . . [their] plans also took account of institutional opinion and hence, at one remove the wishes of sections of the public these embodied.

What the post-war settlement did for the structures and ideology of the education system, then, was to cast central government as its guardian, the maker and keeper of the rules, conventions and limits of educational policy making. It had three key components. It contained the principle of the mandarin voice, of the crucial establishment and protection of a state interest, distinct from that of political parties (even those in power), capital or labour. Secondly, this role should be exercised in the public interest and, thirdly, the nature of the role, and the interpretation of the public interest were broadly defined in technocratic, Fabian terms. The powers the State took to itself in the 1944 Act were relatively limited formally and underused in practice, in part because it was assumed, quite plausibly, that their LEA counterparts held much the same view of their own role (see Brighousee, 1988). As Bogdanor (1979: 166) puts it:

> the DES was not given strong formal powers to secure the implementation of its policies because it was assumed that both central government and local education authorities were managed by men of good will

whose main concern was to improve the service and whose reflective judgements remained untainted by the intrusion of party ideology.

LEAs and their teachers were the major means of putting flesh on the bones of the educational framework implied in the 1944 settlement and were trusted by central government to do so, with its power in reserve to police the boundaries rather than to prescribe the contents of education. To help do this the 1944 Act provided the Minister of Education with the power to appoint a Central Advisory Committee (CAC) to advise *ad hoc* on matters put to it by the Minister. The CAC membership itself (which was changed for each commission it received), largely drawn from the 'Great and the Good', had a great deal in common with the guardians of the post-war settlement. In this situation, as Kogan (1983: 60) puts it:

> the prevailing principles of the governance of education could be those of evolution, interaction, decentralization, and letting things grow at the base, rather than central preconstruction and installation. Innovation would be innate rather than externally-fostered, spontaneous rather than pre-structured, although encouraged by national policies which gave maximum discretion to the prime institutions [i.e. the schools].

Despite the commitment of the mandarinate this post-war settlement did not remain impervious to all the challenges posed by the kind of economic, political and social changes listed at the beginning of this chapter. However, it has never disappeared entirely in all its aspects, and it will be useful to consider briefly how and where the settlement was eroded.

At one level it broke down because of the increasing demands for the amount and range of education. These took two main forms. First, the recognition of the contribution educational credentials could make to life chances raised social expectations and intensified demand. It quickly threatened the principles of restraint and responsibility on the part of all parties that the post-war settlement drew directly from war-time experiences. Not only were the partners to the settlement under great temptation to pursue their own self-interest (which in the area of education were rarely indulged), but the growing 'de-subordination' of civil society alluded to above was bringing different demands to education from a new range of pressure groups. A slow-down in the rate of increase of educational funding in response to a changing world economic situation came rapidly to mean that not all demands could be met. This same economic situation also began to intensify pressure for greater 'relevance' in education. It threatened the full employment basis of the settlement and created pressure for education to contribute to the national (economic) interest rather than to the public interest.

The final and arguably the most important aspect of the breakdown of the post-war settlement was in the area of legitimation. The post-war settlement created an enormous burden of legitimation; by pledging itself to achieve so much, by accepting responsibility to do so much, the State gave itself the problem of delivering what it had promised. In education the post-war settlement centred around increasing and substantiating equality of opportunity, and providing a minimum level of education for everyone. However, though increased expectations led to increased demands, in education, this was rather less of a problem than in other sectors of the post-war settlement. The devolution to LEAs of much of the power to initiate and innovate – as R.A. Butler (1968: 13), architect of the 1944 Act puts it: 'I always envisaged that in secondary education the developments would come from the circumference, that is from the LEAs' – could potentially have created quite excessive demands on the resources of the education system, but this was prevented, or at least inhibited, by two factors in particular. First, while Butler insisted that it would be a great pity if we took away the interest and control from the LEAs, he also believed that 'the Minister of Education will and should always have the whip hand as far as money goes' (ibid.: 22). Secondly, as I suggested above, the LEAs were in effect run on rather similar principles to those guiding the Civil Service that are outlined above. They were not in a position of having to offer promises or fulfil demands in the same sense that politicians were, but were guided rather by similar conceptions of the public interest. It was for the LEA Chief Officers, according to Brighouse, 'an optimistic and deferential age' before 1974, when 'any half-way competent Education Officer could secure not only control of management but also policy itself' (1988: 100). The system worked then because, as Bogdanor puts it, 'the system worked best when only a small number of interests were involved whose rank and file were content to defer to elites and could, therefore, be relied upon to act sensibly' (Bogdanor, 1979: 161). Not only were there similarities of outlook and practice between LEA Chief Officers and Ministry civil servants, but the leaders of both the local authorities and of the teachers, William Alexander and Ronald Gould respectively, could be relied upon to 'deliver' their members. Furthermore, if much was expected of the education system, much was also allocated to it. Expenditure on education rose rapidly in the post-war years and not only to support basic provisions of roofs over children's heads and teachers to stand in front of them. New needs had been identified for education and new claims were made for it. Crucially, both were made by the professionals within the system who also determined the nature of the responses to these needs and claims.

However, while the structure and ideology of the 1944 settlement guided local as well as national education policy, there was no great uniformity of response. Local education policies differed significantly from each other, shaped both by the variations in the immediate problems they faced and by variation in the range of responses from officials and professionals in the service. However, while this produced the kind of both incrementalism and pluralism that Maclure celebrates in the quotation at the head of this chapter, the professional, technocratic and Fabian parameters within which they were developed set broad limits to the kinds of response possible. Oversimplifying hugely, it might be suggested that education policy was shaped by the process of identification of 'local public interest' and its amalgamation into an educational agenda, its translation into a problem or sets of problems amenable to technical solution, and the enlistment of the profession to solve the problems. And if this led sometimes to the 'politics of administrative convenience' (see Hargreaves, 1983), it also set broad limits to both inputs to, and outputs from, the policy-making process. From the centre, the Schools Council operated in a compatible manner. Teacher-dominated, it essentially offered professional advice on the identification and technical solution of educational problems, with the decision as to whether or how to act on this advice remaining firmly in the hands of the teachers, the schools and their local authority employers.

Even the clearest direct intrusion of party politics into education policy making after 1944, the Labour Government's introduction of comprehensive schooling via Circular 10/65 does not represent as major an exception as might initially appear. For while, as one leading authority puts it, 'ministry policy on secondary organisation up to 1965 can be explained in terms of an administrative stereotype: a combination of precedent and pragmatism led the ministry to abandon any plans it may have had for the coherent development of secondary education' (Fenwick, 1976: 156), considerable progress was being made towards comprehensive secondary systems in many local authorities. With no central guidance, already almost 10% of pupils were in comprehensive schools before 10/65 was issued and, as Fenwick (1976: 158) puts it:

> with the advent of a Labour government (in 1964), national and local policies came largely into line, and Circular 10/65 (which asked local authorities to submit schemes for secondary reorganization based on six existing LEA patterns) seemed an acceptable progression of policy to many in education who were not ardent supporters of reorganization.

Furthermore, the policy was driven forward in the Labour Party above all by the National Association of Labour Teachers (ibid.: 156), while the other main sources of the comprehensive policy have been identified as the teaching profession, and social democratic intellectuals very much in the Fabian, reformist tradition (CCCS, 1981). These intellectuals also made a 'talent-catching' as well as an egalitarian argument for comprehensivism.

However, there were three major sources of threat to the effectiveness of legitimation. While the structure of the system could contain and respond to the demands it was created to deal with (and to those it created for itself), it did depend to a degree on the persistence of the economic, political and social conditions under which it was set up. As was mentioned above, at its core was the threat of economic decline with an increased scrutiny of spending, and the changing demands it entailed for education.

This latter point was particularly important. The economic, 'talent-spotting' argument for education became much more prominent than the egalitarian argument. This was in large part due to the influence of the human capital theories which appeared to suggest that investment in education provided much greater pay-off in terms of national economic development than any other kind of investment government could make (see Karabel and Halsey, 1977). However, though it promised much by way of legitimation for the education system, the human capital promise made relatively little impact on the content of schooling, though perhaps rather more in the Further Education (post-compulsory) sector. For what neither the 1944 Education Act, nor the move towards comprehensive secondary schooling, had achieved (or even sought to achieve) was the displacement of the hegemony of a particular class culture in secondary schooling. The public school, Oxbridge traditions remained the model and the criterion for mass secondary schooling (on this, see Dale, 1988a). It was, though, seen as a dead hand on national economic development, and as a major obstacle to the modernization that Harold Wilson saw being forged in the white heat of the technological revolution. It developed into a kind of running sore in relations between a government keen to use education as an instrument of national development and a professionally dominated education service anxious to preserve standards and keep the philistines at bay.

The second threat was built into the post-war settlement. Middlemass's view of the conception of the State was quoted above: 'technocratic rather than party-political, Fabian rather than populist'. This conception may have been fine for the reconstruction of the national system after the war, in providing the places and the teachers for the huge increase in pupils, but, as is clear in a number of social policy areas, it does create major tensions and difficulties. Fundamentally, it is based on assumptions of administrative expertise, and the capacity of administrative and organizational structures to determine and frame processes and experiences effectively. It expects of its 'clients' attitudes of dependence, passivity and gratitude. Yet, especially in education, the more successful this ideology is in achieving its end the more its assumptions about its clients are challenged. So, people learn independence through the education provided for them. They learn how to oppose a system that sees them as passive. They learn to demand as rights what the administrators expect them to be grateful for.

One major, if rather concealed, manifestation of the dissatisfaction with the assumptions of the post-war settlement is to be found among education professionals themselves. Their discontent was triggered in part by what they saw as the shortcomings in the setting up of the comprehensive system. In essence, this was a political rather than an educational move. There was no new educational mandate to match the new pattern of organization. A new educational mandate in consequence grew from the grassroots, and it represented significant reinterpretation of the public interest from that of the post-war settlement. From being realized through social improvement, the motif of the post-war settlement, the new mandate saw the public interest being realized through social critique. Pupils were seen as having entitlements rather than as recipients. The aim of education placed greater emphasis on personal development and less on the development of civic conformity. Schools were to prepare critical citizens rather than conformist citizens, and they were to do it by means of a critical/progressive approach to the curriculum and pedagogy, rather than by extending the public school liberal education to a larger segment of the population (these arguments are developed at greater length in Dale, 1988a, and Dale and Fielding, forthcoming).

The third threat to the post-war settlement was also in part a product of its success. It was not just that achieving greater equality of educational opportunity raised people's aspirations of and through education, it was that the means of bringing about this greater equality of opportunity was such as to emphasize education as a private rather than a public good. 'Equality of opportunity' meant access to a form of education perceived as more worthwhile in itself and as more valuable in obtaining desirable occupational and social positions. The highly desirable shift from ascription to achievement meant that education became crucial in the distribution of life chances, and that individuals were in competition with each other over it. For the aspiring individual, egalitarianism soon reached the point where the benefits of levelling up tipped over into the horror of levelling down. Such an atmosphere made it more difficult to sustain a 'public interest' view of education.

These intrinsic threats began to take on more substance as the nature of the demands on education changed over the decade following the 'noon tide' of the 1944 Act in 1960. They developed into a multiple challenge to the post-war settlement. Economic changes led to greater emphasis being placed on education as an instrument of the national interest rather than the public interest (in either form). Political and social changes produced a less deferential, less tractable, less 'mass' population.

Through the 1960s and early 1970s, economic pressure on education grew as economic decline set in, and it was under increasing pressure to justify its potential contribution to national economic development through the identification and preparation of skilled personnel. At the same time the growth in the rate of increase of educational expenditure was slowing down. As a result, efficiency began to work alongside effectiveness as a criterion of central government policy. The DES was not wholly immune – despite the element of insulation given by its intimate expenditure links with local authorities – from such pressures, though this did not prevent it being upbraided by the OECD in 1975 for its lack of planning capacity. Education became the topic of rather wider public interest. In particular, parents, scarcely more than the suppliers of raw material in the 1944 Act, became more involved. It was not just those keen to use the system as their private escalator of social mobility who were concerned with how the system and its schools worked, though they did represent a largely silent but potentially very important constituency, whose aggregated aspirations have been welded together most effectively by more recent Conservative ministers of education. This growth of interests also included those concerned to enhance rather than undermine education in the public interest, who saw the possibility of parents uniting to defend and improve the quality of education offered to their pupils. These range from individual school PTAs and their national federations whose basic aim appears to be to demonstrate that parents exist as people with an interest in education, to organizations like the Confederation for the Advancement of State Education, and the Advisory Centre for Education, whose target is much more the potential and actual harm inflicted on the service by the top-down administered form of the post-war settlement.

Both these sets of parents, in their different ways, helped bring the issue of the quality of education into prominence, and this has been a major feature of discussion about education for the past 20 years. It was, for instance, central to the attack on both comprehensive education and the dominance of a liberal view of education imposed by the professionals in the face of 'common sense' and 'tradition' developed in the Black Papers. This series of right-wing critiques of education was derided on its first publication in 1969, but its influence increased very quickly through the first half of the 1970s and it played an important part in the preparation of the political/educational agenda. As well as the Black Paper critiques themselves, the attention they received in the Conservative press, and the consequent further stimulus they gave to public scrutiny and criticism of education, contributed rapidly to the erosion of a settlement to which professional control was so important and widespread participation so alien.

On the one hand, the new demands on education required that the system be more responsive to the needs of the clients; on the other hand, they entailed a two-pronged attack on the idea of education in the public interest. This was bifurcated into education in the national interest and education in the private interest.

These contain two rather different sets of views and assumptions about education, which might be called their ideological repertoires, both different from education in the public interest, in either its social improvement or social critique forms. Education in the national interest takes the pupil as raw material to be transformed into an efficient worker by means of a vocation-ally dominated curriculum in an education system whose purpose is the development of the nation's human resources and their retention in a commodity (i.e. available on the labour market) form. For education in the private interest, the pupils are human capitalists and the purpose of education is the maximization of individuals' investment in it (which, aggregated, can only produce greater national wealth). Education is to prepare a population of possessive individualists, of consumers stratified by the value of their investments in their own capacity. Such an objective is in principle indifferent to the content of education. This will be shaped by market preference; the chief criterion is that it forms a basis for stratification by achievement. The difference in the assumptions of the dominant views of education are summarized in Table 1.

Table 1 Ideological repertoires of different views of the purposes of education

View of purpose of education	View of pupil	Objectives of education	Output of education	Appropriate curriculum
Public interest (social improvement)	Recipient	Developing civic responsibility	Good citizens	Traditional Liberal
Public interest (social critique)	Entitlee	Personal development	Critical citizens	Critical/ progressive
National interest	Raw material	Maintenance in commodity form and development of nation's human resources	Good workers	Vocational
Private interest	Human capitalist	Maximization of personal investment	Possessive individualists/ competitive consumers	Indifferent stratification criterion

Of course, Table 1 is not exhaustive, nor are the ideological repertoires as exclusive as it suggests: individuals or groups draw on them selectively. Nevertheless, Table 1 does indicate the nature of conflicting views about education that were competing for dominance in the 1970s, as a result of the breakdown of the post-war settlement under changing economic political and social conditions.

Reconstructing the settlement, restructuring the system, revising the ideology: 1976–88

If Prime Minister Callaghan's speech at Ruskin College, Oxford and the series of events surrounding it – the *Yellow Book*, the Great Debate, the 1977 Green Paper *Education in Schools* – were a watershed in the post-war history of education, then that was, as I have argued above, because the settlement enshrined in the 1944 Act was showing increasing signs of strain and breakdown. In this second half of the chapter I want to detail the responses to that breakdown and their culmination in at least the embryo of a new settlement. It will be my central contention that the nature of the problems facing the education system have changed so much that only the construction of a new settlement has been adequate to enable an effective response. I shall also try to show that this is demonstrated by the failure of earlier attempts at tackling the problem, attempts that involved revising the ideology and re-structuring the system, respectively. Indeed, the response to the breakdown of the settlement can be divided into three phases. The first, which I refer to as 'revising the ideology', ran from the mid-1970s to 1984. Essentially, it involved a series of attempts to deal with developing problems within and by means of the existing structure of education, but with changing ideological emphases, especially on the orientation of schooling and the professional accountability of teachers. The second phase was initiated by the announce-ment of TVEI. This signalled a change in the model of political rationality and a fundamental alteration of the structures of the education system and to the locus of control over it. The third phase, heralded by the Education Reform Bill, which will have become law by the time this book is published, involves a new settlement with a distinctly changed role for the State and a clear reprioritization of the agenda of educational problems. In essence, it creates a market system in education, but a market that is underpinned, guaranteed and protected by a less extensive but much more powerful state involvement.

Revising the ideology: 1974–84

It would be easy but facile to suggest that it was the arrival of Margaret Thatcher at the Department of Education and Science which confirmed the breakdown of the post-war settlement and saw its replacement set in motion. As I argued in Chapter 6, it was the style rather than the content of her stewardship that was more proto-Thatcherite. She did little, however, to slow down the erosion of the notion of education as an instrument of social improvement, in particular by the action which first established her fame/ notoriety, the removal of free school milk for schoolchildren over 7 years of age. This was the first of a series of decisions and actions aimed at limiting the scope – and hence the cost – of the education service. This has brought about the virtual disappearance of the schools meal service, though as Chapter 6 also points out, this trend was checked when free school transport was threatened.

Three themes that were to occupy the agenda of the Ruskin speech and what it spawned began to take seed in the early 1970s. Each signified a departure from the principles of 1944. The first was that of standards. Pressure to improve standards, symbolized by the Black Papers, saw the setting up in 1972 of the Bullock Committee on Reading and the use of English, and the creation of the Assessment of Performance Unit (APU) in 1974. What was significant about Bullock was that it introduced the possibi-lity of external influences on curriculum, pedagogy and standards. Previous committees and commissions on education made up of the 'Great and the Good' could have been taken as representing public views of what education should be doing and where it should be going. Bullock, by contrast, assumed these ends of education, and focused on the means, thereby threatening the citadel of teacher professional control and expertise from without. The APU, though set up within the DES, represented another significant shift, this time in the direction of efficiency by means of monitoring pupil performance in a range of curriculum areas. This monitoring by one partner of another's efficiency and effectiveness was scarcely conducive to maintaining the ideology of teacher professional autonomy.

The recasting of teachers as part of the problem rather than as part of the solution was greatly accelerated by the William Tyndale affair. This is discussed at length in Chapter 8, but here suffice it to say that it did have the effect of confirming for many people fears raised by the Black Papers about the dire consequences of teacher autonomy allied to a socially critical educational ideology. As Gerald Grace (1987: 214) points out:

> The ideological attacks from the Right exaggerated the extent of radicalization of the schools, but they were correct in their basic assumption that the granting of classroom autonomy to teachers in Britain had always been premised on the understanding that teachers would use this autonomy conservatively and not radically. A fear of large-scale radical appropriation of teacher autonomy would be guaranteed to provoke a sense of cultural and political threat which resonated with a long historical preoccupation in the dominant social group in Britain.

Teachers' licence was clearly under threat and a renewal was to face much tighter terms.

The Tyndale affair made a wider contribution to what would become the Great Debate by making front page news of what was constructed by Conservative newspapers as an educational 'scandal'. It placed socially critical education distinctly on the defensive and made it a political liability. The themes of irresponsible and unaccountable teachers were also linked to a national economic decline emphasized by the OPEC price rise. This not only demonstrated dramatically the extent of economic decline, but also the nation's vulnerability and a critical need for steps to be taken to rectify it. The three themes of standards, accountability and economic responsiveness dominated the education debates of the late 1970s, and produced a responding flurry of action and rhetoric. The initial responses were guided by the perceived need for the DES to take greater control over the education system. LEA's were required to provide information about their arrangements for the management of the curriculum to the DES, who, on the basis of responses received, announced that they would move towards creating a national framework for the curriculum. This heralded a spate of papers from HMI and DES on the curriculum that continued through the rest of the Callaghan government and the early years of the Thatcher government (for details of these papers see Fowler, 1988). Significantly, however, these documents contained little, if anything, to suggest a more vocational orientation to the curriculum. Rather, they were concerned to establish a core curriculum entitlement for all pupils, which would include a technological/vocational element as a necessary part of a balanced education, no different in kind from any other. That is to say, these documents represented a refinement of existing traditions and a will for increased central control rather than a major reorientation of the curriculum. Indeed, the DES resisted pressure towards linking 16–19 education more closely to economic needs. As Ted Wragg (1986: 11,12) reports on the basis of his work as specialist Adviser to the Parliamentary Select Committee on Education in 1976:

> the DES seemed singularly unenthusiastic about most aspects of the 16–19 school-to-work debate . . . [their] attitude seemed to be: profess ignorance about the whole thing, mention a ludicrously long time scale like 20 years, talk in telephone numbers about the cost and with luck the whole issue will waft away on the next breeze.

However, the pace of change began to increase and the projected greater centralization of control over education to intensify in the early 1980s. This did not follow immediately on Mrs Thatcher's election in 1979. As I have just pointed out, the 'core curriculuming' continued well into the Conservative period of office, while it has been suggested that Mrs Thatcher's victory was 'less the result of a mandate for change than of a mandate to do something other than continue the current drift' (Hoover, 1987: 258). The same author also reports Sir John Hoskyns, head of the Downing Street Policy Unit under Mrs Thatcher, accusing the traditional élite in 1984 of 'a proprietorial feeling towards the country as a whole, almost as if it were an estate of which they were the benevolent owners' (ibid.: 260) – Middlemass's 'guardians' live on!

However, the ideology of devolved professional control was well and truly shaken during Sir Keith Joseph's tenure of the DES, though much of the significant legislation was not initiated by him. It came rather from the Department of the Environment in the form of a series of measures initially to curtail the expenditure of extravagant local authorities. These measures were the harbinger of a more widespread restructuring of the whole system, but rapidly began to limit local education authorities' freedom of manoeuvre and their ability to avoid the major cuts in educational expenditure which Sir Keith imposed. The Schools Council, in many ways the epitome of a professional service, was killed off and replaced by two new bodies, with membership nominated by the Secretary of State rather than by the professional constituencies. The Secondary Examinations Council controlled the examination system, vetting GCSE criteria and subject syllabuses; it thus had great power, but no LEA or teacher representation. The Schools Curriculum Development Council had LEA representation and acted as a limited, underfunded and centrally directed version of the Schools Council. An indication of the progress made towards central government control over this period is given by Wragg. He quotes Shirley Williams, Secretary of State at the DES, telling the Parliamentary Select Committee in 1976, in response to a question about the failure of £7 million allocated to in-service training to reach its intended target:

> there are problems here which do raise the question of inability of the Department of Education and Science to finance by specific grant or direct grant any form of educational innovation. I will not pursue the matter beyond saying that it is very much a matter for each local authority what proportion of its budget it spends on in-service training, even if the central ministry specifically sets sums aside for that purpose, as indeed we did this year. (Quoted in Wragg, 1986: 9,10)

Wragg goes on: 'By 1984 Sir Keith Joseph had introduced specific educational grants, ear-marked in-service priority areas and driven a 125 train through that particular piece of orthodoxy' (ibid.: 9,10).

A further threat to professional control came not from the centre but from the locality. The Education Act of 1980 opened up schools to parental scrutiny – through the requirement to publish brochures for parents (including examination results), and HMI reports on schools – and to an element of parental choice, with parents given the opportunity to express a preference (though no guarantee was given) for a school other than that to which their child had been allocated by the local authority. All these measures weakened professional autonomy, at the same time as falling rolls were weakening professional organizational/union muscle.

The final element of the early 1980s educational legislation that I wish to mention is the Assisted Places Scheme. This was qualitatively different from the other projects because it represented not so much an effort to wring the last possible drop from a dying system, pending its replacement by something as yet unknown; it contained the seeds of one version of what that something as yet unknown might turn out to be. It was a simple enough scheme. Parents who wished but could not afford to send their 'academically able' children to private schools were to be subsidized by central government to enable them to do so. There is no need to go into the operation of the scheme in detail here (see Fitz *et al.*, 1986) in order to point to its key implications for my argument. First, it set up a direct link between central government, private schools and individual parents; local authorities had no part to play at all. Details of how to apply for places under the scheme were published in local newspapers by the private schools concerned. Secondly, it was a very clear demonstration of a lack of faith in state secondary schools and in the possibility of their ever being improved to the level of private schools.

Restructuring the system: 1984–7

So, over the decade between 1974 and 1984, the education system had undergone great changes. The professionals, the LEAs and teachers, were in a state of shock. Parents had been given a platform if not a voice. Most importantly for our current purposes, the DES had been given unprecedented control over the education service, though it appeared not to be altogether happy with this or to know precisely how to use it; it was certainly still regarded as having fallen some way short of achieving all that was expected of it in implementing the requirements of the Great Debate. It had, though, almost certainly changed sufficiently in substance to alter Stuart Maclure's view of the policy-making process outlined in the quotation at the beginning of this chapter, though perhaps not sufficiently to cause him entirely to revise his view that 'if the policies which emerge are not always sound this is because of human frailty or malice, not because there is anything wrong with the implied relationship between education and politics' (Maclure, 1976). He did after all publish a philippic against 'The Educational Consequences of Mr Norman Tebbitt'! However, the core of my argument, and what makes this second phase of the development of a new settlement so important, is that it is precisely a change in the implied relationship between education and politics that was necessary to bring about fundamental change. For if radical change had occurred, it was by no means sufficient to achieve even the reorientation of education implied by the Great Debate, let alone the new targets set for it by an increasingly confident and increasingly dominant and coherent brand of Thatcherite Conservative policies. And the reason for this lay not in the abilities or the motivations of the politicians but in that relationship between education and politics; the radical educational message could not be delivered through existing political forms and modes of political rationality. What I have in mind here is best expressed, and was indeed inspired, by Claus Offe's distinction between what he called 'conjunctural' and 'structural' modes of political rationality. I can do no better than quote his definitions at some length; the kernel of my argument is that up to 1984, and specifically the introduction of TVEI, Conservative governments had effectively been attempting to implement policies with a supply side (structural mode of political rationality) bias, through the medium of a system still largely following a conjunctural mode of rationality that had grown up alongside the demand-led education system of at least 30 of the previous 40 years:

> Under conditions where the formation and activity of organized interest groups is not regulated by specifically attributed collective status given to the organization and its members, policy makers do not have much control over the intensity and content of specific demands that are being made in the political process nor over the number and identity of organized collectivities by which such demands are being made. At best, *political parties* are able to perform a reconciling function, thus overarching the specific conflicts of interest between organized groups and providing some programmatic directives and priorities to policy makers. Under such conditions of low institutionalization of interest groups – conditions that come closest to the liberal-pluralist model of the political process – articulations of interest and demand have to be

accepted as given from the point of view of the policy maker. His or her objective – and his or her standard of political rationality – would be to serve as many of the specific demand inputs as possible, given the limitations of fiscal and other resources, so as to satisfy a maximum of special interests. This requires, in turn, increasing the efficiency and effectiveness of the governmental use of resources, maximizing predictive capacities, measuring cost/benefit ratios, employing sophisticated methods of policy and budgetary planning, using social indicators and so forth. *Because demand inputs have to be treated as given, the only thing that can and must be rationalized by 'good' policy maker is the efficiency and effectiveness of outputs* [my emphasis]. The working of civil society itself is considered as given – both in the sense that it can be taken for granted and that it is neither feasible nor legitimate to attempt to interfere with its internal dynamic. The political problem is one of compensating for market failures, resolving conflict, supervising rules, and fine tuning. To be sure, there is a considerable range of conflict over the extent and nature of such policies which may be more or less 'interventionist'; but they converge on the notion of the separation between the political and the socioeconomic spheres of social life, which is the underlying notion without which the very term 'intervention' does not make any sense.

This type of political rationality, which we would associate with 'active' interventionist policies aiming at optimal and comprehensive satisfaction of manifest (as well as some anticipated) interest is, however, not the only conceivable type of political rationality. If political parties fail to aggregate and reconcile, on the basis of their respective programmatic orientations, major segments of the electorate, and/or if policy makers find it difficult or impossible to accommodate significant interests due to the lack of sufficient fiscal and institutional resources at their disposal, the inverse type of political rationality is likely to take over. This one follows the imperative of keeping output constant, that is, at levels that are considered reasonable or affordable, while channeling demand inputs in a way that appears compatible with available resources. The variable to be manipulated and balanced, in this case, is not policy outputs, but *the system of interest representation and the modes of resolution of conflict*. It is this standard of political rationality that inspires 'the search for the stable ordered society, for a system where competition, class conflict and political disunity [are] structurally rendered impossible' (Harris, 1972: 66). *The standard of a 'good' policy here to put it in the simplest terms, is not to satisfy demands but to shape and channel demands so as to make them satisfiable* [my emphasis].

The distinction between the two modes of political rationality can be conveniently made in terms of 'conjunctural' versus 'structural' policies. Conjunctural policies would seek to maximize the adequacy of policy *responses* to problems as they emerge and appear on the agenda; the concomitant expectation is that such problems and demands will remain within a range of manageability defined by existing capacities of state action and their continuing improvement. Structural policies, in contrast, become the predominant mode of intervention as soon as this expectation is no longer supported by experience. They are adopted in response to conditions of economic and institutional crisis. In response to such crises, the physical and economic parameters of production and the institutional parameters of interest representation, which together constitute the nature of the problem, become subject to redesign. The shift is from policy output and economic demand management to the shaping of political input and economic supply – from 'state intervention' to 'politicization'. (Offe, 1981: 125–7)

The implications and importance for my argument of this approach are clear. The kind of reform possible under the conjunctural mode of political rationality had reached its limits by 1984. Indeed, in many ways those limits had been reached long before. We might, for instance, see the confusion about the role, authority and mandate of the APU as arising from an attempt to implement a policy assuming structural, 'supply-side' political forms at a time when the definition of a good policy was still based on conjunctural, demand-side assumptions.

Offe's distinction also exposes the relativity of the assumptions upon which explanations of education policy making, like those that Maclure put forward, quite justifiably rested in the mid-1970s. As Offe (1981: 124) puts it:

Pluralist theory tends to explain the existence, strength, and particular articulation of interest organization by reference to properties of the constituent *elements* of the organization: their values, their willingness to sacrifice resources for the pursuit of their interest, their numbers, and so on. That this type of explanation leads at best to a very limited understanding of the dynamics of interest representation becomes evident as soon as we realize that an identical number of interested individuals with identical degrees of determination to defend and promote their interest may produce vastly different organizational manifestations and practices, depending on the strategic location of the groups' members within the social structure and depending on the political-institutional status their organization does or does not enjoy. The concrete shape and content of organized interest representation is always a result of interest *plus* opportunity *plus* institutional status. To employ structuralist language, we can also say that interest representation is determined by ideological, economic, and political parameters.

Not only are there differences in the relative influence of pressure groups, but their very status as pressure groups is not inevitable, natural or normal; rather, it is a function of a specific mode of interest representation, one whose character in the period under review was determined above all by political and ideological factors.

I will now discuss the key characteristics of the structural mode of political rationality for the restructuring of education, and suggest the forms in which they have been implemented.

1. *Shaping and channelling of demands.*   The clearest example is the Technical and Vocational Education Initiative (TVEI). Quite crucially, TVEI symbolized and heralded the replacement of a conjunctural with a structural mode of rationality in the politics of education. It centralized control over the allocation of resources and the recognition of demands, and directed them to clear politically, rather than professionally, selected targets. TVEI is described in more detail in Chapter 9, but its most important feature for our present purpose is the 'bid and contract' system of 'categorical funding' which TVEI extensively piloted. Under this system, central government made resources available for specified purposes, and invited LEAs to submit detailed bids for these resources. The bids then became the basis of a contract between central government and the LEA. A variation on this method is seen in the delegation of control over 25% of the resources of Non-Advanced Further Education to central government, these resources to be released on agreement by central government to the providing institution's (typically a College of Further Education) plans for work-related NAFE. Most significantly, both these initiatives were set in motion not by the DES but by the Manpower Services Commission. The reasons for this and the implications of it are discussed at greater length in Chapters 5 and 9. It is sufficient to note here that though the DES was traditionally reluctant to embrace anything like a structural mode of political rationality (see the quote from Shirley Williams above), under Sir Keith Joseph it took some distinct steps in that direction and, following the success of TVEI as a funding mechanism, has adopted the bid-contract system for the whole of its financing of in-service education of teachers.

2. *Political prioritization of policy targets.*   Rather than the incremental drift that characterizes demand-led policies (and that is welcomed by their proponents), supply-led policies require prioritization of targets. This does not necessarily mean that the prioritization has to be political, though that has certainly been the case in recent years. Targets for education funding have been selected with a clear political purpose in mind. This will be considered more fully in the next section, but a clear example is the diversion of resources into 'non-state' educational purposes such as the APS and the City Technology Colleges.

3. *Control over alternative sources of demand.*   The obvious example here is the effective removal of the LEAs as a source of educational policy making. The first step was decimation of their funding. The second, to be discussed further below, is the marginalization of their major professional functions implied by

the introduction of the national curriculum. In Brighouse's words, the LEAs have become 'eunuchs'. One other means by which demand has been controlled also involves curtailing the power and influence of the professionals. One example is the manipulation of the way schools are governed and managed in such a way as to give much more say to parents and other community representatives (including the local Chief Constable) at the expense of education professionals and elected politicians, both of whom may be seen as sources of additional demand on schools. Rather similar moves are afoot in the higher education sector with the replacement of the professionally dominated University Grants Committee by a University Funding Committee which will be made up of a very much higher proportion of members from industry and commerce, who can be relied upon to channel demand 'sensibly' even if they cannot entirely suppress it.

4. *Keep output constant and affordable.* This was achieved by the further extension of financial controls, culminating in the system of 'rate-capping' which effectively meant that local authorities were financially penalized for spending above a limit set by central government, even where the finance did not come from central government. This has had a quite dramatic impact on the level of educational spending, actual and potential.

5. *Control over the system of interest representation and conflict resolution.* One obvious example here is the effective removal of the organized teaching profession from any formal influence over or consultation about education policy. This is compounded by the abolition of the Burnham Committee and the removal of teachers' salary negotiation rights and the imposition of a contract of employment which lays down the hours they have to teach. It confirms the shift from licensed to regulated professional autonomy which is taken ever further by proposals for the appraisal of their professional performance. A further manipulation of the system of interest representation has already been referred to. It involves the replacement not just of professionals but of those who might be expected to share this experimental, public interest view. So, no more commissions of the Great and the Good. Indeed, no more commissions at all; rather, the nomination of members to bodies like SEC, and the use of short-term, trusted and sound advisers.

6. *Efficiency replaces effectiveness as the criterion of good policy.* The distinction between effectiveness and efficiency is at the heart of the distinction between the two modes of rationality. A most enlightening illustration of this is to be seen in the work of the Audit Commission, a quintessential tool of the structural mode of political rationality. The Commission sees its mission as changing local authorities' culture and criteria of success. It:

> does not merely wish to describe, control or restrain local authorities but explicitly aims to change them . . . specifically, its approach focuses upon 'economy' and a narrow definition of 'efficiency'; greater control

and viability; increased centralization including an enhanced role for chief executives, and a de-emphasis on the role of elected members. Its neglect of effectiveness is caused not merely by the undoubted technical and political difficulties of identifying and determining the impact of local authority outputs, but also more fundamentally as a greater focus on effectiveness could weaken the Commission's attempts to change local authorities. Influencing acceptance of reduced funding and a reduction in the scale of organizations also means cutting back on purpose. Identifying unfilled needs and demands would have the opposite impact. (McSweeney, 1988: 42)

It is difficult to see how LEAs, traditionally the biggest local authority spenders, will be able to resist entirely the tone and target of the Audit Commission's evangelizing zeal, even indirectly. And if it is difficult for LEAs, how much more difficult is it likely to be for schools to step outside those criteria and assumptions as they become responsible for their own finances as is proposed under the system of Local Financial Management of Schools which will also further reduce the ability of LEAs to plan and administer education in their local areas?

It seems legitimate to conclude, then, that the education system has been restructured in a way almost literally unimaginable little more than 10 years

Table 2 Changing roles in the structure of education in England, 1944–88

	1944–74	*1974–88*	*1988–*
National Ministry	Overseers (Chair)	Limited assertiveness (MSC assertive)	Minister's instrument
Political party in power	Reserve power	Electorally opportunist	Dominant
LEA	Active partners (Managing Director)	Squeezed	'Eunuchs'
Teachers	Active partners (Executive Director)	Problems	Proletarianized
Parents	Who?	Constructed as 'natural experts'/ moral guardians	Consumers
Industry	Indifferent (full employment)	Concerned (increasing unemployment)	Consultants

Note: The periodization used is to highlight the key features of my argument. Inevitably and regrettably, it conceals many important changes that took place within and across the periods I have isolated.

before. Powerful central control over what goes on, and what can go on, in education, was installed by the series of legislative innovations briefly outlined above. The shifts in the roles of various groups in the structure of the education system are summarized in Table 2.

However, two major issues remained to be concluded before a new settlement could be established. First, powerful as it was, central control over the system was not complete. Even the bid and contract system pioneered by TVEI left considerable latitude for local interpretations and modification (see Open University TVEI Study Group, in press). Furthermore, the bid and contract system applied to a relatively small area of educational practice only. Alternative sources of influence on the shape and content of schooling may have been emasculated or marginalized, but LEAs and schools were still able to continue rather less disturbed than the shock induced in them by the sound and f·iry of radical reform might have suggested.

The second issue is that of purpose. Restructuring the system to enable central government domination does not determine how that domination will be used, though it channels it in various ways, including, most importantly, making it very difficult to carry on in the existing direction. So what was required to complete the new settlement was a guiding ideology to exploit the restructuring, and it is to that that we now turn.

Reconstructing the Settlement: 1987–9

The cornerstone of the new settlement is the market. The market is to achieve more effectively, efficiently and equitably all that the Welfare State as the cornerstone of the post-war settlement promised and, it is argued, failed to achieve. Further, the market can achieve all these social gains without the major fiscal crises inevitably created by chronically voracious welfare state services and benefits. The market is (to over-summarize) to replace the institutions of the ideological state apparatus.

It cannot, though, replace the repressive state apparatus. Rather, it needs it. The market needs the State to bring into being the conditions under which it can flourish, and it needs it to police and guarantee those conditions. The new settlement is not then premised in the replacement of the State by the market, but on the essential symbiosis of a small strong State establishing and defending the market that funds it.

This strong State/free market basis of the new settlement involves a number of fundamental departures from the settlement it replaces in form as well as content. These are very well described in the passionate commentary on the Education Reform Bill that precedes Volume 59 of the *Political Quarterly*. As its author points out, the Bill:

> is one of the most ambitious exercises in social engineering in twentieth century British history. Yet it is the product, not of a broad social consensus developed through careful enquiry and wide ranging debate, but of the *a priori* certainties of a government returned to power by little

more than two-fifths of the electorate. [Besides this], the methods, and in some important respects, the objectives, have changed. The man in Whitehall is no longer the enemy. He is the instrument of ministerial faith. Ministers still want to extend freedom of choice, but only if they can first make sure that the right choices will be made. They no longer seek to liberate society from the embrace of the central state. They seek to use the central state to re-fashion society, so that the freely-choosing individuals of neo-liberal doctrine will choose to conform to the require-ments of a market order. And in order to push forward the cultural revolution without which that ambition must be vain, they are deter-mined to tame – indeed, if necessary to dismantle – the intermediate institutions which lie, like society's equivalent of the ozone layer, between the state and the citizen. . . . This leads on to the most striking feature of the Bill – the panoply of power which it grants to central government. The Secretary of State will determine the programmes of study needed to implement the curriculum which all schools will be obliged to teach, and will be empowered to change them as he wishes. He will appoint the Curriculum Council which he has to consult before doing so. He will also determine standards of attainment, the ages at which children are tested and the methods of assessment. (Anon., 1988: 3,1,2)

Here is the contrast with the quotation from Maclure that opened this chapter. All that he celebrated in the process as well as the outcomes of education policy making is finally swept away in the new settlement encapsu-lated in current (1988) legislation. The Education Reform Bill proposes an imposed, centralized, doctrinaire, anti-pluralist form of education policy making, that promises policies whose soundness is very much a product not of human frailty or malice but of the relationship between education and politics. I will end this chapter by elaborating somewhat on this proposition.

Education in the new settlement is to serve both its component parts. It is both to become itself subject to market forces, and to be part of the strong state defence of the market. These two requirements are intrinsically far from mutually complementary, and the education system will not be based on the assumption that they are. Instead, it will be a dual system polarized between what I will call market schools and minimum schools. The three basic functions will be divided among these two types of school. Assistance to capital accumulation is taken as guaranteed by opening up education to market forces; recall the ideological repertoire of education in the private interest that assumes that collective good must flow from allowing indi-viduals freely to pursue their private good. Guaranteeing a context not inimical to capital accumulation becomes the paramount function of the state education system, in its minimum school form. The post-war settlement was based on a Welfare State protecting the victims of a market economy from its worst excesses. The new settlement reverses these priorities. It sees the strong State defending the market from any social dislocation and unrest, and individual demoralization and demotivation generated by its operations. Much of the current legislation can be read as directed at precisely that purpose of social control by various means, with the minimum fundamental objective of schools as retaining the whole of the workforce in the commodity form (i.e. available for work when there is no work available for them). Finally, the legitimation function is reduced somewhat as the State hands over more and more of the responsibility for providing education to the market, and makes the education that children receive more the consequence of their parents' choice and less the consequence of state provision.

I will now consider the legislation relating to the two parts of the settlement in education and to the two types of educational provision that will support them.

Before education can be brought into the marketplace and made subject to consumer choice, a range of possible alternatives has to be created. This is to be achieved in two ways – by increasing choice within the state sector, and by increasing the range of realistic alternatives to the state sector. In the former case, in spite of the 1980 legislation, parents had no effective rights to choose their own state school. The current legislation changes this by requiring schools to open their enrolment to allcomers and allowing their numbers to rise to 1979 levels. Thus parental choice, rather than LEA planning, will determine the size of schools (and hence the resources available to them, in so far as those resources are allocated on a per capita basis), and ultimately their viability. This is, of course, a further diminution of the powers and duties of LEAs, who are the major institutional and constitutional victims of the legislation – part of the 'taming and dismantling of society's ozone layer'.

The second means of extending consumer choice is to provide for this creation of alternative forms of school provision. The chief means on offer in the legislation is the possibility of schools 'opting out' of local authority control and becoming 'grant maintained schools', directly funded by central government. Such schools would be in an intermediate category between state schools and private schools. They would be joined in that category by City Technology Colleges. These will be a relatively small-scale innovation, with no more than 20 planned (and only 1 open so far). Their unique characteristics are that they are to be largely funded by industry rather than by government (though levels of funding from industry have so far been much lower than is necessary to establish the schools and considerable government subsidy has been required), with a strong technological bias in the curriculum, and with a selected intake.

The possibility of a range of alternatives in education has thus been created, though whether this is enough to create a market in education is not yet clear. However, legislation has also been directed at increasing the demand for alternative forms of education as well as increasing its supply. The main vehicle for this has been the introduction of parents as consumers. As I suggest in Chapter 8, there is no intrinsic reason why parental involvement in education should be attached to a private interest rather than a public interest view of its purposes. I also suggest there that the Tyndale case was instrumental in enabling the construction of the parent as private consumer. This construction has been reinforced by the legislation requiring schools to publish information, brochures, exam results, and so on; the crucial point is that, as Joan Sallis points out, the nature of this information is such as to encourage parents to *compare* schools rather than contribute to the improvement of the school their children attend (Sallis, 1988: 30).

The very important place accorded to parents in the legislation has two other major consequences. Their freedom to choose schools and the way that it has been enabled, especially using examination results as a basis of comparison, can only increase the importance and prominence of examinations in schools, and make schools more reluctant to experiment with any kind of educational alternative. Secondly, parents are given influence – especially through their potential membership of, and pressure on, governing bodies – over the moral tone of the school. They are clearly seen as much more effective moral guardians of what is right than teachers ever were, and in this way as contributing to the social control function of schools.

They will be able to exercise this influence in the 'minimum' schools as well as in the various forms of semi-private market schools. I refer to these schools as minimum schools because while the market philosophy would ideally have no non-market schools, where there have to be non-market schools their provision should be minimal in order to persuade more people of the value of the extra provisions available in market schools. However, the minimum schools have to meet two other criteria – social control and commodification. In essence, they will be required to attempt less but to do so under much more intensive scrutiny and monitoring. The major means to this end currently proposed are the national curriculum and, especially, the testing of all pupils in a range of subjects at 7, 11, 14 and 16 years of age. The two together will provide a means of controlling schools and ensuring some degree of efficient provision of a minimum education for all pupils. Most importantly, they provide a rudimentary means of overcoming the largest obstacle blocking the efficient and speedy transformation of the education system, the teachers and their traditional commitment to rather different and more extensive forms of education for all. Now that they are unequivocally no longer partners or participants in the formation of education policy, teachers have more than ever to be managed and manipulated. Headteachers are already being encouraged to take management much more seriously and are being awarded salary differentials that further separate them from their staffs. Forms of teacher appraisal are in full swing and can only be expected to be intensified, quite possibly as part of contracts of employment, with more extensive control the price of any salary increase. These measures clearly require further refinement before strong state principles are fully installed in education. However, both aspects of education's contribution to the strong State – social control and commodification – are likely to be made rather easier by legislation compelling some form of training for all unemployed school leavers, on the one hand, and by demographic trends that will see a dramatic fall in the number of 16- to 19-year-olds in the next few years, on the other.

Conclusion

This has been a somewhat gloomy view of the current educational scene in England, but I do not believe it is inaccurate in the interpretation of what is happening as part of a new political settlement based on a strong State and market freedom. However, the prospects are not wholly dark for at least three reasons.

1. The implications of the new settlement are by no means yet fully installed in the education system and there are good reasons to believe they never will be. Industry's response to City Technology Colleges has been exceptionally disappointing from the government's point of view, and they have had to receive major support from the public purse to enable the programme to continue. There is no evidence of overwhelming demand by parents for private education. On the contrary, if the universal opposition to any proposed school closure is anything to go by, the vast majority of parents are happy with their children's education. In any case, allowing market forces to operate essentially oligopolistically is no way to guarantee quality in education. Allowing – requiring – popular schools to continue growing not only involves the closure of other schools (and hence a reduction of choice) but shows no recognition of either the unpopularity of very large schools, or the strictly limited intake policy of the most popular public schools that provide a model for the proposed 'semi-independent' tier; Eton does not take everyone who applies. And, of course, over much of the country there is no choice of secondary school, because there is only one within a realistic travelling distance.

2. In any case, the market does not work effectively as a link between education and the economy. It very obviously does not ensure that adequate numbers of young people will be attracted into engineering or physics teaching, or provide sufficient disincentive for those unwise enough to want to study sociology. It encourages, rather than discourages, ludicrously disproportionate numbers of graduates to seek to enter the City, law or accountancy, a trend that taken to logical limits would see higher education swamped by eventually unemployable undergraduates in law and accountancy, and departments of engineering forced to close down.

3. The legislation, if not the settlement, is essentially double-edged. The powers it gives to central government can be used by any occupant of the office, of whatever political stripe (a fact that has disturbed many government supporters). Even opting out can be used in ways out of line with the present government's preferences. The extent to which a public interest conception of education, broadly conceived, continues to permeate the professional assumptions of those involved daily in the education of children was recently demonstrated in the readiness of the Headteachers of all the (very different) comprehensive schools in one local authority area to use (successfully) the threat of 'opting out' *en masse* to forestall a

proposal to reintroduce selective education in the area.

Recently, in the common room of the Education Department at the Victoria University of Wellington, New Zealand, I saw a cartoon drawn in response to the somewhat similar changes that society is undergoing. It showed the captain of a rapidly sinking ship exhorting his passengers and crew to take a positive attitude to their imminent fate, to see it as a set of challenges rather than a cause for resignation or despair. 'Make use of the unprecedented opportunity to analyze the properties of sea water', he urged them, 'establish under totally realistic conditions just how far you can swim'. The challenges facing education in the public interest are not yet so final or fanatic. Though the perils may be equally threatening, the ship is in no immediate danger of sinking. But its structure must be kept in constant repair. The challenge must anticipated. The pessimism of the intellect must be rigorously tested and the optimism of the will maintained.

PART 4

Two Cases

8 The Case of William Tyndale

It is an interesting comment on both our education system and the way it is reported that the names of far fewer state schools than public schools are widely recognized. When they are recognized, they are more likely to be known because of a 'scandal' than because of any educational reputation they may have achieved. So, probably more people know the name Risinghill, even though the infamy associated with the name led to it begin changed, than know the names of Prior Weston, say, or Sidney Stringer. But I would guess that perhaps the three best known schools in the country are Eton, Harrow and William Tyndale. In this chapter I want to argue that what brought this school to our notice had the effect at least of enabling the current restructuring and redirection of the education system, and hence the politicization of school deviance. William Tyndale Junior School was the subject of a scandal at least as great as Risinghill and far more significant in the reverberations it set up and amplified throughout the educational world. While it will be my argument that rather than being their cause, the Tyndale affair was merely the occasion of the major changes in the English education system which followed it, nevertheless it does seem worthwhile to consider briefly just what was the nature of the scandal that surrounded the school. There are two reasons for this digression. First, maybe the only opportunity to get a clear impression of at least some of the aims and assumptions of an education system as uncodified, incoherent and implicit as the English system was (I shall argue this point more fully below) arises when at least some of those implicit assumptions and norms on which it is based are pushed to such an extent that in order for them to be retained they have to be made explicit. As a result of the Tyndale affair we know more about what kinds of schooling were possible in England. And, secondly, because it was such a dramatic and powerful precipitator of the subsequent changes, because it came to symbolize so clearly much of what the changes were intended to proscribe, it is possible that the form of some of those changes may have been a direct response to what was seen as so dangerous at William Tyndale.

Having said that, it is no easy task to attempt to describe briefly what it took the Auld Inquiry (Auld, 1976) several hundred hours of public hearing to establish.

The first thing that the Tyndale affair shows about the nature of the control of schooling is how far it rested on assumptions of shared values and norms, priorities and practices throughout the education system, rather than on explicit rules. This is most clearly revealed in the claimed impotence of either the ILEA or the managers of the school to act decisively against a teaching staff, the great majority of whom were in what amounted to open rebellion against both managers and authority. Neither the school managers nor the parents, neither the politicians nor the officers of the ILEA, appeared to be able to control what the teachers were doing. Indeed, had it not been for a 'renegade' member of the staff publishing documents critical of the policies and practices of the rest of the staff, it would have been difficult even to find out what they were doing (though it should be said that some of the staff, at least, paid more attention than is probably typical to giving parents information on what they were doing). The Tyndale case showed that, though the sharing of values and norms, policies and practices on which the system rested was in fact monitored by the professional officers of the local authority, when pushed to the limit this monitoring could be overridden or ignored; it also showed that teachers could run the schools in ways that clearly contradicted many of the shared assumptions on which the education system rested. Teachers could be in effective day-to-day control of the schools, and they could use that control in ways not welcome to the school managers or the funding authority.

It was perhaps the way the Tyndale teachers used – or rather the way they were said to have used – the control they established which ensured the school a place in educational history. I shall argue below that schools are expected to serve basic functions in capitalist society at the economic, political and ideological levels. What has come to be assumed was going on at William Tyndale suggests that the teachers there ignored or denied the functions they were – implicitly, of course – expected to perform.

At the economic level they were quite explicit in opposing the centrality of schools' human resource service to the economy. Their job was not to provide 'factory fodder'; they saw themselves as preparing human beings rather than human capital. They sought, too, to undermine the class structure as far as possible in their policies and practice, rather than reinforce it, which they saw as the inevitable outcome of schools' traditional sorting and selection function. The practical outcomes of these policies were a decreased emphasis on 'occupationally useful' skills, a refusal to stratify the pupils on the basis of accepted criteria and the *implementation* of not that uncommon rhetorical claim that the school should serve the most 'deprived' segment of its population.

This approach was complemented at the political level by the encouragement of questioning rather than blind obedience among the pupils, and by the denial of hierarchical relationships both within the staff and between the staff and pupils. This latter, of course, culminated in the famous (or infamous) system of 'total children's rights'.

Perhaps the most important impact the Tyndale affair had at the ideological level came from the teachers' vehement denial of the 'neutrality' of schooling, and their explicitly socialist philosophy. This underlay their policies and practices at the other levels and raised a number of ordinarily unasked questions about the relationships between education and society, teachers and their pupils, and teachers and their employers.

Politicizing education

If we are to talk about the 'politicization' of a process, it is important that we first of all establish its previous 'unpolitical' nature. To talk of the 'politicization' of an aspect of education may seem at least superfluous following the tremendous emphasis there has been in much recent sociology of education on the intrinsically and unavoidably political nature of education. What much of this work is concerned to establish is the political effect of the very claims made for the neutrality of schooling. I will argue below that for a number of reasons it has become much more difficult and even counterproductive of the aims they are intended to achieve, to substantiate such claims about the non-political nature of education. I want here to look forward to that argument by considering very briefly how such claims have been sustained historically, and how more recently claims for education's neutrality became exposed to increasing conflict and contradiction.

The neutralization of education might be seen, at a very abstract level, as being achieved through two linked propositions, the one of which stated that certain aspects of education were 'above' politics, the other of which stated that certain aspects of education were 'beneath' politics. It is a critically important feature of English society that throughout its rapid growth to industrialization, and since, certain values and virtues – a particular view of culture – have remained paramount. It has now become a truism that during this process the aristocracy 'incorporated' rather than confronted the rising bourgeoise, and the part played by the public schools in this has frequently been noted. It is also the case that it was these values, virtues and culture that permeated the state system of education, as much as, or more than, any industrialist values. Attempts to account for the nature of the English education system in terms of a crude industrial, human capital model inevitably end up with a large remainder. The system was penetrated as much by the ideas of those Raymond Williams (1961) calls 'the old humanists' as by those he calls 'industrialist trainers'. What is more, the old humanist ideas had claimed and continued to claim an apparent intrinsic superiority, and to be the 'natural' matter of education. The consequent easy assumption that such values were above politics – with the parallel assumption and defence that those challenging them were in danger of 'bringing politics into education' – lasted until well after the 1944 Education Act; indeed, it is by no means dead now.

However, the dominance of the 'old humanist' tradition, with its placing of education above politics, has been considerably eroded in the past 25 years. A number of associated factors have contributed to this process. Perhaps most important has been the accelerating qualitative change in the workforce requirements of industry and commerce. For most of this century following the major expansion in the need for clerical workers in the early years of the century up until the 1950s, the chief variations in industry's workforce requirements were quantitative rather than qualitative. The increasing rate of technical change – and consequent state intervention in industry – together with the great expansion of the public and private service sectors of the economy altered the employment market, and made the possibility of a close fit between the products of the education system and the needs of industry seem particularly desirable. At the zenith of the influence of human capital theorists in the 1960s, investment in trained labour through education was claimed to yield greater dividends than almost any other kind of investment the State could make. The old humanists' ideals with the objective of producing 'educated gentlemen' were to be consumed in the white heat of the technological revolution and replaced by an education system producing the technocrats that revolution required. Crucially, for almost the first time, the culture of a particular *class* ceased to be equated with the *national* interest in education. Its claim, therefore, had to be made on common ground with its competitors; its natural superiority was gone.

The other major factor bringing about the erosion of the idea of education being 'above politics' was the debate over comprehensive schools. Again, the intention to use education explicitly to pursue particular social/political goals, revealed how it had always and inevitably favoured, though implicitly, other sets of social/political goals. The comprehensive debate was very much more about equality of opportunity and hence about access to the unproblematic old humanist culture of the grammar schools than it was about changing the class character of the dominant culture. This latter theme, though, did come to prominence indirectly in the comprehensive debate through the other major thrust of the pro-comprehensive argument, that talent which the country needed was being wasted, i.e. the efficiency argument. Efficiency is essentially quantifiable. It chimes much better with the technocratic rather than the old humanist view of schooling. And the critical thing about the technocratic rather than the old humanist view of schooling is that it opens up schooling to direction and evaluation on the basis of external criteria, and draws its priorities from outside the education system itself.

It was the comprehensive debate, too, which spotlighted questions about those mundane, day-to-day aspects of school life which can easily be seen as so much matters of administrative routine to be 'beneath politics'. In particular, that debate focused attention at least as much on the *mechanisms* of selection, as on the principles of selection. It thus called into question pre-eminently the objectivity of the 11+ exam and exposed the class nature of educational selection. What had been matters of routine school and classroom organization – streaming is perhaps the best example – had their political implications revealed. I am not, of course, arguing here that some kind of nasty conspiracy was rumbled as an unintended consequence of the desire to introduce comprehensive schools. I am pointing rather to a set of unquestioned beliefs in the political neutrality of educational administration. (It is interesting to note here how easily we talk of educational administrators rather than educational policy makers, and how this is reflected in the creation of university departments of educational administration and management rather than of educational policy studies; if the argument implied in the original title of this paper is correct, that situation may change over the next decade.)

The most extreme claim about the political nature of those mundane aspects of school life ordinarily considered 'beneath' politics is, of course, that contained in Bowles and Gintis's (1976) correspondence theory. Very briefly, Bowles and Gintis argue that the reproduction of the social relations of production depends on the reproduction of a particular kind of consciousness, on workers being 'attitudinally attuned' to the demands of capitalist industry. Their claim is that this consciousness is reproduced through the hidden curriculum, the apparent trivia of school organization and daily classroom life which instil into the potential worker attitudes of docility, punctuality, authority, merit, and so on. This claim may exaggerate the influence of the hidden curriculum, but it does confirm its distinctly political nature.

One other critical point emerging from the foregoing discussion and dialectically related to it is that we are forced to recognize the relative autonomy of education. The pattern of English education cannot adequately be explained by reference to some master plan drawn up over brandy and cigars by the CBI. Nor can it adequately be explained by reference to the efforts of crusading politicians, eager to use the education system as the key machine tool in their own projects of social engineering. The education system has continued to expand throughout this century, with very little direct reflection of the demands made on it by any of its clients, customers or consumers. It has, then, been relatively autonomous in the sense that objectives and techniques generated within the education system have had as much influence on the structure and direction of the education system as have externally imposed objectives and techniques. Education must be seen as an apparatus of the State in that it is state-funded, but this funding has not entailed close control from other state apparatuses or from the designs of industry, trade unions or the electorate.

This certainly does not mean that there were no external constraints on education. Of course, there were many accumulated in the growth of the system. I have described some of these constraints elsewhere (Dale, 1976), particularly those associated with the organization of schooling, the teacher–pupil ratio, and so on. These classroom constraints are complemented by further constraints at other points in the education system. Direct government intervention in teachers' salary negotiations is one obvious example; the system of secondary school examinations is another, while the whole debate over the comprehensive school issue, though it embraced important contributions from teachers' organizations, was one which was essentially carried on outside the education system and imposed its outcomes on the education system (which led, of course, to the claim that this debate 'brought politics into education'). Within these broad guidelines, however, the education system did have considerable autonomy. This autonomy was, though, conditional upon it not being 'abused'. When it was 'abused', as for example in the case of Risinghill, its conditional nature was quickly revealed. Perhaps the most succinct way to conceptualize the status of the education system up until very recent times is to see it as a kind of *licensed autonomy*. An implicit licence was granted the education system, which was renewable on the meeting of certain conditions. Just how these conditions could be met was again subject to certain broad limitations. (An analogy with public house licensing is not entirely inappropriate. Pubs have a licence to operate a certain number of hours per day, but exactly which hours is not so closely laid down, while the renewal of their licence is dependent on their not being too blatantly or regularly 'in trouble'.)

The educational expansion of the decades from the early 1960s to the early 1970s stretched the terms of the education system's licence to new limits. A number of the earlier constraints on the system were disappearing – notable among these was the gradual demise of the 11+ – while some crucial institutions and processes of education were now being controlled much more from within the system than from outside it – I am thinking here of the Schools Council for Curriculum and Examinations, whose existence as a teacher-dominated body was itself testimony to the strength of the forces internal to the educational system – and the Certificate of Secondary Education, an examination demanded by, and controlled by, the teaching profession. Again this does not mean that 'anything went' within education. I have argued elsewhere, and in reference specifically to progressive education, that though this may have indeed been a golden age for educational expansion inspired from within the education system, the particular areas in which education expanded, and the particular forms which this expansion took, were broadly shaped by the dominant social democratic consensus on the nature and place within state activity as a whole (see Dale, 1979). Nevertheless, the overall picture is one of an undoubted expansion of educational provision which was very far from being directly and systematically controlled by government, industry, Jack Jones and Hugh Scanlon, the IMF, or anyone else.

In the second half of the 1970s things were very different. There had been considerable retrenchment in the education service. The particular social democratic consensus based on the Labour Party, the National Union of Teachers and the sociology of education which, (Finn *et al.*, 1977) have so convincingly argued, dominated the education system for the best part of 30 years, has begun to disintegrate, quite conceivably for good. Neither willingly, nor altogether wittingly, the three 'partners' in the alliance described by

Finn *et al* found themselves unable to sustain the basis of their partnership in the face of a new and very different set of economic, political and ideological pressures.

A developing world economic crisis was dangerously accelerated by the dramatic rise in the price of oil announced by OPEC in 1973 and was particularly acutely experienced in Britain. Inflation rates were among the highest in the developed world. Unemployment was at levels unknown since the Second World War. There was a decline in real wages and standards of living. The political response to these circumstances (which has tended to be in practice, if not in rhetoric, bipartisan) was effectively two-fold. On the one hand, emergency measures had to be taken to prevent the situation getting worse. On the other hand, policies had to be introduced, at all levels, to ensure that it could not happen again. Education was not immune from either of these thrusts. As part of the defensive strategy, it had to take its share of the cuts along with all the other social services. Not only this, but there was no guarantee that such cuts would ever be restored entirely, since the escape strategy appeared to require a shift of resources from wealth-consuming to wealth-producing sectors of the society. The message for education was clear in outline, if not in detail; it called for a much more effective implementation of the human capital policy which had been supposed to maintain the white heat of the technological revolution. It had not. The institutional arguments – expansion of numbers of higher education places in science and technology – had been made, but they had not been taken up; the horse had been led to the water but was not drinking. The 'cultural' claims of education were still proving more attractive than the economic. This situation had, of course, been made possible by a relatively buoyant employment market for graduates of almost any variety, and it was market forces which 'rectified' it; the sudden increase in graduate unemployment, perhaps especially the closing down of the 'I can always teach' option, prodded six formers into 'vocational' courses far more effectively than any government exhortation. Nevertheless, a major, and politically unwelcome, consequence of the 'licensed autonomy' of the education system had been made clear, and the political will to bring the system under closer control had been established.

If these changed economic and political circumstances quite clearly implied changed priorities for education, they certainly did not imply that the achievement of the new priorities had to be designed and implemented in particular ways. They could have been achieved in a wide variety of ways. The particular form the educational reforms of the late 1970s took were particularly influenced by the nature of the ideological debate. I have argued elsewhere (Dale, 1979) that the 'golden age' for educational expansion provided particular opportunities for the development of progressive pedagogic as well as curricular approaches, and that with the endorsement given them by the Plowden Report these 'progressive' ideas tended to become, at least rhetorically, the new orthodoxy, though this was very largely confined to the primary school. However, opposition to these ideas, at first lonely and rather derided voices, gained in strength, especially as the underlying economic expansion and full employment which had underpinned the educational expansion began to slow down and stop and, eventually, by the mid-1970s had become a very powerful voice indeed, having been taken on board by at least part of the Conservative Party's education cadre. The line taken by this opposition was not a particularly coherent one, based as it was on opposition to a number of disparate features of school and youth culture of the late 1960s, which it endeavoured to link together into a problem answerable by the single solution of the reimposition of mortal and academic standards. The picture painted showed schools taken over by extreme progressive ideas, which were being peddled by a tight-knit group of politically motivated and irresponsible teachers with the deliberate intention of weakening the nation's moral fibre by the corruption of its youth, and of weakening its international competitiveness by the destruction of its academic standards. The consequence was that half our kids could not write and even fewer could spell, while the mysteries of long division were beyond all but that fortunate but increasingly beleaguered rump in the remaining grammar schools; the Marxists had taken over the universities and football hooligans made it impossible for decent folk to leave their homes.

What the William Tyndale affair did, of course, was to *prove* that this was no mere fantasy. It demonstrated that what we had all felt in our hearts about progressive education when it was being so enthusiastically pushed was right after all. There could no longer be any objection to the necessary measures to tighten up the education service being taken; even the NUT had not supported the Tyndale teachers.

The preceding section can be summarized as follows – the growing economic crisis which came to a head in the early 1970s, together with its political repercussions, established the need for new objectives for the education system; the route to be followed to these objectives was both specified and cleared of major obstacles by the reactions to the William Tyndale affair.

Consequences for schools

We are now in a position to assess some likely consequences of the changes brought about in the education system following the *Yellow Book*/Great Debate/Green Paper exercises which were the public outcome of the processes I have described above. I want to look at the consequences under two main headings, those of control and of content. These, it seems to me, are two areas where a new level of state intervention has been provoked owing to, in the one case, the inability of central government to ensure adequate implementation of its declared policies under what I have called above the 'licensed autonomy' of the education system and, in the other case, the need to create a new balance between the functions of education in a new economic and political situation.

The fundamental shift in the area of control is from 'licensed autonomy' to what I will call 'regulated autonomy'. Control over the education system is to become tighter, largely through the codification and monitoring of processes and practices previously left to teachers' professional judgement, taken on trust or hallowed by tradition. This shift has come to be equated with the move to greater teacher accountability. Undoubtedly, teachers will be called on to provide a more detailed account of their teaching; indeed, one of the first practical reactions to the William Tyndale affair was the doubling of the primary school Inspectorate in inner London and a much closer monitoring by them of what teachers had actually done rather than what their records said they had done. However, it does seem to me that it is dangerous to limit consideration of the greater control entailed by 'regulated autonomy' to questions of accountability for at least two reasons. First, the move to regulated autonomy is not confined in its effects to teachers and, secondly, accountability is both about more than questions of how far, by whom, and with what consequences teachers are to be judged on the basis of their pupils' performance on standardized tests, and about less than its extreme versions implemented in the United States.

More fundamental than the stress on accountability, it seems to me, is a change in the focus of control from the production to the consumption of educational messages. The traditional assumption seems to have been that what was laid down in the syllabus was what was taught in the classroom, and what was taught there was what was learned there. Thus, anyone wishing to control or oversee what was going on in education need only monitor the construction of the curriculum to maintain a fairly tight grip on things. And, certainly, the examination system provided formidable support in the form of evidence of what had been learned. However, not every aspect of the curriculum is publicly examined; though, for reasons I advanced above, this has not meant an enormous proliferation of different curricula. Nevertheless, there has been a continuing expression of concern over the performance of schools and it has focused not so much on what is *taught*, on getting the curriculum right, as on what is learned. This concern is most clearly expressed in the area of reading and arithmetic. There is little doubt that these 'subjects' are very widely *taught* (though the possibility that they could be ignored was one of the hares started by Tyndale), but increasing (though rather sketchily evidenced) concern has been expressed over how well they are learned. This has raised critical questions about the transmission of the messages, which has involved calling into questions both teachers' competence ('do they get sufficient training in teaching reading?') and their priorities ('is enough attention being paid to standards of literacy and numeracy?'). So we have moved from a situation where control over the accurate transmission of appropriate messages was assumed to be guaranteed by control over their production, to a situation where it is assumed that it can only be guaranteed by monitoring their consumption.

What seems to be at issue in the accountability area, then, is the bureaucratization of teachers' professional judgement. Under the system I have described as licensed autonomy, the major source of teachers' authority was that they could expect to be backed up by their employers and their representatives as long as they stayed within certain implicit boundaries of curriculum, pedagogy and evaluation. What they did within these boundaries was a matter for their professional judgement, and this professional judgement was the justification for their actions. Now I am aware that teachers' historic fear of inspectors is not unjustified, but I think it can be argued that the widespread change in label from Inspector to Adviser (the ILEA, ironically, was one of those retaining the Inspector title) did signal a real change in the role (baldly, from an emphasis on policing those implicit boundaries to an emphasis on exploiting the possibilities they provided). And it should be recognized at this point that much of the difficulty in implementing 'expansionist' or progressive reforms which has been so exhaustively documented will also be encountered in the process of implementing reforms which appear to be regarded (though not entirely justifiably to my mind) as comparatively reactionary. While it may be that there is a greater in-built affinity within the education system for stabilizing rather than expansionary reforms, it is undoubtedly the case, for instance, that individuals appointed to key positions because of their ability and desire to forward an expansionary policy are still in those positions, and might be expected to be as much of a stumbling block to the attempts to regulate the system as were those traditionalist headteachers we know so well as obstacles to curriculum reform in schools.

It is clear, however, from the setting up of the Assessment of Performance Unit, that one important outcome of its work could well be to replace teachers' professional judgement as the rationale for their practice, with a series of standardized tests which will monitor pupils' progress over a very wide area of the school curriculum. This would provide a routinization and homogenization of the system, and would place all teachers in the traditional position of secondary school subject teachers of teaching to a particular assessment of their pupils. The effects of this would be particularly felt in the primary school, where everything the teacher does could be subject to such a monitoring process, over which teachers seem unlikely to have even as much influence as they have presently over secondary examinations.

This development has been seen by some people as yet another example of 'deskilling', of the 'proletarianization of professional work', but it seems to me that this misconstrues what is at issue somewhat. The bureaucratization of teaching implied by the greater central regulation of the education system combined with a vulnerable market situation has the effect of putting the teachers once again in a conventional employee situation from which they had been strenuously and not unsuccessfully striving to escape during the expansionary years. Effectively, the core element of their claims to professional status has been denied, while at the same time the possibility of introducing machinery to deal with teacher incompetence has been raised for almost the first time in the Green Paper. It is clear that this will have a considerable impact on the teacher unions, especially on the traditionally more 'professional' NUT, and this is, indeed, one of the reasons that I suggested that the break up of the dominant social democratic consensus might be permanent.

This process of the routinization of control of the education system does not end with its effects on teachers. The government of schools is at present under scrutiny, too, following the report of the Taylor Committee, with its somewhat corporatist suggestions for representative school management bodies. Whatever the details of the final outcome, it seems highly likely that schools will become increasingly opened up and answerable to bodies (such as parents) traditionally regarded as having only at most an indirect influence on the workings of the school. This confirms, and possibly extends into non-academic areas, one of the key messages of the present change in the control of schooling, that schooling is too important to be left to the teachers.

It is clear that this could have many consequences for what is to count as deviance in schools. Definitions of, and responses to, deviance are unlikely totally to evade the extension of codification of school life. One consequence of codifying procedures rather than relying on notions of 'good practice' is that it means that changes in the procedures are likely to require further codification. One particularly likely candidate for legislation, it seems to me, may be corporal punishment. In many areas, decisions over its use are taken out of the hands of headteachers, but in many others it remains a matter of their, and their colleagues', discretion. The logic of the argument I am making would suggest that, at least, headteachers will be required to justify how they exercise their discretion to 'lay' bodies, and that, at most, legislation outlawing the use of corporal punishment in schools will be introduced.

The formal if not the actual effects on both teacher and pupil deviance of its politicization through greater control are likely to be quite significant. They are clearest at the level of the teachers. Here, both what is to be done and the consequences of failure to do it are laid down much more systematically than before. It will be very much more difficult if not impossible for the next Tyndale situation to arise. The Tyndale teachers could claim that they were doing nothing that was anywhere officially proscribed. They were dismissed for going on strike and not for incompetence, and it certainly seems possible that attempts to dismiss them on grounds of incompetence would have created some major reaction among teachers and put the NUT in a very embarrassing position. It was then, but soon will not be (and may not even be now), a plausible defence against incompetence and abuse of professional authority to claim that competence was impossible to define and that one teacher's interpretation of what constituted effective teaching was as good as another's. Of course, it is not suggested that definitions of deviance can be confined to the breaking of laid down rules; it is suggested that an enlarged area of teacher deviance will be formally codified, and hence that the classification of some deviant teacher behaviour will change from 'maverick' to 'disobedient'. This will have some effect on the process of labelling pupil behaviour deviant. It will not, though, have so much effect on what behaviour is to be labelled deviant; that will result from the changes in the content of schooling called for by the move from licensed to regulated autonomy and by the circumstances which precipitated it, and it is to this that I now turn.

I suggested above that the reaction to the economic crisis of the early 1970s did not call forth new policies for education so much as it reiterated the existing commitment to increasing the human capital production function of education, while placing extra emphasis on the need to ensure more effective implementation of that policy. That is true as far as it goes, but it does neglect one major new influence on the education system which that crisis threw up, namely unemployment, particularly but not only among school leavers, on a scale unprecedented since the Second World War.

It is the dual response called forth by the economic crisis – the attempt simultaneously to prevent things getting worse and provide the basis for warding off future crisis – which broadly framed the changes in the context of education which were proposed in the *Yellow Book*/Great Debate/Green Paper exercises. Thus we are not talking of anything as simple as 'increasing the relevance' of education in considering these changes – not, that is, unless we are prepared to talk of the relevance. If we accept the argument put forward above about the nature of education's three core functions and of their intrinsic mutual incompatibility, we should expect some of the new proposals to conflict with others, and that no smooth, universally appropriate new way forward has been laid down.

One thing that does seem fairly clear is that both strands of the new proposals depend for their effective implementation on the relegation of the ideological function of education from the pre-eminence it was beginning to establish. It tends to be regarded as a luxury we can do without; in times of crisis we must come to grips with the real problems of the world. In fact, though they are set down in a somewhat mocking manner here, the aim of such sentiments becomes relatively easy to achieve. The withdrawal of the taken-for-granted expectation of a job for everyone, whatever they have studied at school or university or wherever, in itself diverts students and pupils (and their teachers, wishing to do the best for them) away from 'the frills' and into the more vocationally relevant courses. Thus, quite apart from the attempts to increase the effect of externally over internally generated priorities and processes in education – which, of course, tends to have the effect of strengthening the economic and socialization functions of education relative to its legitimating function – the need for legitimation wanes as the salience of the credentialling function paradoxically waxes during the period of increasing unemployment.

This requires some development. Crucially, the argument is that in a time of full employment, where everyone moves easily into a job, the possession of particular educational qualifications has less marginal value than it does in a time of high unemployment. To put it crudely, it is a shift from a sellers' to a buyers' market. This is not to claim that there was not always tremendous competition for desirable jobs, and that qualifications played a part in employers' selection processes. It is rather to argue that lack of specific qualifications was not such a handicap in times of full employment, and that it was a very important factor in the continuing prominence of the ideological function of education. Similarly, it does not imply a complete neglect of its function on the part of the education system; but it does mean that it performed that function in ways maximally compatible with the continuing ascendancy of ideological function. This is a large part of the explanation of the failure of the huge growth of expenditure on education, and on higher education in particular, to play the part it was designed to play in advancing the technological revolution.

What we are seeing now, then, can be interpreted, at a rather abstract level, as an attempt to bring about a double shift in the way that the education system performs its economic function. The two, linked components of this shift are both directed at bringing about a greater specificity in the economic function of education. They entail, on the one hand, a move from the provision of credentials to the provision of qualifications and, on the other, a move from allocation to placement, i.e. the move is in the direction of a system that will *place* people in specific slots on the labour market on the basis of their *qualifications*, and away from a system that *allocates* people to a particular sector of the job market on the basis of their *credentials*. The consequences of this on the ground are obvious and already visible: greater emphasis on vocational courses, attempts verging on the desperate to demonstrate the vocational relevance of higher education courses, broader arts courses and narrower science and technology courses.

One particularly important consequence is the creation of what might be called 'para-educational' institutions, such as the Manpower Services Commission. These represent a new and decisive development in the education system. They are set up outside the control of the existing system, almost in exasperation and frustration at the failure of that system to 'come up with the goods'. They are also, however, a response to the quite new aspect of the problem confronting the education system, that of very high youth unemployment.

However, it is perfectly plain that the number of jobs available to school leavers varies quite independently of the qualifications they possess, and a major task for the education system becomes the control of the problems created by this situation. Crucially, what the schools are expected to do is to instil the patterns of motivation appropriate to potential workers in capitalist enterprises in pupils who see such a status as unlikely ever to be achieved. The supply of such motivation is, of course, precisely what schools are assumed to provide in Bowles and Gintis's (1976) correspondence theory. It has always seemed to me, however, that the motivation appropriate to the very different kinds of work in capitalist societies is much more frequently provided in the work situation itself than anticipated effectively in school. As has been pointed out, the 'discipline' record of British industry is not one that offers much support to Bowles and Gintis's (1976) argument (see Miliband, 1978).

I have argued elsewhere that the hidden curriculum essentially socializes pupils into a set of values, a particular system of rewards, of authority and of hierarchy (Dale, 1977). These could be assumed to be specified in the forms of particular patterns of motivation in the eventual workplace. However, in a situation where such motivation cannot be supplied in the workplace, because there isn't one available, then the schools might be expected to do just what Bowles and Gintis claim they do anyway. What, indeed, might be required is a codification of the features they ascribe to the hidden curriculum to fill the motivation gap created by widespread youth unemployment. Supplying values whose appropriateness can be confirmed in the work situation is no longer sufficient; an orientation to work, even when there is little likelihood of work being available, has to be supplied. Thus, a further broad shift we are seeing is that from the provision of proved values to the provision of specific motivation.

The management of education

The Tyndale affair has been widely regarded as a management problem. It is seen as posing questions both about how conflict between individuals and groups can be settled, and about what institutional machinery is most likely to bring about this desirable end. Yet, as in so many other areas, what happened at William Tyndale served to bring concentrated attention to bear on a problem which was far from novel, through a dramatic demonstration of some of the more extreme difficulties the problem might entail.

It was already clear before 1975 that the basis of the management of the English education system, enshrined in the 1944 Education Act, was in a rapidly advancing state of decay. The social, economic and educational context of 1944 had been transformed by the late 1960s, placing an increasingly unabsorbable strain on the assumptions on which the system was based. The two most crucial assumptions were those of a balance of power, and a supra-political consensus. The 1944 Act sought to create a balance between central and local government and the teaching profession, as we saw in the last chapter.

As Bogdanor (1979: 158) further states:

> Were any element in the system to seek to use its formal powers to the full, the system could not work. Mutual constraint, as in the Hobbesian universe, is the precondition of success, and the war of all against all would make progress in education impossible. There must, therefore, be limits on the degree of politicization of the education service if it is to operate successfully.

There are at least five shortcomings to be noted with respect to this system of education management. First of all, it quite clearly does not reflect at all accurately the situation in the system it was set up to control. The comprehensive schools issue alone, culminating in the Tameside judgement, knocks the props out completely from under a system premised on the exclusion of party politics from educational matters and some sort of permanently available central-local consensus. Secondly, as Bogdanor also points out, the system is ineffective in directing the education system into new pathways. Since 1944, the potential contribution of education to both individual and national economic prosperity has been widely acknowledged, but a system which rests on no one party taking an undue initiative in its direction has responded only slowly to the challenges contained in the role of education in the development of human capital. (This is not to suggest that the system of education management alone is responsible for this failure, very far from it.) Thirdly, again as noted by Bogdanor, such a system is able to operate much better in periods of expansion than in periods of retrenchment, when squabbles between the parties to the consensus over the distribution of even scarcer resources may become inevitable. Fourthly, in recent years there has been evidence of a change in the style of education management, at both national and local level, towards a 'managerialism' emphasizing efficiency rather than broadening access (see David, 1978a), with the DES coming under the influence of a 'manpower planning ideology' (see Tapper and Salter, 1978). At a local level this has been accompanied by a growth in the size of local authorities following the 1974 reorganization of local government, and by the introduction in many of them of a system of 'corporate management' drawn from industrial and business use and intended primarily to increase efficiency (see Cockburn, 1977). Finally, the assumptions have been challenged by an increasing desire for participation in the control of the education system by many of the groups affected by it but excluded from influence over it. As Bogdanor (1979: 161) puts it:

> in particular the move towards greater participation in education has done much to undermine traditional arrangements. For the system of consultation worked best, when only a small number of interests were involved whose rank and file were content to defer to elites, and could, therefore, be relied upon to act 'sensibly'.

(And what did William Tyndale do to that?!) As David (1978b) has shown, pressure towards greater participation in the control of education was already building up in the late 1960s. At that time such pressure was associated with radical efforts at securing greater community control over schools; it is interesting that such moves were nowhere near as successful as the articulation of 'parent power' to a much more conservative political stance in the late 1970s, and it is difficult to avoid seeing an effect of William Tyndale here. What the Tyndale case was used to demonstrate was the importance of parents having some say in what was going on at their children's school, rather than an example, albeit rather flawed, of an attempt to set up a school more responsive to its local community than to perceived national priorities.

It is fairly clear that the Tyndale affair did have some effects in the area of the management of education. It served to deliver the final blow to the 1944 system by demonstrating that its several shortcomings could jointly lead to disaster. It had, perhaps, two particular effects in this area. First, it appeared to show that the pursuit of national economic goals could not merely be ignored but actually frustrated in a system where clear central leadership was absent; in this way it made the path to greater DES intervention in the education system much smoother. And, secondly, it greatly enhanced the likelihood that the progress of parent participation in schooling would be articulated in a conservative rather than any kind of progressive or radical philosophy of schooling.

Teachers' classroom autonomy

The assumption that the education system was governed by a more or less implicit consensus about aims and objectives, strategies and tactics had considerable effects at the level of the management of individual schools, too. For, as Pateman (1978) argues, where the goals of schooling were expressed in terms of implicit understandings rather than explicit targets, this:

> increased the power of both teachers and inspectors. In the case of teachers it made it difficult for them to be held to account by either parents or managers with whom it was possible, if desired, to play a 'catch us if you can' game. In the case of inspectors, it required of them a hermeneutic understanding of the schools, the efficiency of which they were assessing. . . . Education, like medicine and the law, had its mysteries to which teachers and inspectors were privy, and parents and politicians were not.

This approach is developed further in Dale and Trevitt-Smith (1976). In a consensual situation teachers' classroom autonomy has plenty of space to develop – in such a situation:

> the extent to which a school board can hold teachers or a school to account for its performance is strictly limited, since by definition its members are not expert and can at best only claim to be able to identify cases of gross incompetence, gross inefficiency and plain corruption – and even here they may well feel constrained to rely on the advice of the head teacher or an inspector.

Two common explanations of the Tyndale case, one from 'sympathetic liberals' and the other from more cynical radicals, become pertinent here. A common argument from people not unsympathetic to the Tyndale teachers is that what they were attempting was fine in theory (and some versions go on to indicate that similar things are being done with impunity in other schools) but they just were not very good at carrying through these admittedly very difficult practices and policies. Chaos inevitably ensued, to a degree that was interfering with any kind of effective education of the children. The more cynical view suggests that what happened to the Tyndale teachers merely confirms what we knew all along, namely that all the talk about professional autonomy was just a hoax – when it is put to the test, when someone actually treats it seriously, then its bogus nature is immediately revealed.

Both these arguments seem to be too simple and to ignore some of the complexities of the situation. The first argument assumes the persistence of a consensus about education, according to Pateman (1978), a logical precondition for teacher autonomy '. . . when the ends of education cease to be consensual . . . the claim to professional freedom logically collapses. For in such a situation there is no longer a neutral professional dealing in expertly-assessable means', albeit one that has changed over the years and is now represented, in primary schools at any rate, by what might be called 'Plowdenism'. John White (1977: 62) puts this very clearly:

It is one of the ironies of this case that they were, after all, only putting into practice in a radical form the theories that had been pumped into them in their own training and which have, between Hadow and Plowden, become the official gospel of the primary world.

Two points need to be made about this. First, the teachers at William Tyndale saw themselves as going well beyond Plowdenism – in April 1975 Brian Haddow had attacked 'the late 1960's style of informal progressive repression', advocated the abolition of 'pointless structure' and called for more egalitarian systems for staff and children. (The teachers' view on progressive education are set out in Ellis *et al.*, 1976). Thus, 'incompetent Plowdenism' seems an ineffective charge to lay at their door. Secondly, I have argued elsewhere (Dale, 1979) that the period of dominance of the Plowden consensus was already very much on the wane, and was yet another educational phenomenon whose end was hastened rather than directly brought about by its being dragged into the Tyndale affair. Effectively, then, teacher autonomy was being treated under a form assuming a consensus regime some time after a consensus could in fact be established. Hence the conditions for the kind of teacher autonomy premised on consensus were absent; it was only a matter of time before their absence was discovered.

The other pat response to the Tyndale affair – its exposure of the hoax of teacher autonomy – also rests on a number of rather fragile and vague assumptions about the nature of teacher autonomy. Essentially, they make the exercise of teacher autonomy far too voluntaristic, indeed far too easy. What they miss is the situated nature of teachers' classroom autonomy, and even, indeed, its political nature. Only its suppression is seen as a political act; its practice by teachers in situations like that at William Tyndale is seen rather as the expression of inalienable professional rights. Yet Pateman's argument shows that it is only in the relatively narrow – and in a sense self-defeating – context of working within a consensus framework that the assertion of teacher classroom autonomy (if that means doing something different from what is officially expected of them, which it usually implicitly does) is anything other than a political challenge which must be interpreted and acted on as such.

Oddly similar in some ways to this cynical interpretation of the Tyndale affair is the more popular and more right-wing view which sees the teachers as abusing their power and deserving everything they got. This account, too, turns on a particular interpretation of teacher autonomy. There are very many, very widely recognized constraints on teacher autonomy, some of which it is impossible for individual teachers to overcome (such as the teacher–pupil ratio, the inability of schools to choose whom they will teach and so on), others of which it is possible, if very difficult, to overcome (such as the expectation that children will be taught the 3R's or that they will not be tortured). Teachers have an implicit mandate to combat ignorance and indiscipline and they have to carry it out in particular circumstances (such as the teacher–pupil ratio, external examination demands) which themselves entail certain constraints. Within these constraints, teachers are relatively free to carry out their duties as they will. They are only relatively free since, first, they remain at the bottom of a hierarchy of authority and subject to the immediate control of their headteacher and, secondly, the ways in which they exercise the freedom available to them are subject both to the constraints of the classroom situation, its 'hidden curriculum', and to the assumptions about what it is to be a teacher, which they distil from their own pupil experience, their teacher training and their teacher experience. One result of this, for instance, is to make a cognitive style of individualism very prominent among teachers. It is for this reason, rather than any lack of imagination or initiative on the part of teachers, that what autonomy teachers have has both tended to be minimized in much writing about teaching, and to have had so confirmatory, rather than disruptive an effect on the education system. Consequent to this modifying of possible autonomy, it was possible for teachers to be granted a 'licensed autonomy' within the education system without danger of this leading to a revolutionary, or even radical, transformation of the system.

What the Tyndale teachers appear to have done, however, and what led to the·charges of abuse of autonomy, was to step outside the implicit and internalized guidelines as to how what autonomy they had should be used, as much as to extend the area of autonomy itself. In exercising their autonomy, the Tyndale teachers both ignored their mandate (by reversing the priorities it contained) and ignored the prescriptions for practice contained within the sedimented common sense of the teaching profession. This dual negation in the exercise of their professional autonomy is the basis of accusations of its abuse.

The effects on educational policy of this perceived abuse of their autonomy by the Tyndale teachers have derived from the two sides of that negation. Steps have been taken to ensure both that the mandate (to teach certain subjects like maths and reading) is actually made mandatory (through specification of the remit of the APU) and to reinforce the already potent effect of experience and professional common sense (through more frequent and more detailed monitoring of teachers and school activities). It has led to an increasing emphasis on how educational knowledge is *consumed* at the expense of how it is *produced* – symbolized in the waxing of the Assessment of Performance Unit while the Schools Council wanes. It has led to a recognition of the political nature of teachers' classroom autonomy in a period when there is no clear consensus on educational goals, and a consequent attempt both to specify the aims and objectives of the education system more clearly and more explicitly, and to routinize teachers' accountability for the performance of their (newly specified) roles. What is involved is the replacement of teachers' professional judgement by bureaucratic accountability. No longer will teachers be able to use their professional expertise to play 'catch me if you can'; they will now have to play 'jumping through the hoops'.

The influence of the teaching profession

The effect which the Tyndale case had on teacher autonomy was not, however, limited to the moves to limit teachers' classroom autonomy just outlined. The affair also had a notable effect on the whole standing of the teaching profession and on its power and influence in the corridors and conference rooms where education policy is made. This is particularly important, for it is possible to distinguish two rather different conceptions of teacher autonomy which are frequently combined, with consequent confusion and lack of clarity. The first conception of teacher autonomy, which we might call the weak conception, would limit it to the free exercise of acknowledged expertise in executing in the school and classroom educational programmes designed elsewhere, over which teachers should have no greater say than anyone else. It is this conception which underlay the discussion in the previous section. The second, 'strong' conception would include the creation as well as the execution of educational programmes within the scope of teacher autonomy, on the basis that the teachers are the experts about education and that they alone, or they best, can decide what should be taught as well as how to teach it. Now these issues are the subject of a continuing philosophical and political debate which is not strictly relevant here. What is relevant is that the Tyndale affair had an important effect not only on the weak conception of teacher autonomy, an effect which, as we saw in the previous section, led to it being curtailed, but also on the strong conception. This is not because the Tyndale teachers were in any way closely associated with those levels of the teaching profession which exercise its influence over educational policy, or because they were in any way attempting directly to bring pressure to bear on national educational policy themselves. Far from it. They were, in fact, repudiated by their union, the National Union of Teachers, which represented not them, but the deputy head, Mrs Chowles, at the Auld Inquiry and, though they received some initial support from their local association of the NUT in the form, for instance, of asking other local primary schools not to enrol children removed from William Tyndale, this appears not to have continued in the same way.

The two conceptions of teacher autonomy broadly divide the two major teacher unions, with the NUT holding very much more to the strong conception than the NAS/UWT. Some idea of what this strong conception involves can be gained from the remarks of Max Morris, a former president of the NUT, and still a very influential figure in teacher politics, who is reported as saying at an NUT executive committee that:

> The TUC [of whose General Council the NUT's secretary is a member] had ignored the views of the teacher unions over (the) Taylor (committee Report) [which may be summed up in the General Secretary's reference to it as 'a busy body's charter'], the views of the workers in the industry concerned. The TUC would never presume to ride roughshod over the wishes of one of the industrial unions – the miners, for instance – about developments in their industry [the TUC had asked the government for swift implementation of the Taylor Report]. (*The Teacher*, 20 December 1978: 8)

In a similar vein of 'what's good for teachers is good for education' are Morris's comments to the House of Commons Expenditure Committee:

> Every improvement in teachers' conditions is inevitably an improvement in the education of children in our schools. Equally every improvement in educational conditions within schools improves teachers' conditions. The two things go together like that.

It should be added that Bogdanor (1979: 162) also quotes Terry Casey, General Secretary of the NAS/UWT, stating to the same committee that:

> one tends to look at educational problems from what seems to me a very rational point of view, that the interests of teachers in the end are completely consonant with the interests of the education service.

It has been and continues to be, however, increasingly difficult to sustain this approach for a number of reasons, several of which appeared to be strengthened by what happened at William Tyndale. One basic cause was the generally declining economic state of the country. This inevitably led to ever more severe cuts in budgets for education, affecting both resources and staffing. The zenith of the NUT's influence had been reached, inevitably, in the decade of rapid educational expansion from the late 1950s on, and such contraction not only closed off possible avenues of further expansion, but made it very difficult even to maintain the *status quo*. Again the Tyndale affair had no direct effect on this, but the atmosphere it created made it very much easier for such cuts to be implemented. That atmosphere had a similar effect on the teaching profession retaining its central role in educational decision making. As has been hinted above, the DES was very keen to give a more decisive lead to the education service, to bring it more into line with perceived national priorities, and 'clipping the teachers' wings' seems to have been regarded as an important part of this. Before Tyndale, though, this would have been politically very difficult to achieve, given the very entrenched and apparently well legitimated position the teaching profession held. Tyndale, together with other evidence (such as the alleged decline in literacy) of 'the failure of the schools to do what the nation required of them' made this 'wing clipping' much more feasible. It did this through creating a situation where the scapegoating of the education system for the nation's parlous economic condition could be converted into the scapegoating of the teachers, and thus absolve all other levels of the system from responsibility. Thus, the educational policy makers and implementers emerged from the attacks on the system they directed scot free, while the reputation of the teaching profession received a very damaging blow.

As well as being squeezed from the one side by the more aggressive stance being taken by central government, the NUT's influence was also being pressured from the other side by the development of 'parent power', and once more this development was far from being hindered by the Tyndale affair.

So, notwithstanding the NUT's explicit repudiation of the Tyndale teachers, what they were popularly interpreted as having done has made a significant contribution to the erosion of the teaching profession's influence on education policy. Its wings *have* been clipped by the DES – note, for instance, the Schools Council's new (1978) constitution which effectively removed it from teacher control. It has been forced onto the defensive both by cuts in educational budgets and by falling rolls, with the pressure they put on the maintenance of teachers' jobs. And the public reputation of the teaching profession has not been as low for a long time, something which has further weakened its ability to defend its influence and its interests; this is symbolically reflected in a public mention, however tentative – in the Green Paper – of the possibility of setting up machinery to sack incompetent teachers, a further erosion of teacher power which the effect of Tyndale made it much more difficult to resist.

It should by now be clear that the role attributed to the William Tyndale affair in respect of changes in the control of schools and the accountability of teachers is essentially a facilitative one. What happened at the school did not initiate or cause these shifts, whose consequences are not yet clear, but whose broad aim quite clearly is to restructure and redirect the education system. Both the successful completion and an intended outcome of this process involve cutting back the influence of the teachers at both classroom and policy levels.

While the broad direction of change had nothing to do with the Tyndale affair, some details of the route taken might, without distortion, be regarded as attributable to it. So I might best conclude this chapter by pointing out two fairly major features which are not entailed by the overall nature of the restructuring and redirection which the change of educational priorities is bringing about, but where the public representation of the William Tyndale case had a particularly potent impact. First, I think it made a major contribution to the articulation of 'parent power' to a conservative rather than a progressive or radical educational programme. There is little in the phenomenon of parent power itself which would necessarily predispose it in that direction or that would necessarily lead to it being in opposition to, rather than in association with, 'teacher power' (though on this latter point the approach of the teaching profession is clearly crucial); the example of what happened at Tyndale might be seen to have pushed it powerfully in that direction.

Secondly, the scapegoating of the education system for the nation's economic failures need not necessarily have led to the teacher sector of the system taking all the blame. If blame was there to allocate – which seems highly dubious, and to be itself a function of the uneven development of the various levels at which the system operates – it seems at least plausible that it might be laid at the doors of at least some of the other parties to the education partnership. As it is, following William Tyndale (and also the Bullock Report, which looked to the improvement of teachers for an improvement of reading standards), it is the performance of teachers which is being monitored and not that of any other part of the system.

9 The Technical and Vocational Education Initiative

The Technical and Vocational Education Initiative [originally known as the N (New) TVEI] was announced by the Prime Minister, Margaret Thatcher, in the House of Commons on 12 November 1982. She announced that 'in response to growing concern about existing arrangements for technical and vocational education for young people expressed over many years, not least by the National Economic Development Council', she had asked 'the chairman of the Manpower Services Commission together with the Secretaries of State for Education and Science, for Employment, and for Wales, to develop a pilot scheme to start by September 1983, for new institutional arrangements for technical and vocational education for 14–18-year-olds, within existing financial resources, and, where possible, in association with local authorities.'

That announcement came like a bolt from the blue to all the most directly interested parties. Neither the DES, the local education authority associations, the teacher professional organizations, nor even the MSC had been consulted before the announcement was made. It created an enormous furore not only by the manner of its delivery but also by what it appeared to threaten. The reference to 'new institutional arrangements', and to collaboration with local authorities 'where possible', gave rise to considerable fears that a new kind of institution was intended – or rather that something like the old technical school was to be revived. There were some grounds for these fears. David Young (then chairman of the MSC, now a Cabinet Minister, and together with Sir Keith Joseph and Norman Tebbit credited with producing the original plan) made it clear that MSC were in the last resort (if local education authorities did not cooperate in the scheme) prepared to set up their own schools, which he thought might even be called 'Young' schools (*Education*, 26 November, 1982).

However, local authority resistance crumbled very rapidly (though complaints about lack of consultation continued) and their collaboration in the scheme was assured with Mr Young's announcement that the membership of the National Steering Group to be set up to run the initiative 'would reflect the key part the education service would play in the pilot projects' (*Education*, 1982).

The TVEI scheme emerged as:

a pilot scheme; within the education system; for young people of both sexes; across the ability range; voluntary. Each project must provide a full-time programme; offer a progressive four-year course combining general with technical and vocational education; commence at 14 years; be broadly based; include planned work experience; lead to nationally recognised qualifications. Each project and the initiative as a whole must be carefully monitored and evaluated. The purpose of the scheme is to explore and test ways of organizing and managing readily replicable programmes of technical and vocational education for young people across the ability range. (MSC, 1984).

In his letter to all education authorities in England and Wales, inviting them to submit applications, David Young amplified this framework by indicating that the general objective was to 'widen and enrich the curriculum in a way that will help young people prepare for the world of work, and to develop skills and interests, including creative abilities, that will help them to lead a fuller life and to be able to contribute more to the life of the community'. Secondly, he suggested that 'we are in the business of helping students to "learn to learn". In a time of rapid technological change, the extent to which particular occupational skills are required will change. What is important about this initiative is that youngsters should receive an education which will enable them to adapt to the changing occupational environment.'

Sixty-six LEAs applied to be included in the project and 14 were chosen (the originally planned number was enlarged to ensure better geographical coverage). A central feature of the scheme is that these authorities then signed contracts with MSC for the delivery of the project outlined in their application. These projects were all drawn up to match the guidelines contained in David Young's letter, but they differed considerably from each other in philosophy, numbers of schools involved (though most schemes included between five and eight schools and colleges of further education) and the number of pupils to be involved (though the funding basis assumed five annual cohorts of 250 pupils per authority). Some of these differences and their implications are elaborated more fully below. Each local project is responsible to a local steering group made up of representatives of both sides of industry, educational interests, voluntary organizations and so on. The steering groups report to the TVEI Unit in the MSC and to the local authority.

Twice as many Conservative as Labour authorities applied; Labour authorities refused to submit bids on the grounds that the scheme would both be divisive by reintroducing some form of selection into comprehensive education, and have a narrowing, excessively vocationalizing effect on the curriculum. These have been the dominant criticisms of the TVEI scheme throughout its short history. At first, the pilot nature of the scheme received a great deal of emphasis. Critics in the House of Commons (where questions on TVEI were answered by both the Employment and Education ministers) and elsewhere were typically told not to become too anxious or worried about what was after all only a small pilot scheme. And yet, scarcely 3 months after the announcement of the first group of pilot LEAs and before the projects had started, it was announced that the scheme would be extended, with another £20 million in addition to the original £7 million available to bring in another 40 or so (in the end 44 more authorities were accepted) LEAs in September 1984. And then, in October 1984, a further extension of the scheme was announced to start in September 1985. The indications are that all those who apply in this round will be successful, leaving only a residue of Labour authorities opting out, on broadly the same grounds as they originally gave.

TVEI does not follow any of the three main routes of bringing about major educational change in Britain, either in the nature of its aims or in its methods. It is neither a programme drawn up by and in consultation with practising educators, aimed at improving the content and/or delivery of (parts of) the school curriculum (the Schools Council model); nor does it follow the Plowden Advisory Committee model, where representatives of a wide range of appropriate interests join with the 'great and the good' to scrutinize, and recommend a series of more or less major changes; nor does it follow the model of legislative change, which encouraged comprehensive schooling, for instance, or raised the school-leaving age. Rather, it might be argued, it follows a business or commercial model, moving resources into a new 'line' when the existing one is proving ineffective. At the centre of its aims is improving the service to a particular group of customers, clients and consumers – it does not seek to improve the service to those already seen as (too) well catered for. Its mode of operation is executive rather than legislative or advisory. And it is singularly unencumbered either by the professional experts, or by the 'great and the good' – there are no latter-day Lords Vaizey or (Michael) Young in TVEI.

TVEI, then, is a political intervention, in the sense that it was introduced into the educational system from outside, albeit with the acquiescence or even encouragement of the Secretary of State for Education (though without even the knowledge of his department officials, or any other part of the educational apparatus, national or local). Though in the end the cooperation of the majority of LEAs was secured – at least to the extent of making themselves contractually accountable for disposing of very large sums of money for specified purposes (though, as I shall show below it cannot be assumed that these purposes were necessarily inimical to them) – it is clear from David Young's comments quoted above that the scheme would have been introduced anyway (though whether it could have succeeded without the cooperation of the education service is a matter of fascinating, if now futile, debate).

Another crucial feature of TVEI is its size and scope. It now involves the majority of education authorities (though, not, of course, the majority of schools or pupils) in the country and provides unprecedentedly large amounts of money for those involved. Its objective is not merely the improvement or updating of a particular aspect of the school curriculum – although this is undoubtedly part of its intention – but the redirection and restructuring of the school experiences of a large proportion of pupils. This redirecting and restructuring is aimed at bringing schools into a closer relationship with the world outside them, especially, though not exclusively, 'the world of work'. This will involve making 'the vocational' rather than 'the academic' the central purpose and criterion of what a considerable proportion, if not all, children learn in school. In both these aspects, then, its extra-educational, political origins, and its funding and ambitions, TVEI is quite unlike any curriculum innovation we have seen in this country before.

TVEI also differs from what has gone before in the pattern, process and pace of curriculum change it involves. It represents an obvious and deliberate break with the essentially incremental, apparently haphazard, pattern which had typified educational change. It represents as much a break with, as continuity with, existing provision, seeking to renew or even replace it as much as building on it. Its size and its ambitions also push it towards being comprehensive rather than piecemeal.

The accepted pattern is challenged, too, through its operation at the margins of the school, both financially and educationally. That is to say, TVEI gains maximum 'bang for a buck' from all its funding being devoted to additional items, and none of it to the continuing basic cost of running the school, which accounts for nearly all the funding it receives, leaving very little available for 'development'. Educationally, its funding and the conditions attaching to it mean that, at least formally, the school has to adjust to the innovation rather than the other way round.

The process of change is not wholly dependent on persuasion and the marshalling of voluntary effort in the schools involved. LEAs and schools are contractually accountable for implementing the changes they propose to introduce. They must be able to demonstrate that the material and human resources they have bought with TVEI money are being used, at least preferentially, with the pupils, and for the purposes, specified in the contract. A second major difference is that formal authority for the direction of the project is vested not in the schools, the LEA or the MSC alone, but in the local steering group (on which, of course, all three parties are represented, along with both sides of industry). A third difference is that the projects are also monitored by members of an advisory team within the TVEI Unit. All those appointed so far have had extensive experience within the education service, and they appear to see their role as supportive and advisory as much as evaluative.

Finally, it is clear from the timetable outlined above that the TVEI has been introduced at quite unprecedented speed. Scarcely 9 months after the first, entirely unheralded announcement, the scheme was operating in 14 LEAs, who had had 2 months to prepare their applications and who learned that they had been successful barely a term before the programmes had to start. The pace has hardly relaxed since then, certainly in the schools, as the implications of those very rapid decisions became transformed into timetable, resource, administrative and pedagogic problems, all requiring almost immediate responses.

The background to TVEI

Its unique, secret and personal origins make it difficult to point with any conviction of accuracy to the sources and diagnosis that lay behind the TVEI proposal. Nevertheless, it is possible to infer a good deal about that diagnosis. It has two main elements. One is that what is taught in schools has to be changed. The other is that the process of changing what is taught in schools has itself to be changed. Both these elements were, of course, central to the 'Great Debate' on education of 1977, and they remained important, though not exclusive, components of the diagnosis which 5 years later produced the TVEI.

The influence of the teaching profession over what went on in education had already begun to decline before the institution of the Great Debate, under the influence of falling school rolls (and consequent loss of union 'muscle'), the ideological onslaught on the alleged consequences of a teacher-dominated system, encapsulated in the Black Papers, and a general feeling of dissatisfaction that education had failed to deliver what it had promised, socially, politically and economically, and for which it had claimed ever-growing funds. In particular, the education system had at the very least done little to forestall or inhibit the country's economic decline. And this apparent failure of the education system was laid very much at the door of the teachers, especially following the William Tyndale affair, which led to teachers being identified as the major culprits in this situation. This was possible in large part because of the 'licensed autonomy' which gave them great influence over the kinds of changes that should take place in the education system (see Chapter 8).

A clear recognition of the perceived need to curtail 'teacher power' was inscribed in the very format of the Great Debate. As Bates (1984: 199) puts it:

the Great Debate reflected a trend towards defining and limiting the boundaries of teacher autonomy. The very initiation of a public debate on education, involving the unprecedented consultation of industrial organizations and parents as well as educational organizations, served as an explicit reminder to the teaching profession that the curriculum was not solely their responsibility to determine. . . . Thus the Great Debate, irrespective of its content, simply as a means of intervening in education helped to change the political context in which educational issues were discussed.

That teachers' licensed autonomy affected not only the process of educational change, but also its content was, of course, a central theme of the Great Debate. A clear tension was discerned there between teachers' professional interest and the interests of the wider society, and especially of industry. This professional interest led to an over-emphasis on the academic and a matching neglect of the vocational aspect of schooling.

The argument that it is essential to change this emphasis, and the stress on the 'need' to being education and industry closer together, to attach the former more closely to the needs of the latter has, of course, been the object of a 'recurrent debate' (Reeder, 1979) in English education over the course of this century. This is not the place to go through that debate (which is developed more fully in Reeder, 1979 and Esland and Cathcart, 1981, while useful accounts of American experience which suggests that education is called in to solve a range of social and economic problems, are given in Grubb and Lazerson (1981) and McGowan and Cohen (1977).

Beck has convincingly argued that through the second half of the 1970s industry's contribution to this recurrent debate took a dual form. On the one hand, larger employers and, significantly, the Department of Industry were putting forward the criticism that the education system's longstanding academic bias 'had played a major part in creating and maintaining the situation in which wealth creation, the profit motive and engineering were accorded less status in Britain than in most other manufacturing countries' (Beck, 1983: 221). On the other hand, a campaign against alleged declining standards and discipline, generated mainly in the press, pointed to the negative consequences for pupils' attitudes to work and authority of progressive teaching methods, teacher autonomy and certain aspects of comprehensive reorganization.

However, it was quite clear that it was not enough merely to advise, counsel and tinker. Stripped of its academic bias, the education system would not automatically revert to some pristine 'economy-friendly' state; a positive alternative was required. This alternative, heavily implicit in the Great Debate, and explicit before and after it, remains vocational education.

The problem is that vocational education is a very slippery and ambiguous concept. This is because it is defined in opposition, or contrast, to what it is hoped it will supplant. Thus vocational education is called on in the Great Debate and Green Paper to save a system with an inappropriate curriculum bias, low standards, and insufficient and ineffective links with industry. Hence vocational education comes to be associated with three quite distinct purposes, making pupils more able to get jobs, making them better performers in jobs, and making them more aware of the world of work, and of the workings of the economy which awaits them.

The term 'vocational education', then, covers three different and separate – though not necessarily mutually incompatible – aspects of the diagnosis produced by the Great Debate. It is to counter (a) the teacher-based progressive ideology which allegedly leads to a neglect of, or even contempt for, rigour and standards, and produces pupils with attitudes inimical to the

disciplinary and moral requirements of many employers, who prefer therefore to offer jobs to older, more mature and more 'stable', if less qualified,
people; (b) the fact that the things that pupils are taught at school are
inappropriate, and often do not equip them to do the jobs they are offered; (c)
the fact that they do not know enough about the world of work, and especially
about the economic importance of industry. This applies almost as much to
those who will enter other economic sectors as to those who will remain
unemployed (see Moore, 1984). As an answer to all these shortcomings a
more vocationally-oriented education consequently becomes even more
difficult to define and to prescribe in detail.

The diagnosis contained within or implied by the Great Debate does not,
however, exhaust the diagnosis which underlies TVEI. There are at least two
factors which led to the need for its supplementation. First of all, though the
diagnosis was at least superficially clear, very little had happened between
1977 and 1982 to shift schools in the required direction; many of the criticisms
contained in the Great Debate and Green Paper still held good. And,
secondly, over that period there had been a quite dramatic increase in youth
unemployment, as well as continuing expansion of 'high-tech' industry.
Both these factors were incorporated into the diagnosis which we can infer
underlay TVEI.

It is clear that the work that the MSC had done in response to youth
unemployment influenced the thinking behind TVEI. (This is not to say that
because TVEI is located in the MSC it automatically parallels MSC's policies
for young people post-school in school. It is clear that TVEI is not 'YTS in
the schools' – though many critics originally assumed that it would be.)
Essentially, the recognition that youth unemployment was too important
and, certainly in the wake of the Toxteth riots, too potentially dangerous to
be left to the market, produced a dual response. On the one hand, it greatly
intensified moves towards providing far more training. This was an original
purpose of the MSC, which became less prominent during the period of the
Youth Opportunities Programme, but resurfaced again very powerfully in
the New Training Initiative and the Youth Training Scheme. This latter
scheme was held by many (see Farley, 1986) to contain the seeds of the
comprehensive training programme which it was held Britain, in contrast to
its competitors, and especially West Germany, had never had. The possibility
that this kind of training could be built into a single, coherent 14–18 scheme,
certainly seems to underlie some TVEI projects.

The other part of the MSC response to youth unemployment is 'vocational
preparation'. This consists of programmes aimed at attuning young people to
the world of work, though they may never experience it directly themselves.
It is a series of solutions to what Offe (1984: 99) calls 'the problem of
institutional "storage" of the portion of the social volume of labour power
which (because of conjunctural and structural changes) cannot be absorbed
by the demands generated by the labour market'. The problem is essentially
one of keeping the unemployed employable, of keeping them available for
employment when employment is not available for them. It is tackled in two

main ways. One is through programmes of ersatz work experience (see Watts, 1983). In projects of vocational preparation this work experience is a vehicle not so much for learning skills or applying knowledge learned in school, but for learning something of what it feels like to be employed. The other main response is the development of programmes of 'social and life skills'. One aspect of these programmes stresses the importance of acquiring non-academic, interpersonal skills which are useful in getting and keeping jobs, especially white collar jobs; content focuses on how to behave at interviews, how to take and give messages and instructions, and so on. The other aspect stresses adjustment to a likely long period of unemployment, coping with its impact on personal, social and family relationships.

The other major strand of influence of the MSC's experience in youth training and youth unemployment is rather more difficult to pin down. It is essentially a new kind of pedagogy, rooted in the work of the Further Education Unit, whose publications have done much to define this approach. There is space here to do little more than list some of these shifts, but it is worthwhile to do so because they are evidently beginning to affect the work of TVEI schools, especially through the introduction into schools of courses leading to qualifications of the Business and Technician Education Council, the City and Guilds of London Institute, the Royal Society of Arts, and other bodies whose work had previously been confined to the post-compulsory sector. This 'new FEU pedagogy' involves, then, among other things, a move towards teaching courses rather than subjects, 'experiential' and 'problem solving' rather than 'academic' learning, criterion – rather than norm-referenced assessment, competence rather than age-related courses, the introduction of profiling on a wide scale and qualifications that are 'work-related'. These features are not, of course, being taken on wholesale by schools (though it is important to note the desire of B/TEC and CGLI to gain very much more than a foothold in the pre-16 curriculum; see 'Schools to be offered new practical curriculum', *TES*, 6 January 1984), but it is clear that some of them, especially perhaps profiling (which is part of all TVEI projects), are being introduced across a range of schools.

One final aspect of the experience of the MSC's youth programmes, which cross-cuts all those discussed so far should be mentioned at this point. This is the connection between practicality and relevance, and student motivation. Those 'turned off' schools by an academic diet are frequently reported as blooming when carrying out relevant or practical work, and to become 'different people' on work experience.

The third major strand of the diagnosis which appears to underlie TVEI is the educational consequences of the pace and nature of technological change. Again, the issues are well known, and by no means exclusive to TVEI, and I will do no more than mention them here. The educational implications of the pace of technological change have usually been derived from an assumption that it will mean that very few people are likely to stay in the same job, or even the same broad area of work, all their lives. There is a consequent need for 'education for flexibility', and specifically an emphasis on 'generic' rather than 'specific' skills. This does not seem to have been nearly such a prominent feature in TVEI, however, as those associated with the *content* of technological change, and especially the growth of Information Technology (IT). There are at least three assumed consequences of this growth that are built into the diagnosis. First, it is held that future employment prospects are likely to be most propitious in IT-based industry and commerce. Secondly, even those who are not employed in IT-related jobs will live their lives in a society where relationships of all kinds, and especially of individuals to institutions, will be transformed by IT. And, thirdly, teaching and learning themselves will make ever-increasing use of IT, altering both what it is possible to teach, and how it is possible to teach it. These three features combine to place a heavy emphasis on IT in TVEI.

The three aspects of the diagnosis which I have identified so far – the legacy of the Great Debate, the rise of youth unemployment, and the consequences of technological change – are by no means exclusive to TVEI. They are, rather, part of the *zeitgeist* and I have merely tried to indicate the particular emphases which seem to underlie the specific TVEI diagnosis. However, there is one further element which underlies much of the distinctiveness of the TVEI diagnosis and it is peculiar to TVEI. This derives from David Young's close personal association with the Jewish charity ORT, the Organization for Rehabilitation through Training, which, it is clear, provided something of a model for TVEI:

> ORT's philosophy is to incorporate job specific training into a broad education beginning at the age of 14, with an emphasis on the individual pupil. . . . The British ORT trust [of which David Young was an original trustee] was founded in 1980 out of a concern that schools here were failing to develop the potential of a large proportion of their pupils, and a desire to make education more relevant to the world outside, by developing practical and marketable skills. (Hofkins, 1984: 180)

Putting TVEI into practice

While most of the elements of the diagnosis which produced TVEI were common currency, they had had rather little impact on the education system. Privately sponsored programmes like Project Trident, which concentrated on providing work experience for school pupils, and Young Enterprise, which aimed to show them how business worked, had had some impact (see Jamieson 1986), but neither they nor any more official efforts seemed likely to bring about the kind of redirection of the education system called for in the Great Debate and Green Paper.

There are a number of reasons for this. Among the more important are:

1. The DES's constitutional position prevented it from making central interventions in the school curriculum. It had therefore to rely on what it could

achieve by means of advice, persuasion and whatever pressure it could bring to bear.

2. The funding base of schools made them less vulnerable to the kind of incursions that the MSC had been able to make into the curriculum and structure of colleges of further education.

3. It is by no means certain that the DES's own field representatives and organic intellectuals, the HMI, were convinced either of the correctness of the diagnosis or of the value and appropriateness for schools of the approaches contained within MSC youth programmes.

4. The schools and teachers had always quite explicitly opposed attempts to divert them in a more employment-related direction. They, too, did not accept the diagnosis, which they felt made them scapegoats for the nation's economic decline.

Thus, while the problem of the kind of education required by the diagnosis outlined above was being taken seriously, and a range of possible solutions was available, the problem of school, teacher and education system auto-nomy and accountability remained. There was not in the existing framework a way of reorienting schools in the desired direction. That is why the MSC had to be given the job of delivering TVEI.

What the education service was confronted with when TVEI was announced, then, was a broadly familiar package to be delivered by quite new means to a body operating with a style, expectations, and under a set of constraints, quite different from those it was used to (see Chapter 5). How the LEAs and schools reacted to this situation, and the effect of that reaction on the shape of TVEI in practice, will make up the remainder of this chapter.

For the essential point is, of course, that being acquainted with the origin and framework of the project does not necessarily tell us a great deal about how it works. It certainly does not tell us conclusively and comprehensively what TVEI is. This is so for the general reason that practically every study ever published of an educational or curriculum innovation concludes that the form it actually takes is different from what was intended, that the process of implementation itself alters the shape and emphasis of the project. It is also true in the particular case of TVEI both for the reason that, as suggested in the last section, the diagnosis is a fairly broad and flexible one, which does not entail or specify particular remedies for particular problems, and that there was no pressure from MSC for LEAs to conform to particular kinds of programme in their submissions. They had, of course, to fit in with the guidelines, but there was a clear acceptance, and even encouragement, of the diversity across the local projects; this is demonstrated clearly in the first 14 projects selected, which differ very considerably from each other in their interpretation of the common guidelines, their institutional arrangements, and so on. Even where the same subjects appear near universally, like Technology or Business Studies, the level and content through which they are to be approached differs across the schemes.

'What TVEI is, then, in any particular LEA or school, is the outcome of continuing interplay between the requirements of participation in the initiative, as spelled out in the authority's contract with the MSC, and what existed before, and continues to exist alongside, TVEI in the authority and schools. TVEI has to be accommodated to the existing patterns of practice; however great the sums of money involved in any particular local project may appear as extra funding, they are a very small proportion of the overall budget, and certainly not sufficient to cause an LEA to completely reorganize itself as the condition of accepting TVEI money – though this is rather less true at the level of the school.

It will be useful to go very briefly through the structures and processes through which the design and implementation of local TVEI schemes have to pass to get an idea how, and how far, the broad guidelines of the initiative are shaped to meet local requirements, conditions and traditions. The obvious place to start is the LEA's decision to prepare an application for participation in TVEI. It seems that in each of the three rounds of TVEI there was in some authorities a great deal of discussion over whether to bid for TVEI or not. As I stated above, the main grounds of opposition (apart from the initial, and continuing, anger over the manner of announcing the scheme) were that the scheme was divisive and that it would have a narrowing effect on the curriculum. One further objection was that the money came from the MSC, which led to fears of a takeover of the school system similar to that which it was felt MSC was carrying out in the further education sector. The continuing strength of these objections is apparent in the fact that 21 LEAs in England and Wales and 4 in the north of Scotland are still (1986) refusing to submit bids for TVEI money. So why did the majority of LEAs apply to take part in the scheme? After all, the initially hostile reception to the scheme was practically universal. The answer is, undoubtedly, because of the money. Though some LEAs were already carrying out TVEI-like projects, and others were eager to do so, it is unlikely that so many of them would have volunteered to take part in a scheme with the aims of TVEI if there had not been such large sums of money involved. At a time of falling rolls and declining funding for education, most authorities felt that they could not afford not to bid for the TVEI money, and they invested much time and effort in preparing their bids in an extremely short time. The extent to which local authorities were *only* 'doing it for the money', i.e. the nature of their commitment to the principles of TVEI, varied considerably. There are some missionaries among the first round of TVEI authorities, and also perhaps some who were hoping to be able to 'take the money and run'.

Differences between the various schemes deriving from the nature of the authority's ideological commitment to it became wider through the process of the preparation of the bid. At least three rather different models, with different consequences for the eventual shape of the scheme, appear to have been followed. In some authorities, the initial approach from MSC was passed to the authority's senior officer dealing with further education, because he or she was the person responsible for all contact with MSC. This led in some of those cases to the scheme being drawn up within the further education section of the LEA and consequently inscribed with at least some of the elements of the FEU pedagogy mentioned above. A different pattern, and one which I suspect was much more common among the second round authorities who had a little longer than the first round to prepare their bid, was to devolve responsibility for drawing up the scheme to a consortium, or competing consortia, of heads in the authority. These groups were obviously likely to be primarily committed to getting what they could out of the scheme for the schools. A third pattern was for the authority to select the schools to take part in the scheme first, and draw up a proposal in collaboration with them. A further dimension of difference within this pattern comes from the different criteria used to select the schools. Some TVEI schools have been included because they have demonstrated that they could make it work, others because they are thought to need a new challenge. In some cases it has been used to equalize provision across the authority by bringing extra resources to the worst-off schools, in others it has been used to smooth school amalgamation. In yet others, TVEI funds have gone to the schools in the areas of the most powerful councillors.

So, just as the guidelines did not clearly imply or promote any particular kind of scheme, nor did they suggest any 'profiles for the TVEI school'. In this situation, though their initial motivation may have been the money, when it came to preparing the applications which showed how the money would be used, local authorities fitted the requirements of TVEI to their own particular circumstances. How they did this varied with the way the bid was prepared, but typically TVEI money provided solutions to other problems in addition to that of changing the provision of technical and vocational education according to a specified set of guidelines.

It should not be assumed, however, that LEAs have been able to take on TVEI without cost, that they are doing nothing they would not have done anyway, given the funding. At the simplest level, it seems highly unlikely that any LEA would have been willing to suggest, or able to get away with, such an uneven distribution of such large resources across its schools. The concentration of those very significant extra resources within, in most cases, a very small proportion of their schools, has undoubtedly created major problems for LEAs. It seems unlikely, too, that LEAs would voluntarily have surrendered even that part of their control of what goes on in their schools which is required by participation in TVEI.

TVEI's reception in the schools largely parallels that in the LEAs. Initial suspicion of its background and purpose mixed with morale levels depressed through the 1980s by curtailment of funding and poor career prospects leave schools uncertain about what was required, and also about what they might have to concede. In this situation, TVEI represented for most schools almost the only prospect of funded curriculum development at all, let alone of such lavish funding, and like the LEAs, this made it difficult for those identified by whatever processes the LEA used as TVEI schools to say no to participation in the project. As with the LEAs it is difficult to point to a typical school reaction to TVEI. Some of those involved were clearly very anxious to be included in the scheme, others were wary of it; some staffs were divided on it, while others were agnostic. The motives of schools were as varied as LEAs, but again the money and resources involved were critical factors.

The TVEI schools have, though, had to change in a number of ways, and while certainly almost every one of them I have consulted insists they are doing nothing they would not anyway have wanted to do if the funding had been available, it is not so clear that the *particular* changes entailed by TVEI would have been at the top of their priority list, or that, given a free hand, they would have spent the available money in precisely, or even broadly, the same areas.

At one level, indeed, the most immediate and obvious impact of TVEI on schools has been the vast amount of extra work it has involved for staff, especially, but not only, those directly involved in the project. They have been involved not just in 'new' or 'additional' projects, like attempting to mitigate sex-stereotyping, or creating a profiling system, but also in what they would, pre-TVEI, have recognized as hard core curriculum development, in drawing up new courses to fit in with the local interpretations of TVEI. And though this has in some schools reinforced any divisiveness inherent in TVEI, in rather more it has provided a boost to morale, and rekindled the professional fires of a large group of teachers, many of which had been dampened, apparently for good, by the depressed state of the profession in the years before TVEI came on the scene.

In the end, the surest guide to what comprises TVEI in any particular LEA or school is what that LEA or school was like before November 1982. But though LEAs and schools have not been forced to do anything they would not have wanted to do, given the funding, this does not mean that they are spending TVEI money as they would have, given a free hand. To this extent, at least, the initiative has succeeded in shifting the pattern of education in the schools involved in it.

The TVEI effect

Both the structure and the ideology of TVEI constrain the breadth of possible interpretations of the TVEI guidelines. They do not do this in a denotative way, however, and the scope for possible interpretations of the guidelines remains wide. The most important effect of the structure and ideology is that they make treating TVEI as merely a piece of curriculum reform, in the narrow sense of changing the subjects taught to a particular group of students, extremely difficult. Conceiving of, and delivering, an acceptable interpretation of TVEI almost necessarily involves a combination of factors. Critical differences between TVEI schemes come not only from their empha- sizing different aspects of the guidelines – such as subject development, profiling or work experience – but from the particular combination of those aspects in each school. This combination is a key component of what I will call the 'TVEI effect', and its precise formulation is shaped by the reaction to, and interpretation of, the TVEI guidelines, and the resources available in the changing context of each school.

The TVEI effect, what TVEI means within any school, is not produced only by each school's interpretation and combination of the set guidelines, however. It is also a function of the *salience* of the scheme within the school. This is made up of a number of factors, which will be discussed below. Like the combination of TVEI guidelines adopted within a school, the salience of TVEI results from the reaction of the headteacher and staff to the introduction of the scheme in the context of a particular school at a particular point in its history. The combination of TVEI guidelines and the scheme's salience within a school are mutually influential, whether mutually supportive or mutually hostile, and their relationship, together with the effect on the scheme of any changes in what is going on in the major part of the school, gives the TVEI effect its internal dynamic and determines the nature of the school's response to external factors.

In this final section of this chapter, then, I first of all consider something of the range of variation in the interpretation of some of the guidelines. I then go on to look at the idea of the salience of TVEI in the school, and finish by suggesting some of the key conditions within schools under which the guidelines are interpreted and the salience determined.

Most obviously, introducing TVEI into a school might be expected to involve some change in what is taught, either through the introduction of new subjects to the curriculum or in the modification of existing subjects. There is, however, considerable variation in the extent of change in what is taught, from the introduction of a whole new slate of 'TVEI subjects' that did not previously exist in the school, to the use of TVEI resources to teach existing, and unmodified, syllabuses more effectively. It is important to recognize that the degree of subject change brought about by TVEI is not the only nor necessarily the most important index of its effect on schools. Though we would be right in assuming that it will typically be a central component of the TVEI effect, it is possible to conceive of a potent TVEI effect being achieved in a school with little modification of pre-TVEI syllabuses.

A key 'non-subject' aspect of the TVEI is profiling. Though the guidelines speak only of 'records of achievement', in the great majority of TVEI schemes that requirement is met by something called 'profiling'. The possible variations of practice under that heading are very wide. Some schemes have adapted 'off the shelf' existing forms of profiling, while others have devised their own, often at great cost in teachers' time and effort. A variety of possible uses of pupils' profiles exists. They can be summative or formative, for teacher use only or available to parents and students too, and so on; but the major distinction in their contribution to the TVEI effect is between those (relatively few) schemes where that contribution is substantive, where profiling is a key organizing axis of the whole scheme, and those where it is limited to a more or less important service function.

The contribution of work experience to the TVEI effect can be appreciated in a rather similar way, in that its extent and nature vary with the degree to which the two periods of work experience that students must undergo in the course of the 4-year scheme are integrated into the scheme as a whole, or treated as a quite separate part of it. It is possible for the curriculum as a whole and the period of work experience to be organized in full recognition of the mutual benefit they could provide; or it is possible for the organization of work experience to be seen as just another chore entailed by taking the TVEI money and using it for things that are really important. The reaction to, and integration of, work experience can, indeed, stand for the perceived place and importance of 'links with industry' as a whole within TVEI schemes.

Residential education's contribution to the TVEI effect also varies with the nature and extent of its integration into the scheme as a whole. This applies to both of the two main forms it appears to have taken: the 'outward-bound' form, where the 'adventure and self-reliance' medium is a more central part of the message than the actual context in which it takes place; and the 'curriculum enrichment' form, where students are brought into contact with aspects of their subjects that lie outside the ability of the school to provide.

Besides the guidelines contained in the contract there are some other necessary accompaniments of bringing TVEI into a school, which may be important components of the TVEI effect. One of these, which has already been mentioned, is the prominence of the scheme in the school. Another very important one, which it is easy to take for granted, is the need for schools to spend in a relatively short time relatively large sums of money (though the precise amount of money available for spending by schools and the precise degree of control they have over that spending vary). This presents both technical and political difficulties. The technical difficulties arise as much as anything from schools' sheer inexperience of disposing of large sums of money in a short time in the most appropriate way. This inexperience, together with the short time-scale, may indeed lead to a conservatism in spending the money, i.e. a tendency to spend it on somewhat more advanced equipment for teaching essentially the same content. More time for deliberation, and the consideration of alternatives, may have led in some cases to rather more 'radical' uses of the money.

The political problems associated with the distribution of the extra funds may also tend to push it into a similarly conservative direction. Any distribution, whether it is of equipment or additional salary points, is likely to be perceived as threatening by one or other subject departments or groups of staff within a school, and again there is some pressure towards changing as little as possible, 'doing more of the same', or introducing initiatives that cross the whole curriculum.

The magnification of the TVEI impact in the school through monitoring and marginality clearly enhances its prominence. This relates to what I have called the 'salience' of TVEI in the school. This contributes a great deal to the TVEI effect. It is made up of three components: identity, integration and compass. Identity refers both to the amount and to the nature of what is known about the scheme within the school. The public identity of a school's TVEI scheme can be found in the way the scheme is publicized to the staff and to the pupils and parents. It appears perhaps most clearly in the way TVEI is 'marketed' to pupils and parents. Is it separately identified in the options booklets? Is there a preferred target audience implicit in the way the scheme is described (and especially in the subjects it is possible to take alongside TVEI)? How far is its technical and vocational nature stressed, and especially its 'job-getting' potential? The clarity, popularity and divisiveness of the TVEI identity within a school are rooted in part in the kind of public face presented. They are also rooted in the less public aspect of TVEI in practice, which itself derives from the kind of changes entailed by the way the school interprets and combines the guidelines.

Together with its identity, the extent of its integration into the school as a whole determines the 'profile' of TVEI in the school. It is possible, for instance, for TVEI pupils, their parents and those who teach them not to be aware of their TVEI status. The degree of integration of TVEI into the school is associated with the degree of separateness of the TVEI group(s). This is a function of the number of hours they spend being taught as a separate group, the number of teachers teaching them, whether or not they are a group for non-TVEI purposes – especially whether they are a distinct registration group – and whether or not they have their own accommodation. The extent of TVEI's integration into a school is associated not only with the degree of isolation of those directly involved in it. It is also determined by the spread of information about it among those teachers not directly involved, whether they are made aware only of what they 'need' to know for the smooth operation of the scheme – which in many cases will be nothing – or of the broader details and ramifications of the scheme as a whole as it develops.

What I am calling its 'compass', the degree to which it penetrates and affects the workings of the rest of the school, is another part of its salience, but it is not directly linked to the height of profile. The compass of TVEI in a school comes about through a combination of articulation and infection. Articulation refers to the changes necessarily implied for the rest of the school by TVEI; for instance, in the timetable, or the need to construct viable classes in particular subjects. Infection refers to the 'voluntary' reactions in the rest of the school to TVEI. These can be positive – as might occur, for instance, in a decision to profile whole year groups and not just the TVEI/pupils – or negative, as might occur in the refusal of departments teaching 'core' subjects to accommodate any changes in approach implied by the introduction of TVEI; such as, for instance, a shift from English to 'communications', or Mathematics to 'numeracy'.

It is crucial to realize that the form taken by both components of the TVEI effect, the combination of the guidelines and its salience, emerges, and continues to change, through a complex process of negotiation between what was before TVEI and what might emerge as a result of it. These negotiations, explicit and implicit, between head and staff, co-ordinator and departments, members of the same department and so on, do not take place in a neutral arena. That arena is defined and marked by the history of previous negotiations, which are unique to each school. TVEI both heightens the importance of some facets of that history, and brings new aspects of it into play, as well as filtering the effect of external events into and on the negotiations. Among the especially prominent conditions of negotiation over TVEI are:

1. The generally low level of morale within the teaching profession, following some years of declining funds, falling rolls and apparent decreasing public esteem. This meant a warm welcome for almost anything that promised extra funding and the possibility of professional development.
2. Considerable resistance among both the leadership and the rank and file of the teaching profession to a narrowly defined 'vocational education' – the preparation of factory fodder – and to anything that threatened the principles of comprehensive education.
3. The heightening of this resistance through the apparent attribution to teachers of blame for national decline in the debates that prefigured TVEI, where teachers appeared as scapegoats, as part of the problem rather than part of the solution.
4. The existence of a growing pressure towards some kind of differential reward for different performance in the payment of teachers.
5. The possibility that some subjects might disappear from the curriculum with declining staffing levels.
6. Apprehension over the effects of the entry of the MSC into the area of further education.
7. A heightened awareness of competition between secondary schools, possibly involving their very survival, as a result of falling rolls.

Not all the factors apply in all cases. More importantly, they do not all carry equal weight. For instance, the need for extra funds in most cases outweighed any reservations about TVEI. It did not remove those reservations, though, and a common pattern of acceptance of TVEI into a school is to attempt to do it with minimum infringement of those reservations. But that is only one form of response, albeit fairly typical. The main point is that whatever the orientation towards TVEI, however significant the various conditions of negotiation may be, TVEI is never merely imposed on schools. It is always accepted on certain implicit or explicit conditions based largely on the existing history, ideology, structure and location of the school, to produce a TVEI effect unique to that school.

Conclusion

I have argued here that although TVEI varies immensely across authorities and schools, it does not vary infinitely. The variations are constrained by the origins of the initiative and the problems it was created to solve. These led to it taking on a particular broad structure and ideology, both of which allowed a very wide range of local variation. The nature and extent of that variation are shaped in the schools into the unique TVEI effect by their own history and the conditions under which TVEI was accepted into the schools. In the end, although it may be changed or even transformed by TVEI, the surest guide to understanding TVEI in a school is what the school was like before.

References

Althusser, L. (1971). Ideology and ideological state apparatuses. In *Lenin and Philosophy and Other Essays*. London: New Left Books.

Anderson, D., Lait, J. and Marsland, D. (1981). *Breaking the Spell of the Welfare State*. London: Social Affairs Unit.

Anon. (1988). Commentary. *Political Quarterly*, **59**, 1, 1–5.

Archer, M. (1979). *Social Origins of Education Systems*. London: Sage.

Auld, R. (1976). *William Tyndale Junior and Infants School Public Inquiry: A Report to the Inner London Educational Authority*. London: ILEA.

Bates, I. (1984). From vocational guidance to life skills: Historical perspectives on careers in education. In I. Bates, J. Clarke, P. Cohen, D. Finn, R. Moore and P. Willis, *Schooling for the Dole*, pp. 170–219. London: Macmillan.

Beck, J. (1983). Accountability, industry and education: reflections on some aspects of educational and industrial policies of the labour administrations of 1974–9. In J. Ahier and M. Flude (eds), *Contemporary Education Policy*, pp. 211–32. London: Croom Helm.

Berg, L. (1968). *Risinghill: Death of a Comprehensive School*. Harmondsworth: Penguin.

Bogdanor, V. (1975). Defending equal rights. *Times Educational Supplement*, 28 May.

Bogdanor, V. (1979). Power and participation. *Oxford Review of Education*, **5**, 2, 157–66.

Bosanquet, N. (1981). Sir Keith's reading list. *Political Quarterly*, **52**(3), 324–41.

Bourdieu, P. and Passeron, J.-C. (1977). *Reproduction*. London: Sage.

Bowles, S. and Gintis, H. (1976). *Schooling in Capitalist America*. New York: Basic Books.

Boyle, E. and Crosland, A. (1971). *The Politics of Education*. Harmondsworth: Penguin.

Boyson, R. (1975a). More power to parents. *Times Educational Supplement*, 28 May.

Boyson, R. (1975b). *The Crisis in Education*. London: Woburn Press.

Brighouse, T. (1988). Politicising the manager or managing the politicians – Can the headteacher succeed where the Education Officer failed? *Educational Management and Administration*, **16**, 97–103.

Bull, D. (1980). Time to reform school transport. *Where*, **159**(July), 8–11.

Butler, R.A. (1968). The 1944 Education Act in the next decade. In P. Bander (ed.), *Looking Forward to the '70s: A Blueprint for Education for the Next Decade*. London: Colin Smythe.

166   *The State and Education Policy*

Centre for Contemporary Cultural Studies (1981). *Unpopular Education: Schooling and Social Democracy in England since 1944*. London: Hutchinson.

Cockburn, C. (1977). *The Local State*. London: Pluto.

Corbett, A. (1969). The Tory educators. *New Society*, 22 May, 785–7.

Corrigan, P. (1979). *Smash Street Kids*. London: Macmillan.

Corrigan, P. and Frith, S. (1975). The politics of youth culture. *Working Papers in Cultural Studies*, **7/8**(Summer), 231–9.

Cox, C.B. (1981). *Education: The Next Decade*. London: Conservative Political Centre.

Dale, R. (1976). *The Structural Context of Teaching*. E202 Unit 5. Milton Keynes: Open University Press.

Dale, R. (1977). Implications of the rediscovery of the hidden curriculum for the sociology of teaching. In D. Gleeson (ed.), *Identity and Structure: Issues in the Sociology of Education*, pp. 44–54. Nafferton Books.

Dale, R. (1979). From endorsement to disintegration: progressive education from the Golden Age to the Green Paper. *British Journal of Educational Studies*, **27**(3), 191–209.

Dale, R. (1988a) Comprehensive education in England. Paper presented to the Conference on Reform in Secondary Education, Madrid, April.

Dale, R. (1988b). Implications for progressivism of recent changes in the control and direction of education policy. In A.G. Green and S.J. Ball (eds), *Progress and Inequality in Comprehensive Education*, pp. 39–62. London: Routledge and Kegan Paul.

Dale, R. and Fielding, M. (forthcoming). Introduction to Part II. In R. Meighan and C. Harber (Eds), *Educational Management and Democratic Practice*. Ticknall: The Education Now Publishing Cooperative.

Dale, R. and Trevitt-Smith, J. (1976). From mystique to technique: completing the bourgeois revolution in education. Unpublished paper. Open University.

Dale, R., Esland, G., Fergusson, R. and Macdonald, M. (eds) (1981). *Education and the State*, Vol. 1: *Schooling and the National Interest*; Vol. 2: *Politics, Patriarchy and Practice*. Lewes: Falmer Press.

David, M. (1982). Sex, education and social policy: Towards a new moral economy. Paper presented to Westhill Sociology of Education Conference, Birmingham, January.

David, M. (1978a). Parents and educational politics in 1977. In M. Brown and S. Baldwin (eds), *The Year Book of Social Policy in Britain 1977*, pp. 87–106. London: Routledge and Kegan Paul.

David, M. (1978b). The family – education couple: towards analysis of the William Tyndale Dispute. In G. Littlejohn *et al.* (eds), *Power and the State*, pp. 158–95. London: Croom Helm.

Deem, R. (1981). State policy and ideology in the education of women, 1944–80. *British Journal of Sociology of Education*, **2**(2), 131–44.

Donald, J. (1981). Green Paper: Noise of crisis. In R. Dale, G. Esland, R. Fergusson and M. Macdonald (eds), *Education and the State*, Vol. 1: *Schooling and the National Interest*, pp. 99–113. Lewes: Falmer Press.

Eccleshall, R. (1977). English conservatism as ideology. *Political Studies*, **25**(1), 62–83.

Eccleshall, R. (1980). Ideology as commonsense: The case of British conservatism. *Radical Philosophy*, **25**(Summer), 2–8.

Ellis, T., McWhirter, J., McColgan, D. and Haddow, B. (1976). *William Tyndale: the Teachers' Story*. London: Writers and Readers Publishing Co-operative.

Esland, G. and Cathcart, H. (1981). *Education and the Corporate Economy*. E353 Unit 2. Milton Keynes: Open University Press.

Esping-Anderson, G., Friedland, R. and Wright, E.O. (1976). Modes of class struggle and the capitalist State. *Kapitalistate*, **4/5**(Summer), 186–220.

Farley, M. (1986). Trends and structural changes in vocational preparation. In R. Dale (ed.), *Education, Training and Employment*, pp. 73–94. Oxford: Pergamon Press.

Fenwick, I.G.K. (1976). *The Comprehensive School 1944–1970*. London: Methuen.

Finn, D., Grant, N. and Johnson, R. (1977). Social democracy education and the crisis. *Working Papers in Cultural Studies*, **10**, 147–88.

Fitz, J. (1981). The child as a legal subject. In R. Dale, G. Esland, R. Fergusson and M. Macdonald (eds), *Education and the State*, Vol. 2: *Politics, Patriarchy and Practice*, pp. 285–302. Lewes: Falmer Press.

Fitz, J., Edwards, A.D. and Whitty, G. (1986). Beneficiaries, benefits and costs: An investigation of the Assisted Places Scheme. *Research Papers in Education*, **1**, 3.

Fowler, G. (1981). The changing nature of educational politics in the 1970s. In P. Broadfoot, C. Brock and W. Tulasiewicz (eds), *Politics and Educational Change*, pp. 13–28. London: Croom Helm.

Fowler, W.S. (1988). *Towards the National Curriculum: Discussion and Control in The English Education System 1965–1988*. London: Kogan Page.

Frankel, B. (1979). On the state of the State. *Theory and Society*, **7**, 199–242.

Frith, S. and Corrigan, P. (1975). The politics of youth culture. *Working Papers in Cultural Studies*, **7/8**, 231–42.

Gold, D., Lo, C. and Wright, E.O. (1975). Recent developments in Marxist theories of the capitalist State. *Monthly Review*, Part I (October), Part II (November).

Grace, G. (1987). Teachers and the State in Britain: A changing relation. In M. Lawn and G. Grace (eds), *Teachers: The Culture and Politics of Work*, pp. 193–228. Lewes: Falmer Press.

Gramsci, A. (1971). In Q. Hoare and G. Nowell-Smith (eds), *Selections from the Prison Notebooks*. London: Lawrence and Wishart.

Grubb, W.N. and Lazerson, M. (1981). Vocational solutions to youth problems: The persistent frustrations of the American experience. *Educational Analysis*, **3**(2), 91–103.

Habermas, J. (1976). *Legitimation Crisis*. London: Heinemann.

Hall, S. (1979). The great moving right show. *Marxism Today*, January, 14–20.

Hall, S. (1980). Thatcherism – A new stage. *Marxism Today*, February, 26–8.

Hargreaves, A. (1983). The politics of administrative convenience: The case of middle schools. In J. Ahier and M. Flude (eds), *Contemporary Education Policy*, pp. 23–58. London: Croom Helm.

Harris, R. (1980). The revolt of the Lords. *Spectator*, 22 March, 12–13.

Hofkins, D. (1984). ORT: Confidence through skills. *Education*, **163**(5), 100.

Hogan, D. (1979). Capitalism, liberalism and schooling. *Theory and Society*, **83**, 387–413.

Hogg, Q. (1947). *The Case for Conservatism*. Harmondsworth: Penguin.

Holland, G. (1986). The MSC. In S. Ranson and J. Tomlinson (eds), *The Changing Government of Education*, pp. 88–99. London: Allen and Unwin.

Holloway, J. and Picciotto, S. (1978). *State and Capital: A Marxist Debate*. London, Edward Arnold.

Hoover, K.R. (1987). The rise of conservative capitalism: Ideological tensions within the Reagan and Thatcher governments. *Comparative Studies in Society and History*, **29**(2), 245–68.

Hussain, A. (1976). The economy and the educational system in capitalist societies. *Economy and Society*, **5**, 4, 413–34.

Jamieson, I. (1986). Corporate hegemony or pedagogic liberation? In R. Dale (ed.), *Education, Training and Employment*, pp. 23–40. Oxford: Pergamon Press.

Jessop, B. (1982). *The Capitalist State*. Oxford: Martin Robertson.

Johnson, R. (1979). Three problematics: Elements of a theory of working class culture. In C. Critcher, J. Clarke and R. Johnson (eds), *Working Class Culture*, pp. 201–237. London: Hutchinson.

Joseph, K. (1974a). Time to stop the rot. *Times Educational Supplement*, 1 November.

Joseph, K. (1974b). The pursuit of truth or relevance? *Times Educational Supplement*, 15 November.

Joseph, K. (1979). The class war. *Guardian*, 18 July: p. 7.

Karabel, J. and Halsey, A.H. (1977). *Power and Ideology in Education*. New York: Oxford University Press.

Katz, M.B. (1980). Reflections on the purpose of educational reform. *Educational Theory*, 30(2), 77–87.

Kellner, P. and Crowther-Hunt, Lord (1980). *The Civil Servants: An Enquiry into Britain's Ruling Class*. London: Raven Books.

Kogan, M. (1971). *The Government of Education*. London: Macmillan.

Kogan, M. (1975). *Educational Policy Making*. London: Allen and Unwin.

Kogan, M. (1978). *The Politics of Educational Change*. London: Fontana.

Kogan, M. (1983). The case of education. In K. Young (ed.), *National Interests and Local Government*, pp. 58–75. London: Heinemann.

Kogan, M. and Packwood, T. (1974). *Advisory Councils and Committees in Education*. London: Routledge and Kegan Paul.

Kogan, M. and van der Eyken, W. (1973). *County Hall*, Harmondsworth: Penguin.

Laclau, E. (1977). *Politics and Ideology in Marxist Theory*. London: New Left Books.

McCulloch, G. (1986). History and policy: the politics of TVEI. *Journal of Education Policy*, 1(1), 35–52.

McCulloch, G., Jenkins, E. and Layton, D. (1985). *Technological Revolution: the Politics of School Science and Technology in England and Wales since 1945*. Lewes: Falmer Press.

McGowan, E.E. and Cohen, D.K. (1977). Career education – Reforming school through work. *Public Interest*, 46(Winter), 28–47.

McSweeney, B. (1988). Accounting for the Audit Commission. *Political Quarterly*, 59(1), 28–43.

Mackenzie, R.F. (1970). *State School*. Harmondsworth: Penguin.

Maclure, S. (1976). Politics and education. *Oxford Review of Education*, 2(1), 17–25.

Manpower Services Commission (1984). *TVEI Operating Manual*. London: MSC.

Manzer, R. (1970). *Teachers and Politics*. Manchester: Manchester University Press.

Mayntz, R. (1979). Public bureaucracies and policy implementation. *International Social Science Journal*, 31(4), 633–45.

Methven, J. (1976). What industry wants. *Times Educational Supplement*, 24 October.

Middlemass, K. (1986). *Power, Competition and the State, Vol. 1: Britain in Search of Balance 1940–61*. London: Macmillan.

Miliband, R. (1968). *The State in Capitalist Society*. London: Quartet.

Miliband, R. (1978). A state of desubordination. *British Journal of Sociology*, 29(4), 399–412.

Moore, R. (1984). Schooling and the world of work. In I. Bates *et al*. *Schooling for the Dole?* pp. 65–103. London: Macmillan.

O'Connor, J. (1973). *The Fiscal Crisis of the State*. New York: St Martin's Press.

Offe, C. (1973). The abolition of market control and the problem of legitimacy 1. *Kapitalistate*, 1, 109–116.

Offe, C. (1975a). Further comments on Muller and Neususs. *Telos*, 25(Fall), 100–11.

Offe, C. (1975b). The capitalist state and the problem of policy formation. In L.J. Lindberg, R. Alford, C. Crouch and C. Offe (eds), *Stress and Contradiction in Modern Capitalism*, pp. 125–44. Lexington, Mass.: Lexington Books.

Offe, C. (1976). 'Crisis of crisis management': Elements of a political crisis theory. *International Journal of Politics*, **6**(3), 29–67.
Offe, C. (1981). The attribution of public status to interest groups: Observations on the West German case. In S. Berger (ed.), *Organizing Interests in Western Europe: Pluralism, Corporatism and the Transformation of Politics*, pp. 123–58. Cambridge: Cambridge University Press.
Offe, C. (1984). *Contradictions of the Welfare State*. London: Heinemann.
Offe, C. and Ronge, V. (1975). Theses on the theory of the State. *New German Critique*, **6**, 137–47.
Offe, C. and Wiesenthal, H. (1980). Two logics of collection action: Theoretical notes on social class and organizational form. In M. Zeldin (ed.), *Political Power and Social Theory*, pp. 67–115. Greenwich, Conn.: JA1 Press.
Open University TVEI Study Group (in press). *From National Guidelines to Local Practice*. Milton Keynes: Open University Press.
Papagiannis, G., Kleese, S. and Bickel, R.N. (1982). Towards a political economy of educational innovation. *Review of Educational Research*, **52**(2), 245–90.
Pateman, T. (1978). Accountability, values and schooling. In A. Becher and S. Maclure (eds), *Accountability in Education*, pp. 61–94. Slough: NFER.
Ranson, S. (1985). Contradictions in the government of education. *Political Studies*, **33**(1), 56–72.
Reeder, D. (1979). A recurring debate: Education and industry. In G. Bernbaum (ed.), *Schooling in Decline*, pp. 115–48. London: Macmillan.
Russell, T. (1978). *The Tory Party*. Harmondsworth: Penguin.
Sallis, J. (1988). *Schools, Parents and Governors: A New Approach to Accountability*. London: Routledge.
School Without Walls (1978). *Lunatic Ideas*. London: School Without Walls and Corner House Bookshops.
Short, C. (1986). The MSC and Special Measures for the Unemployed. In C. Benn, and J. Fairley (eds), *Challenging the MSC: on Jobs, Education and Training*, pp. 40–51. London: Pluto Press.
Tapper, T. and Salter, B. (1978). *Education and the Political Order*. London: Macmillan.
Taylor, W. (1985). Productivity and educational values. In G.D.N. Worswick (ed.), *Education and Economic Performance*, pp. 101–12. Aldershot: Gower.
Therborn, G. (1978). *What Does the Ruling Class Do when it Rules?* London: New Left Books.
Thorn, J. (1981). Enemies on left and right. *Times Educational Supplement*, 25 September.
Tracey, M. and Morrison, D. (1979). *Whitehouse*. London: Macmillan.
Watts, A.G. (1983). *Education, Unemployment and the Future of Work*. Milton Keynes: Open University Press.
Weinstock, A. (1976). I blame the teachers. *Times Educational Supplement*, 23 January.
White, J. (1977). Tyndale and the left. *Forum* **19**(2), 59–61.
Williams, G. (1981). The government's educational policy during the first Parliamentary Session. *Education Policy Bulletin*, **8**(2), 127–44.
Williams, R. (1965). *The Long Revolution*. Harmondsworth: Penguin.
Willis, P. (1977). *Learning to Labour*. Farnborough: Saxon House.
Wilson, M. (1977). Grass roots conservatism: Motions to the Party Conference. In N. Nugent and R. King (eds), *The British Right*, pp. 64–89. Farnborough: Saxon House.
Wolfe, A. (1981). The ideology of US conservatism. *New Left Review*, **128**, 3–27.
Wolpe, A.-M. (1976). The official ideology of education for girls. In M. Flude and J. Ahier (eds), *Educability, Schools and Ideology*, pp. 138–59. London: Croom Helm.

Woods, R. (1981). Margaret Thatcher and secondary reorganization. *Journal of Educational Administration and History*, **13**(2), 51–61.

Wragg, T. (1986). The Parliamentary version of the Great Debate. *Perspectives 26: Ruskin Plus Ten*, pp. 6–14. Exeter: Exeter School of Education.

Wright, E.O. (1977). *Class, Crisis and the State*. London: New Left Books.

Wright, N. (1976). Teacher politics and educational change. In G. Whitty and M. Young (eds), *Explorations in the Politics of School Knowledge*, pp. 244–56. Nafferton: Driffield.

Wright, N. (1977). *Progress in Education*. London: Croom Helm.

Author Index

Alderson, J., 55
Althusser, L., 24, 54
Anderson, D., 87
Anderson, M., 19
Apple, M., 1–20
Archer, M., 34, 45
Arnot, M., 18
Astuto, T., 19
Auld, R., 126

Bates, I., 151
Beck, J., 152
Becker, H., 85
Berg, L., 46
Bernstein, B., 18
Bogdanor, V., 83, 97, 98, 100, 138, 144
Bosanquet, N., 87–8
Bourdieu, P., 3, 42
Boyle, E., 43, 78
Boyson, R., 77, 83, 84
Brighouse, T., 98, 100
Bull, D., 93
Burnham, W., 6, 19
Butler, R.A., 100

Carnoy, M., 7
Cathcart, H., 152
Clark, D., 19
Cloward, R., 19
Cockburn, C., 40, 139
Cohen, D., 152
Corbett, A., 78
Corrigan, P., 42, 46
Cox, C.B., 93

Crosland, A., 43
Crowther-Hunt, N., 56

David, M., 86, 139
Deem, R., 86
Donald, J., 85

Eccleshall, R., 81, 82, 83
Ellis, T., 141
Engels, F., 1
Esland, G., 152
Esping-Anderson, G., 43

Farley, M., 153
Fenwick, K., 101
Finn, D., 130
Fowler, G., 91
Fowler, W., 107
Frankel, B., 44
Freire, P., 9
Friedman, M., 77
Frith, S., 42, 46

Gintis, H., ix, 3, 18, 19, 25, 129, 137
Gold, D., 43
Grace, G., 107
Gramsci, A., 10, 12, 26, 53
Grubb, W.N., 152

Habermas, J., 48, 63
Hall, S., 6, 10, 19, 20, 77, 84
Halsey, A.H., 102
Hargreaves, A., 101
Harris, R., 83

Hayek, F., 77
Hogan, D., 18, 26
Hogg, Q., 82
Hopkins, D., 155
Holland, G., 72
Holloway, J., 43
Hoover, K., 108
Horne, D., 19
Hunter, A., 20
Hussain, A., 47

Jamieson, I., 157
Jessop, B., 43, 73–4
Joseph, K., 77, 80, 88, 89

Karabel, J., 102
Kellner, P., 56
Kogan, M., 43, 54, 79, 100

Laclau, E., 24, 54
Lash, S., 18
Lazerson, M., 152
Levin, H., 18

Mackenzie, R., 46
Maclure, J., 94, 110
MacSweeney, B., 115
Manzer, R., 43
Marx, K., 1
Mayntz, R., 56
McCulloch, G., 66
McGowan, E., 152
Methven, J., 80
Middlemass, K., 99
Miliband, R., 26, 80, 137
Moore, R., 152
Morrison, D., 85
Mouffe, C., 14

O'Connor, J., 31
Offe, C., 27, 29, 30, 32, 35, 43, 45, 47,
    48, 53, 58, 63, 73, 110–12, 153

Omi, M., 19

Papagiannis, G., 71
Passeron, J-C., 18, 42
Pateman, T., 140, 141
Picciotto, S., 43
Piven, F., 19

Ranson, J., 70
Reeder, D., 74, 152
Ronge, V., 47, 48
Russell, T., 78, 82

Salter, B., 43
School Without Walls, 85
Shor, I., 19
Short, C., 67

Tapper, E., 43
Taylor, W., 68, 71
Therborn, G., 28, 34
Thorn, J., 83
Tracey, M., 85
Trevitt, J., ix, 140

Urry, J., 18

Weinstock, A., 80
White, J., 141
Wiesenthal, H., 58, 63
Williams, G., 91
Williams, R., 62, 80, 127
Willis, P., 18, 42
Wilson, M., 78
Winant, H., 19
Wolpe, A-M., 86
Woods, R., 79
Wragg, T., 108, 109
Wright, E., 36
Wright, N., 40, 84

Subject Index

Assisted Places Scheme, 91, 109
Audit Commission, 114–15
authoritarian populism, 5–10, 77

Black Papers, 104
bureaucratic rationality, 34–5
Business and Technician Education
Council, 154

capacity of education systems, 65, 71–4
capitalism, x, 1
and the state, 25ff
City and Guilds of London Institute, 154
City Technology Colleges, 118, 120
conservatism, 6–9, 76–93
contradictions between functions of
education, 13, 31–2, 46–8
correspondence theory, ix, 1, 47, 58, 137

Department of Education and Science, x,
54, 56, 147
compared with MSC, 66–73
OECD report on, 57

economies, 10
Education Act 1944, and post war
settlement, 96ff
education politics, 24
Education Reform Bill, 117–20
education as a state apparatus, 32ff, 53–74
education systems, agenda of, x, 31–2,
95–7
control of, 40–4, 58ff
educational standards, 5

educational vouchers, 5

fiscal crisis of the state, 31
free market, 4, 7, 116–20
Further Education Unit, 154

gender relations, 2
Great Debate (on education), 45, 85, 105,
136, 151, 152

ideology, 2–19
industrial needs (of education), 5, 7, 46
industrial trainers, 80–1, 127

licensed autonomy (of teachers), 15, 38,
129, 132, 133

management of education (and William
Tyndale), 138–40
mandate of education system, xi, 66–71
Manpower Services Commission, 81,
137
compared with DES, 66–73
'market' schools, 117–21
Marxism, 10–12
'minimum' schools, 117–21
moral entrepreneurs, 85–7

National Association of Schoolmasters,
144
National Union of Teachers, 40, 130,
132, 134, 135, 143–5
neo-marxist theories, ix
'new' sociology of education, 23–4

old humanists, 127–8
Old Tories, 81–4
Organization for Rehabilitation through
    Training, 155

Plowdenism, 141, 149
pluralism, 112
political economy of education, 24
political rationality, modes of, 110–14
politics of education, 10–18
    contrasted with education politics, 24
pressure groups, status of, 110–13

race relations, 2
Rank and File Teachers, 40
Reagan administration, 5, 6, 7
regulated autonomy (of teachers), 133
Ruskin College speech (J. Callaghan),
    45, 105

State, ix, 11–13, 20ff, 53–7
    theories of, 11, 26–7
    core problems of, 27ff, 46, 47–8

state apparatus, 35–6
strong state, 116–20
structural functional sociology of
    education, 23

teachers, 16–17, 36–8
    classroom autonomy, 140–3
    criticisms of, 4
    licensed autonomy, 15, 37, 132, 133
    regulated autonomy, 15, 133
Technical and Vocational Education
    Initiative (TVEI), x, xi, 16, 65–73,
    147–64
    TVEI effect 159–63
technological rationality, 35
Thatcherism, 5, 6, 7, 14, 76–93

Whitehouse, Mary, 85, 86
William Tyndale Junior School, xi, 41,
    46, 127–46
world economy, x